STORIED & SCANDALOUS ST. LOUIS

STORIED & SCANDALOUS
ST. LOUIS

A HISTORY OF
**BREWERIES, BASEBALL,
PREJUDICE,** AND **PROTEST**

JO ALLISON

Globe
Pequot

GUILFORD, CONNECTICUT

Globe Pequot

An imprint of Globe Pequot, the trade division of The Rowman & Littlefield Publishing Group, Inc.
4501 Forbes Blvd., Ste. 200
Lanham, MD 20706
GlobePequot.com

Distributed by NATIONAL BOOK NETWORK

British Library Cataloguing in Publication Information available

Library of Congress Cataloging-in-Publication Data

Names: Allison, Jo, author.
Title: Storied and scandalous St. Louis : a history of brewing, baseball,
    prejudice and protest / Jo Allison.
Description: Guilford, Connecticut : Globe Pequot, [2021] | Includes
    bibliographical references and index.
Identifiers: LCCN 2021019921 (print) | LCCN 2021019922 (ebook) | ISBN
    9781493059171 (trade paperback) | ISBN 9781493059188 (epub)
Subjects: LCSH: Scandals—Missouri—Saint Louis—History—Anecdotes. |
    Social problems—Missouri—Saint Louis—History—Anecdotes. | Saint
    Louis (Mo.)—History—Anecdotes. | Saint Louis (Mo.)—Social life and
    customs—Anecdotes. | Saint Louis (Mo—Social conditions.
Classification: LCC F474.S257 A55 2021 (print) | LCC F474.S257 (ebook) |
    DDC 977.8/66—dc23
LC record available at https://lccn.loc.gov/2021019921
LC ebook record available at https://lccn.loc.gov/2021019922

♾™ The paper used in this publication meets the minimum requirements of American National Standard for Information Sciences—Permanence of Paper for Printed Library Materials, ANSI/NISO Z39.48-1992.

For my three generations: Dave, Brooke, and Lindsay

CONTENTS

CONTENTS

CONTENTS

ACKNOWLEDGMENT

I tender thanks and warmest regards to the staff of the Missouri Historical Society, who scrambled to provide articles and images amid a pandemic.

INTRODUCTION

n 1900 and 1910, St. Louis, Missouri, was the fourth largest city in the country. (And it was fourth largest in 1870, likely because of fudged census numbers.) In the 1920 Census, it slipped to sixth place because other cities had drawn more immigrants in the nineteen-teens. But St. Louis still held a place in national lore. For years, it had been the westernmost metropolis, known for its manufacturing, beer, railroads, music, baseball, World's Fair, and romance with the Mississippi. The undercurrent to all that history is the stories less often written but more often talked about.

This particular set of tales were the talk of the city—and sometimes the country—from St. Louis' founding in 1763 to the mid-twentieth century, 1950. Someone in St. Louis can likely catch you up on the latest. In the process of replaying those stories, we learn about place and time, and we learn that we aren't so different today: We love a good story, the better if it's true.

COLONIAL DAYS:
THE ROMANCE OF
THE REMOTE

I n 1763, France lost the battle with England for the large chunk of North America east of the Mississippi River. Desperate to maintain his country's commerce west of the Mississippi, the French governor in New Orleans needed someone to promote the fur trade with Native Americans. Chapter 1 raises the question of what might have motivated Pierre Laclède to take that job, beyond the opportunity for riches. The answer is the Scandal That Started It All.

Laclède's outpost of St. Louis became the nexus of the global fur trade, connecting the tribal suppliers with exporters and manufacturers in cities to the east and across the ocean. One of the most legendary fur entrepreneurs was Manuel Lisa, and chapter 2 tells the story of his exploiting a powerful trade strategy: bigamy.

THE SCANDAL THAT
STARTED IT ALL

The city of St. Louis, as you can guess
from the name, was originally French.
And the common story of its founding starts
in that most French of American cities: New
Orleans.

The only existing portrait of Marie Thérèse
Chouteau. *Missouri Historical Society Collection*

ILLICIT ROMANCE IN NEW ORLEANS

In 1757, those in the know in New Orleans society were gossiping that a handsome young emigrant from France, one Pierre Laclède, had begun keeping company with the estranged wife of one René Chouteau.

What we know about the woman, born Marie Thérèse Bourgeois, is that she was attractive but stern, strict but kind. A smart businesswoman when resources came her way. Independent. Daring. Her parents had likely arranged Marie Thérèse's marriage to Chouteau, who owned an inn and tavern. There is some evidence it became an abusive relationship.

New Orleans was Roman Catholic, and the Roman Catholic Church did not condone divorce and certainly didn't recognize divorcees remarrying. So, when René and Marie Thérèse's marriage crumbled, René's solution was to move to France, leaving Marie Thérèse alone in New Orleans with their infant son, Auguste.

Auguste was about seven when his mother apparently fell in love with Pierre Laclède.

Pierre had arrived in New Orleans from France a couple of years earlier. He was a younger son in a family of officeholders and intellectuals—and a prize-winning swordsman. In New Orleans, he took up commerce and found himself attracted to the still-legally-married-but-abandoned Marie Thérèse Chouteau.

By 1758, New Orleans society noted that Marie Thérèse gave birth to a second son, Jean Pierre, though René Chouteau was still in France. It was generally known that Pierre Laclède was the baby's father. Laclède was apparently also the father of Marie Thérèse's next two children, daughters Marie Pelagie and Marie Louise.

This is the point at which Laclède's business partner, Gilbert Antoine Maxent, got the monopoly for trade in the upper Mississippi region, anticipating that Pierre Laclède would take on the rigors of the actual work. We can guess that Laclède saw more than commercial gain. Moving the family, which he could not acknowledge, out of New Orleans society undoubtedly seemed like a good idea to him and Marie Thérèse. For one thing, there was always the possibility that René Chouteau would return to New Orleans from France.

For the time being in 1763, Marie Thérèse would stay behind in New Orleans because she was pregnant with the fourth of Laclède's children. But they made plans for her and the children to join Laclède in the wilderness after the child's expected birth in the spring of 1764.

Marie Thérèse Chouteau did send one precious part of her family ahead with Laclède in 1763: fourteen-year-old Auguste Chouteau. He apparently had picked up his mother's common sense along with intellectual habits from the man who functioned as his stepfather.

FOUNDING A CITY

aclède and young Auguste made the difficult journey upriver with men hired by Maxent, looking for a likely spot to establish a fur trading post on the still-French west side of the big river. In between the settlement of Ste. Genevieve, which flooded badly, and the mouth of the Missouri, Laclède and Auguste noted bluffs rising on the west side of the Mississippi. At low water, a stone shelf extended into the river and offered a welcome landing spot. On top of the bluffs, small rivers flowed, and the land opened up to western vistas. Pierre Laclède had found his outpost. According to disputed tradition, he laid out a grid of streets in his head.

He and Auguste retreated back across the Mississippi to the French fort in Illinois country, one that the new British owners were undoubtedly headed toward. Laclède gathered supplies and talked up his fur trading network. By February of 1764, the ice in the Mississippi melted early, and Laclède sent Auguste and a large work crew to the bluffs across the river to begin construction according to plans Laclède provided from memory.

By April, Laclède arrived on the bluffs himself to find cabins and storage sheds. Although others who lived in the area might have had some moniker for the place, Laclède and Auguste named their collection of sheds and muddy paths St. Louis. Presumably that designation would sit well with the current king of France, Louis XV, who revered his sainted-by-the-church predecessor, Louis IX.

Meanwhile, St. Louis undertook its first housing discrimination action—something it would repeat 150 years later in a flurry of Jim Crow activity. Auguste had apparently just laid out the site for the first family home when a collection of Native Americans of the Missouri Tribe arrived, announcing they would like to join the new settlement. The full village from 180 miles west arrived: entire families, dogs, and horses. Possibly a lot for a fourteen-year-old to face.

But Auguste thought fast. He might well have spent time talking to the men, even as he found work for the women. He had goods to trade, after all, and he offered them if the women would consent to dig out what would be the basement for a major building. That task underway, Auguste sent a workman off to Illinois to fetch Laclède.

Laclède must have hurried back across the river to begin negotiations. His argument, as it has come down to us in Auguste's memoir (written when he was elderly), was couched in concern for the Missouris—that they were settling too close to their traditional enemies, the tribes both to the north and to the east in Illinois territory. The natives said they were settling in the village like ducks and geese on open water. Laclède said they would be sitting ducks for eagles and other birds of prey.

Encouraged by many gifts, the tribe heeded the warning and moved on, possibly back to their village to the west, on the Missouri River.

So, 1764 proceeded, and the village grew. The major building, with its newly dug basement, would serve as both business office and home for Laclède and his illegitimate family. That was good because Marie Thérèse and her four younger children—sister Victoire was the newest arrival— joined their father and half brother later that year.

And more imperial news arrived. It seemed that France, burdened by its war debts, had sold its remaining North American lands west of the Mississippi to Spain. The Spaniards wouldn't arrive to govern the city for a good while yet, but that made it all the more urgent to establish French dominance in the fur business.

The young settlement of St. Louis grew as the French commander from the Illinois side moved his forces across the river to avoid the British. When the Spanish finally arrived, they were happy enough to encourage the French inhabitants to continue what they were doing: maintaining good relations with various Native American tribes and growing the fur trade.

AN ODD DOMESTICITY

The village slowly prospered. Pierre Laclède built a fine house—separate from the original building, which was given over to public use. He gave the new structure to Marie Thérèse Chouteau in trust for her children, specifically writing that the gift reflected his appreciation for the work of his "clerk," Auguste Chouteau, and Laclède's affection for her other four children. In addition to the house, Marie Thérèse received three Black slaves, two Native American slaves, and land that could be farmed in the common fields west of town.

The large limestone house occupied the northern half of the block between First and Second Streets, Market and Chestnut. If you could see the foundation today, it would be beneath the Gateway Arch.

Laclède lived in the house as well and had his business office there. His own Native American slaves presumably lived on the extensive property.

However, the new domesticity was not what you might expect. There is no indication that Laclède and Marie Thérèse lived together as husband and wife. She did not perform the usual social duties of a Creole wife, hosting parties and such; she maintained her own financial profile, managing by herself the resources she had been given. A widow—or abandoned wife—with property in that time had advantages married women could only dream of. Even in New Orleans, she had given herself the title Veuve (Widow) Chouteau, in the 1763 Census, to claim those advantages.

The fact that Laclède lived in the house does not necessarily indicate a romantic relationship. There were no business offices of any kind in early St. Louis. All enterprises operated out of private homes, and Laclède had to run his fur trade from somewhere. There also were no hotels or apartments in

8

the village. Unmarried men took lodging where they could, and the original property owners likely all rented to boarders. Madame Chouteau certainly did.

The early governor of the area, Louis St. Ange de Bellerive, lived in her house—with his slave/family. In the early 1800s, when her children had long since moved out, Widow Chouteau's home hosted a store and an apothecary along with her living quarters.

And, when Laclède died, the executors who tallied his belongings had only the one room to inventory. He was a special boarder, perhaps, but only a boarder in the house he had gifted to Marie Thérèse.

Furthermore, in an age when families were large, the five Chouteau children each had anywhere from nine to thirteen children themselves. When Marie Thérèse Chouteau died in 1814, at age eighty-one, she had close to fifty grandchildren, most living nearby in St. Louis.

So, the relationship between Laclède and Marie Thérèse carries overtones of mystery as well as scandal and romance. There is the undeniable fact that Marie Thérèse followed Pierre Laclède into a wilderness and an uncertain future. She may have correctly surmised that there would be less social fallout from their relationship than in New Orleans society. But the fact that it worked out to her financial advantage—and even more advantages for her children—was no certainty in 1764.

THE HUSBAND RETURNS

If Marie Thérèse moved to the wilderness out of fear of René Chouteau's return, she had played that card right. Just before she and the children moved into their new house, word reached the northern outpost that René Chouteau had returned to New Orleans.

Chouteau obviously didn't find his wife and son where he'd left them, and he apparently didn't look very hard for the next seven years, over which time he became a baker. Always pugnacious, René spent some time in jail because he had slandered another baker by insisting the man put poison in pastries. Free by 1774, he started legal proceedings to force Marie Thérèse to return to him. But Marie Thérèse never returned to New Orleans, and the slow exchange of letters ended with René Chouteau's death in 1776.

Pierre Laclède and Marie Thérèse Chouteau were free to marry. But they didn't. Historians speculate that Laclède's business fortunes had soured about this time, and he chose not to leave debts that would burden a family. It would have been a short marriage anyway. Pierre Laclède died in 1778 after a business trip, while traveling upriver from New Orleans to St. Louis. He was forty-eight years old.

THE NEXT GENERATION GROWS

L aclède had bought out the business interests of his partner, Maxent, and then couldn't repay the debt. Auguste Chouteau bought up many of Laclède's possessions, including most of his huge library—which we recognize as classics today. The relatively cheap prices indicate a prior arrangement between Laclède and Maxent to make one last provision for Laclède's loved ones, a way to allow Marie Thérèse, Auguste, and Laclède's four children to inherit what he could not leave them legally.

Auguste Chouteau also bought property that Laclède owned on one of the creeks running through town. Laclède had built a mill on the creek, damming it up to form a large lake. The water would become Chouteau's Pond, the general neighborhood, the Mill Creek Valley. We will hear more of the latter.

Madame Chouteau went on to become a successful businesswoman, managing her own property—with the "help" of slaves, of course. It also helped, no doubt, that she had two sons who were equally successful. Auguste Chouteau made Laclède's business thrive and, within six years, established a trade monopoly with the Osage Tribe. Never flamboyant nor even outgoing, he was known for his calm handling of emergencies, his intellectualism, and his business astuteness and integrity, which won friends among Native Americans as well as associates across the United States and Canada. He was also known, as we will see, as a tough slave master.

Always at the center of St. Louis society, Auguste was continuously in office of some sort until his retirement, serving as colonel of the local militia during the war of 1812. He fought for the election of Thomas Hart Benton as one of the new state-of-Missouri inaugural senators—largely because Benton was willing to assist in maintaining the old Spanish land grants. Auguste died in 1829. (There is more about the legendary Benton to come.)

And, of course, there were the Laclède children—none of whom bore the Laclède name. Jean Pierre Chouteau is known to history as Pierre Sr. Like his half brother, Auguste—and often working with him—Pierre Sr. made a fortune trading with the Osage Tribe to the west. When President Thomas Jefferson took control of the area with the Louisiana Purchase in 1803, he made Pierre Sr. head of Indian Affairs for the northern part of the vast territory, noting the influence he and his brother had with Native Americans as well the variety of white nationals. That would have included French, Canadian, British, Spanish, Swiss, and even American émigrés.

As a result of the family's prominence, the Chouteau name has coursed through St. Louis history for generations—along with the names the daughters and granddaughters married: Gratiot, Papin, Cabanné, Pratte.

The name of Pierre Laclède, meanwhile, faded from the minds of St. Louis citizens. It is recalled now in a street name, in the names of a gas company, a brick company, and a steel company. The surest reference is the relatively new Laclede's Landing, a nine-block entertainment area centered on some of the oldest buildings left along the riverfront.

THE FIRST FAMILY FIGHTS

In fact, conflict was brewing over the years among the many descendants of Auguste Chouteau and the even more numerous descendants of Pierre Laclède. These included an attempt to rewrite the history of the city's founding—although none of them questioned that it had been either Chouteau or Laclède.

One man descended from Auguste is said to have "restored" Auguste's gravestone in the early twentieth century to make him seem older—and therefore more likely the founding father. Turns out he couldn't change Marie Thérèse's birthdate as well, so the original story stands.

A historian documents the occasional rivalry between the "legitimate" descendants of Auguste and the "illegitimate" descendants of Laclède. He recalls a luncheon in the 1940s attended by St. Louis elite of Chouteau ancestry in which one woman asked another, "Are you one of the bastards?" He reports a Laclède offspring saying, "I would rather be the illegitimate descendant of a French nobleman than the legitimate descendant of a New Orleans baker." (van Ravenswaay)

The twenty-first century has given us historians who claim that neither Pierre Laclède nor Auguste Chouteau deserve as much credit as they've gotten for the founding. A short list of officials and other businessmen were active in the new site from early on, they claim. And the site had surely been home to nameless pioneers.

Back in the nineteenth century, the next generation of traders, including a good number of Chouteaus, spread their influence, often maintaining a native family and a "civilized" family—the subject of the following chapter.

2

BIGAMY AS
BUSINESS STRATEGY

Manuel Lisa didn't fit in well with the French
society of the Chouteaus' St. Louis. For
one thing, he was Spanish. For another, he was
self-confident to the point of arrogance.

Lisa left New Orleans and his Spanish
immigrant parents to pursue his ambitions first
in the Northwest Territory that became Indiana. There he learned of a young widow named
Polly Charles Chew. The Chew family had been
attacked by a tribe in their frontier home; the

Manuel Lisa, fur trader,
explorer, bigamist. *Missouri
Historical Society Collection*

husband, Samuel, had been killed. Polly and a child had been captured and were later ransomed. Lisa is said to have felt sorry for them and married Polly, moving her and her daughter to the far side of the Mississippi. They settled in St. Louis by 1799.

And the rivalry with the Chouteaus was on.

The fur trade required native hunters to trap the various animals—beavers in particular—and preserve the hides. (To be precise, the Native American women did the preserving.) The natives would then trade the pelts for the new products that the white men offered. On the domestic side, the natives had learned to appreciate iron pots, blankets, cloth, and beads. On the more militant side, they valued knives, guns, and ammunition. And, of course, there was the white man's liquor.

While tribes in eastern parts of North America continued to fight against the white men taking their land, tribes in the West fought each other, their long-held animosities newly fueled by white politics. The French and Spanish had little interest in taking over native lands. Instead, they wanted the tribes to remain on those lands, busily trapping so the merchants of St. Louis could send the pelts to Europe for handsome sums of money. The job of the succeeding governors of St. Louis was to choose the men who would conduct the trade with the various tribes, avoiding or exacerbating tribal feuds as convenient. Sometimes those men were chosen because of the gifts or benefits they could provide the government or because they asserted that they could guarantee peace with a specific tribe. The Chouteaus even maintained a fort at their own expense among the Osage.

The Osage were not the far west tribes we sometimes associate with the fur trade; they were a dominant tribe in the plains, occupying what would become the states of Missouri, Arkansas, Kansas, and Oklahoma. Pierre Chouteau Sr. spent considerable time in these "near-by" Native American lands, trading and building relations.

THE LEGENDARY
MANUEL LISA

Manuel Lisa wanted action in the fur trade, and he soon got it, going over the local governor's head to receive a piece of the Osage trade that the Chouteaus had license to.

The language limited Lisa's trade to the area where the Osage were living at the time. But Pierre Chouteau Sr. had a trick up his sleeve. By convincing a large Osage group to move closer to the Arkansas River, Pierre established trade on fertile new land, a move beneficial to the Osage and therefore the Chouteaus. And a blow to Manuel Lisa's profits.

The continual bickering and string of contract disputes between Lisa, the Chouteaus, and a number of other traders took a new turn when the Spanish turned the huge region northwest of the Mississippi back over to the French—who promptly sold it to US president Thomas Jefferson just before Christmas 1803.

And, as is well known, Jefferson just as promptly called on Meriwether Lewis and William Clark to explore the new land. The Native Americans of the upper Missouri River lived in a land rich in pelts beyond the Osage and their kin. It was also a land full of danger.

Manuel Lisa didn't hesitate to push into the new territory. His adventures and achievements were the stuff of Western legend for years thereafter. If the Chouteaus were the first citizens of the St. Louis settlement, Manuel Lisa was the first citizen of the waterways of the Louisiana Purchase. One historian says he was "brilliant, aggressive, and litigious. 'Black Manuel' was an eagle among hawks." (Primm)

Lisa negotiated in tense situations with unfriendly tribes. He managed difficult men in more difficult physical terrain. He is said to have encouraged tribes friendly to him to make war on tribes friendly to the British. He was as diplomatic with tribal leaders as he was difficult with the governors and leading citizens of St. Louis.

And he made lasting ties with at least one tribe as many fur traders before him had: He married a Native American woman.

He was, of course, still married to Polly Chew Lisa, who maintained the family home in St. Louis, with her daughter by Samuel Chew and more young children by Manuel Lisa.

AND THE
LEGENDARY MITAIN

isa's new wife's name was Mitain, and she was a member of the Omaha Tribe. Her father was influential in the land north of where the Platte River flows into the Missouri, in the eastern part of modern Nebraska. We often read that white men married the (unfailingly beautiful) daughters of "chiefs." That is not simply an artifact of romance: In fact, that was the pattern. Native American clan leaders chose daughters to marry fur traders to build strategic alliances.

Edwin James, a man who chronicled an expedition in the early nineteenth century, wrote an account of Mitain and Manuel Lisa's marriage as an example of the Native American cultures he explored. He wanted to prove that "maternal fondness appears also to be not less exquisite than we perceive it to be with civilized mothers"—as if he were surprised that "savage" women could be as loving toward their children as the white women he always labeled the "civilized wives." (James)

The explorer says that Lisa "found it necessary to take as a wife a woman from an important Omaha lineage." He indicated that Lisa, despite his prestige in the area, had lost ground just before this time to other traders and needed to regain it. Not only were the fur traders in competition among themselves, but they were substantially worried in 1812 by the new war between Britain and America, given that the British still maintained relationships with various tribes. Marriage to an Omaha "princess" was the ticket, although some of his own writings reveal that Lisa "found such arrangements distasteful." (Thorne)

19

Nevertheless, Lisa picked his bride with an eye to promoting trade and offered the Omaha tribal leader a list of promises. He would live near the Omaha lands part of each year. That was easy enough since he had established Fort Lisa about ten miles north of present Omaha, Nebraska; it was some sixty miles south of the tribe's village. Lisa would "have [his and Mitain's] children made known to the white people" in order to continue trade between whites and Omahas after his death. It is clear that the tribe—and Mitain—knew Lisa had a white wife in St. Louis.

In exchange, he would have their furs. A Lisa biographer puts the trader's presumed reasoning bluntly. "That season Lisa literally wedded the Omaha nation to the American cause, and, incidentally, their yearly catch of beaver and buffalo to his trading establishment by taking to wife Mitain." (Oglesby) The Omahas promptly took up the cause of their new tribesman, went into battle against a tribe allied with the British, and won—bringing two scalps back to Lisa.

The surviving story of the marriage of Manuel Lisa and Mitain indicates that she took the vows seriously, expecting a lifelong union. He expected less, it turned out.

Lisa and Mitain married in the winter of late 1814, and they had a daughter, named Rosalie, in 1815. Lisa would have been at his fort in the fall and early winter of that year, Mitain getting used to his frequent comings and goings. In addition to directing trading operations, Lisa was involved in securing the alliance of various tribes to the US government and escorting various chiefs to St. Louis. There, the Native Americans would meet with William Clark, of Lewis-and-Clark fame and now governor of the territory.

Lisa's sojourn in the spring of 1817 was a turning point in his marriage to Mitain. As he got ready to leave for St. Louis, he insisted on taking his daughter Rosalie with him to "the country of the white people." The explorer recounted that Mitain agreed after some argument, and Lisa's party set sail, only to see that Mitain had changed her mind. She ran beside the water, "crying and screaming . . . and appearing to be almost bereft of reason." (James)

Lisa's party kept paddling and left Mitain on the riverbank. The explorer says she returned home to give away all her possessions, cut off her hair, and remain inconsolable.

Lisa arrived in St. Louis on June 13, 1817, with valuable cargo and his daughter. We have to wonder what Polly Chew Lisa thought of the new arrival. We do know that many frontier women were used to the dual-marriage arrangements—and used to dealing with Native Americans, for that matter. One historian says that Lisa placed Rosalie with a white family, implying that the child didn't join the Lisa household. It could have been that Polly had her own difficulties. Of the children she bore Manuel Lisa, at least one may have died by then.

Meanwhile, Mitain had delivered another child to Lisa, a son named Christopher. Mitain and Christopher nearly lost their lives before Lisa returned. The explorer James recounts the story of Mitain working in a field outside the fenced area of the fort. She had the young child in a "cradle-like board," which she had leaned against a tree as she and her companions worked. A Sioux war party approached, and Mitain initially fled, but she "returned full in the face of the Sioux" to retrieve the baby. She ran to the fence and threw the child in the board as far as she could onto the fort property.

Tradition has it that she was wounded in the following fight, sustaining disfiguring cuts to her face. But she and Christopher survived. At least four of the women "were tomahawked" and died according to James.

Lisa returned for the 1817–1818 season, without Rosalie, of course, but presumably pleased to see his young son alive. No untoward news reached the fort that winter, and Lisa found out only when he returned to St. Louis in the spring that Polly had died in February. By August of that year, 1818, the last of Polly's children, a five-year-old daughter, died as well.

Lisa surely mourned his losses. But his burden was lightened by another marriage, this one an even more surprising match.

Mary Hempstead Lisa married Manuel Lisa and journeyed with him to Native American lands— where she met his Omaha wife. *Missouri Historical Society Collection*

ENTER A PRESBYTERIAN

isa, a Catholic Spaniard, immersed in the Bourbon cultures that preceded the Louisiana Purchase and American occupation, in short order married a New England–born Presbyterian—who likely spoke neither French nor Spanish. The widowed Mary Hempstead Keeny had moved to St. Louis, along with her father, mother, and sister, to be near her brothers, early American émigrés to the frontier.

Her brother Edward Hempstead was a fiery young lawyer who became part of the Creole fur trader circle, a group that included the Chouteaus and Lisa. He and two of his brothers had moved to the St. Louis frontier from Connecticut and were in on the early action. When their fellow Americans took over with the Louisiana Purchase in 1804, Edward became the attorney general of the district that included St. Louis. He was twenty-four years old. He went on to hold impressive elective offices in the new territory.

Despite these achievements, Edward Hempstead's family had one major difference with the St. Louis elite: the Hempsteads were Presbyterians.

Protestant churches sprang up in Louisiana Purchase areas once populated only by French or Spanish Roman Catholics—or by people who simply didn't care about religion one way or another. But St. Louis resisted. If any Protestant denomination had an advantage, it was the Presbyterians, fueled by support from Edward Hempstead's family. He had written home to his folks, warning them of the "town's lack of religious interest," but his father, Stephen, a veteran of the American Revolution, brought his wife and two daughters west anyway.

They were dismayed at what they found. Stephen called St. Louis "the most immoral place I ever knew" and noted that the "Sabbath [is] a day of trade and desecration." (van Ravenswaay) The family bought a farm five miles north of town to escape some of the degradation and dedicated Sundays to gatherings of the few Protestants around. When the First Presbyterian Church was founded in November of 1817, one of the first members was Stephen's daughter, Edward's sister, Mary.

Mary Hempstead Keeny had been widowed back in Connecticut and was in her thirties when the church was founded. She would have known the French Creole elite well. Her sister, Susan, had married Henry Gratiot when she was fifteen, in 1813. (Henry was the son of Charles and Victoire Chouteau Gratiot—therefore the grandson of Marie Thérèse Chouteau and Pierre Laclède.) Edward had married into the French families as well.

Manuel Lisa certainly was a member of the Creole business elite, although it is said he kept a low social profile at times, given that his fiery presence wasn't much appreciated in the more sophisticated French circles. So, it is not surprising that he and Mary would have met. It is perhaps surprising that what records we have of such things indicate a real affection between the two.

Manuel and Mary married in August of 1818 at the hands of the new Presbyterian minister—just before the death of his daughter by Polly and with his daughter by Mitain presumably being raised by some other white family in the town. The newlyweds moved into a finely furnished brick house on Main (First) Street. And in the fall, Lisa headed northwest, perhaps to see Mitain and tell her of the new wife in the family.

We don't know for sure how Mary Lisa felt about Mitain, but she may well not have approved. The second Presbyterian missionary to arrive in the town in 1816, one Reverend Timothy Flint, railed against racial "amalgamation." (Corbett) The Presbyterian Church in Missouri actively tried to Anglicize Native Americans, as a means to saving their souls. French Creole wives might have accepted bigamy as a business practice, but it is unlikely that Presbyterian ones did.

Mary's forbearance was about to be tested. In the fall of 1819, Manuel Lisa did something no other trader had done at that point in time—at least that we have record of. He took his white wife with him to Fort Lisa for the start of the trading season. We have no record of why Mary wanted to make the arduous trip, but she is remembered as the first white woman to visit in the Native American lands. Maybe she wanted to judge the missionary imperative for herself. Maybe she was looking for a child.

THE WIVES MEET

Fort Lisa was where Mitain resided, of course, with Lisa's son, Christopher. So, Lisa sent a messenger ahead, ordering Mitain to take the lad and return to her village some sixty miles north.

The winter went reasonably well once the Omahas and other Native Americans got over the novelty of a white woman. But at some point, Lisa sent for Mitain and demanded two things: that she consider their relationship ended and that she turn over their son.

The explorer who was so impressed by the quality of Native American motherhood reported the conversation in detail, perhaps embroidering Mitain's language in translation. At first, Mitain insisted that she would remain with her son, that if Lisa indeed took him, she would follow. "I can find some hole or corner into which I may creep, in order to be near him and sometimes to see him. If you will not give me food, I will nevertheless remain until I starve before your eyes."

Lisa, as you'd expect, offered "a considerable present" if Mitain would just go away and leave Christopher. Mitain insisted that she had kept her part of the bargain; she had been faithful and borne two children in five years. She argued that she could have married an Omaha chief, but having had two children by Lisa, "what Omaha will regard me?" Mitain went to the heart of the matter. "Ours was not a marriage contracted for a season, it was to terminate only with our lives. Is not my right paramount to that of your other wife; she had heard of me before you possessed her. It is true her skin is whiter than mine, but her heart cannot be purer toward you, nor her fidelity more rigid."

We have to wonder if Mary heard all of this.

Lisa, of course, did not relent. We don't know the timing, don't know if he took possession of Christopher by force. But we do know that the matter reached the official ears of a Major O'Fallon. Our explorer reports, happily, that the major ordered "the restoration of the child to its mother and informed the trader that any future attempt to wrest it from her should be at his peril."

Mary and Manuel returned to St. Louis that spring without the child, but Lisa had contracted some illness during the winter. Soon, he made out his will, making some provision for his only two remaining offspring, Rosalie and Christopher, although it is not obvious whether his son received anything.

Manuel died on August 12, 1820. The Hempsteads steeled themselves and went to a Solemn High Mass in the St. Louis cathedral. Lisa was buried in a Hempstead plot.

We know that Rosalie lived with Mary for a time. Mary, known as "Aunt Manuel," boarded with her brothers' families at times until she died at age eighty-seven. Rosalie married a Baptist preacher, lived in Illinois, and died at age eighty-nine in 1904.

We don't know what happened to Christopher, except that he likely lived with the Omaha. He and his mother may have had some notoriety. In 1833, European visitors exploring the frontier reported seeing a woman that fit Mitain's description, notable because of the scar on her face left by her encounter with the Sioux.

THE MANY WIVES WHOSE NAMES WE DON'T KNOW

The story of Manuel Lisa and Mitain is indeed dramatic, and that is likely why it has come down through time. But it is only one of many.

Take for example, the Chouteau clan. A. P. Chouteau was Pierre Sr.'s oldest son. He went to West Point, had a brief military career, and married his first cousin, Sophie Labbadie. They had eleven children, so he must have spent some time in St. Louis. But most of his time was spent trading and living with the Osage on the Verdigris and Arkansas Rivers. He had Osage wives. In the plural.

As did his brother, Paul, who is listed as having two white wives along with Osage wives. And as did his half brother, Francois Gesseau Chouteau, who is credited with founding Kansas City.

Various other traders were known to move seasonally between their St. Louis families and their country wives. One of the more interesting traders was a trader named André Roy.

Roy had a white family who lived near St. Charles, a considerable town just northwest of St. Louis on the Missouri River. He had another family in an Ioway Native American village on the Des Moines River. When he died in 1794, he made provisions for all his children but insisted that the Ioway children move to St. Charles to claim their inheritance.

The two children and their mother, Angelique, did that. In fact, they moved close to Madame Roy, the white wife, and lived there the rest of their lives. Both Madame Roy and Angelique remarried quickly, and the Roy siblings apparently were close. They reportedly had similar status and economic success in the community.

GENTLEMEN AND HONOR IN THE BLOODY NINETEENTH CENTURY

They called it Bloody Island. For good reason.

During the first half of the 1800s, geology and men's hang-ups about "honor" provided for shockingly violent duels on a sandbar in the middle of the Mississippi River. By the time the sandbar was moved out and dueling lost popularity, important community leaders had died on the island.

But fights over "honor" did not end. Gentlemen took to the courts—and in 1882, to the *Post-Dispatch* newsroom—to settle feuds.

ROWING OUT
TO INFAMY

Here's how the honor game might play out. The first St. Louis duel involving a fatality grew out of the day in 1810 when one man went to deliver a challenge for another.

That year, an attorney named James Graham accused one Lt. John Campbell of cheating at cards. Campbell felt it necessary to challenge Graham to a duel over the insult. Dr. Bernard Farrar was to be Campbell's "second," so he sought out Graham.

Thomas Hart Benton, one of Missouri's first two senators and a deadly duelist. *Missouri Historical Society Collection*

This was part of the honor code. The seconds did the actual communication about details, made sure the weapons were equivalent, paced off the distances, and so forth. It is sometimes said the seconds had the responsibility to try to prevent bloodshed, but that must have been a fool's errand most of the time.

Ironically known for his medical skill and compassionate bedside manner, Dr. Bernard Farrar was recognized as the first permanent physician west of the Mississippi. A biographer says of Dr. Farrar that he "excelled particularly in tact, and seldom erred in prognosis . . . He was bold and decided in character and prompt in execution." All of this is said amid praise of Farrar's riding long distances to get to patients and his skill in treating them. (Scharf) But the same characteristics of boldness led Farrar to a duel.

There is some evidence that Graham and Dr. Farrar were actually friends themselves when the doctor walked in to deliver Campbell's challenge. But the friendship splintered when Graham dismissed Campbell's challenge because "Campbell was not a gentleman." Farrar was furious—this is where his tact abandoned him—and supposedly replied that it was impossible he could be the friend of a man who was not a gentleman when it came to honor. (van Ravenswaay) And with that, Farrar promptly challenged Graham himself.

We have no record of any further involvement in the duel by the Lt. Campbell who started it all. In December of 1810, the men and their seconds piled into small boats and rowed out to the sandbar that as yet had no name. As agreed beforehand by the seconds, each man was allowed three volleys.

Farrar sustained a minor graze in the buttocks at some point, but each of his own shots hit Graham, one in his leg, one in his hand, and one in his side. Farrar switched roles, became the prompt physician, and rushed to help Graham. But the ball that had entered Graham's side lodged against his spine. Despite Farrar's efforts, Graham died four months later.

Dr. Farrar went on to fight in the War of 1812 as both a physician and a soldier. He died in 1849 while fighting another kind of battle, a horrific cholera epidemic that we will explore in an upcoming chapter.

If this duel and the ensuing death seem to have arisen from a minor insult, we have more evidence that tempers and an inflated sense of honor are a bad combination. Let us set the physical and political backgrounds that made St. Louis duels noteworthy—and deadly.

A DEADLY TOWHEAD

The geology first: Sandbars popped up in the Mississippi all the time. Called "towheads," they would emerge as an underwater bump silted up. (Recall that the river is often called the "muddy Mississippi" because of the amount of silt the water carries. Mark Twain lovingly said that the Mississippi was "too thick to drink and too thin to plow.") (Primm) Over time, the towhead would attract plant life and fast-growing cottonwood trees; a small forest might grow on one. Some of the towheads got big enough to change the course of the river.

One particular Mississippi towhead evolved late in the 1700s between Illinois and Missouri, in sight of the citizens of St. Louis. Maybe one state or the other would have claimed the growing piece of land if it had seemed to have any economic value. But neither state did, meaning that neither state's laws applied to anything that happened on the mile-long by five-hundred-foot-wide sandbar.

Geological events unfolded, and the island—as yet unnamed—got large enough to block access to St. Louis' wharves. At the same time, the less sturdy shore across the way on the Illinois side was collapsing. What sounds like bad news for Illinois was actually good. It meant that the Mississippi would essentially shift its deep channel to the Illinois side, literally leaving St. Louis "high and dry."

You might be surprised to find out who rode to the rescue: Robert E. Lee.

In 1837, General Charles Gratiot was head of the Corps of Engineers—the Gratiot who was a grandson of Pierre Laclède and Marie Thérèse Chouteau. He sent one of his best men, then US Army captain and army engineer

Robert Edward Lee to address the situation, years before Lee became a general of the rebel armies in the Civil War. Lee came up with a plan: a series of underwater dikes stretching from the head of Bloody Island to the Illinois shore.

It was an immense job. Some four hundred underwater structures were built, in effect creating a man-made towhead, one that would connect the island to the Illinois side and allow the river to flow deeper and faster on the Missouri side.

It worked. By 1854, the river had moved westward and Bloody Island eventually connected itself to the Illinois shore; you pass over it today as you access the Poplar Street bridge to cross the Mississippi into St. Louis from the east.

But for the years between 1800 and 1857, Bloody Island remained the destination for mayhem and death.

GENTLEMEN AND HONOR

entlemen's duels followed a code. Two men disagreed over some matter, usually involving a public insult. One would decide to challenge
the other. The man challenged could name the weapon, likely a dueling
pistol by the 1810s. The challenged man could also name the distance the
two would stand apart when the firing began.

That was important. Sometimes the distance apart was related to the
offense: The greater the insult sustained, the closer together the men stood.
And the closer together they stood, the more likely one or both would die.
Smoothbore dueling pistols weren't very accurate at any distance. But at five
or six feet, it was hard to miss.

The day having been decided, their seconds would join the "principals"
in rowboats and head to Bloody Island, lush or latent, as the season dictated.
In the St. Louis duels, each principal brought his own physician as well.
That seems like a good idea, given the results.

Nationally, 1804 saw the country's most famous duel, between then
Vice President Aaron Burr and former Secretary of the Treasury Alexander
Hamilton. Hamilton, as the musical tells us, was killed. Duels, like the one
between Burr and Hamilton, had distinctly political origins. And that meant
the newspapers of the day were invariably involved.

In St. Louis, Joseph Charless ran the *Gazette* (which became the *Missouri
Republican*) and from its pages opposed what he called the "little junto,"
which included the old French families and their American attorneys. That
meant all the Chouteaus and their families by marriages, particularly the
Gratiots; the elder Gratiot's new friend, Thomas Hart Benton; Manuel Lisa,
who was blessedly out exploring most of the time; the Hempsteads, Lisa's

Protestant in-laws; William Clark, of Lewis-and-Clark fame and some-times-governor of the territory; and Dr. Bernard Farrar. Most of these men were united in their endless battle to secure their land claims issued under Spanish rule; many had an interest in the fur trade.

Gazette editor Charless was joined in opposition to these men by Judge J. B. C. Lucas and his son Charles; lawyer Rufus Easton; and politicians David and Joshua Barton. These men had land interests as well, but their claims were newer and depended on another geological oddity.

In late 1811 and again early in 1812, major earthquakes struck in what is now southeastern Missouri, spilling into Tennessee, Kentucky, and Arkansas. The quakes, many times larger in reach than the San Francisco earthquake less than a century later, destroyed the town of New Madrid (just north of the Missouri boot heel) and did significant damage in St. Louis. The upheaval briefly caused the Mississippi River to seem to "flow backwards" with the waves that propagated upstream.

Hard on the heels of disaster came the politics, with Congress authorizing compensation for affected landowners. Rufus Easton, one of the junto's opposition, was a territorial delegate to Congress and pushed for passage of the act.

A photograph of a miniature of Charles Lucas, who died in his second duel with Thomas Hart Benton on what would become known as Bloody Island. *Missouri Historical Society Collection*

However, word moved slowly back then to outlying communities. Members of Easton's circle appeared across the territory to buy up damaged property—probably to the delight of devastated owners who hadn't yet heard that they would be compensated by Congress. The land speculators profited nicely. Charles Lucas, the judge's son, successfully defended his claim to 640 acres, which he named Normandy. At the time, it was just rural land a few miles northwest of the town of St. Louis. Now, it's a close-in suburb in St.

Louis County that you drive through if you use Natural Bridge Road to get from downtown St. Louis City to Lambert International Airport.

Aside from the dubious nature of the land speculation, Easton's group was claiming land that many of the junto thought they controlled through the Spanish land grants. The scene was set for personal and political animosities to spill onto Bloody Island.

THE TENNESSEE BRAWLER AND THE POLISHED SCION

The name Thomas Hart Benton echoes through Missouri history, partly because there were two related men who shared that name. To halt the confusion immediately, let us note that the younger Benton, the elder's great-great-nephew, was a well-known painter; his once-controversial mural decorates the Missouri Capitol in Jefferson City.

We are chronicling Thomas Hart Benton the elder, the politician who moved to St. Louis in 1815 because a duel had soured his professional career in Tennessee. Although—duel is not quite the word and soured is an understatement when you're talking about a future president. Then General Andrew Jackson and Lt. Colonel Thomas Hart Benton had worked together raising troops for the War of 1812. Each man had exceptional qualities that would lead to them serving together in the US Senate and working together even more closely when Jackson became president in 1829. But neither could count patience, calm, or the ability to turn the other cheek among their attributes. One historian says, ". . . in capacity for blind fury, utter recklessness, and iron-willed determination, neither man had a superior." (Smith)

The relatively short version of the story is that two of Jackson's officers were readying for a duel, and Benton's brother, Jesse, was a second for one of them. In arguing over arrangements, Jesse, apparently not the calmest of men either, ended up challenging one of the officers—who was seconded by Jackson. The resulting duel was an unusually awkward affair, and Jesse ended up with an embarrassing but medically insignificant wound. Thomas Benton, who had been out of town, objected loudly and publicly, and that was enough. Andrew Jackson announced he would "horsewhip Tom Benton on sight." (Smith)

It would be an interesting matchup. Jackson was tall, but thin. Thomas Hart Benton has been described in terms of an NFL tackle. The fight never got to the dueling field. The two men, along with brother Jesse, and two large friends of Jackson met in a tavern in Nashville for something closer to a brawl. Shots were fired, the whip was brandished, and daggers and a sword cane were wielded to some effect. Thomas Benton, stabbed several times, fell down a flight of stairs, and Jackson sustained two pistol ball wounds. The future president bled enough to soak two mattresses and barely survived.

Benton recovered from his knife wounds and decided to take his law practice west, apparently realizing that the state of Tennessee wasn't big enough for two out-size personalities. In St. Louis, he immediately met and lodged with Charles Gratiot Sr., son-in-law of Pierre Laclède and Marie Thérèse Chouteau. Soon enough, Benton joined Edward Hempstead, Mary Lisa's most accomplished brother, in a law practice.

All this put Benton solidly in the "little junto" camp so opposed by *Missouri Gazette* editor Joseph Charless. Charless soon had reason to be even more irritated because Benton began editing a competing paper, the *St. Louis Enquirer*. In the courtroom, Benton, like Hempstead, was dramatic and aggressive. And to be expected, Benton crossed paths with Charles Lucas, son of Judge J. B. C. Lucas, ally of the Charless faction.

Jurors surely found Charles Lucas and Thomas Hart Benton a study in contrasts. Lucas was smooth, soft-spoken, incisive, orderly. And maybe even more self-assured than Benton. Observers thought Lucas was on his way to becoming a leading attorney in the state, even though he was only age twenty-four in the summer of 1817.

Back in October of 1816, he and Benton had essentially called each other liars in their closing statements in a Circuit Court case. Benton lost the case and challenged Lucas to a duel. Lucas responded that decisions at the bar were no reason to resort to possibly deadly private disputes. But the next summer, in the August election, it was Lucas who made it a private dispute.

Benton was getting ready to cast his ballot when Lucas questioned whether Benton had paid his taxes.

In the less democratic ways of the time, only white male taxpayers could vote, and Lucas may have had information that Benton hadn't listed his only property, three slaves, as of the deadline for voting. Benton reacted by saying he didn't have to answer to "any puppy who may happen to run across my path." (van Ravenswaay)

That did it. Lucas issued the challenge a few days later, delivered by another of the anti-junto crowd and Lucas' second, Joshua Barton. Benton was furious with the timing, because he'd just lost his friend and business partner, Edward Hempstead. (Hempstead had fallen from his horse some weeks before collapsing and dying in the courtroom.) Benton was headed to the Stephen Hempstead house just outside town when Barton arrived. But Benton accepted before he left for the funeral. Barton and Benton's second, a Col. Luke Lawless, drew up the agreement for a meeting on the island at six o'clock the next morning. Lucas wrote a farewell letter to his father to be delivered after the event.

That morning, Benton and Lucas stood thirty feet apart on land that would be known as Bloody Island very soon. At that distance, a man would have to be good with a smoothbore dueling pistol to make a true shot. Benton was known to be good, Lucas not so much so. Both fired on command.

Benton appeared unhurt, but blood bubbled from a wound in Lucas' throat. Lawless, Benton's second, asked if Lucas, the challenger, was satisfied, to which the younger man managed to agree. But Benton wasn't. Everyone was stunned. The challenged man didn't have the right to demand that the fight continue. Lucas told Barton to reload his pistol, but Lucas' doctor objected. Thirty feet away, Lawless, also a judge, was arguing with Benton, who finally agreed to another meeting if Lucas couldn't continue. Lucas agreed, was helped to his feet, and fainted. Benton probably tried not to limp to his boat; the men now noted that Lucas' shot had grazed Benton's knee.

Lucas' friends and Benton's friends engaged in what we would call "trash talk" over the next several weeks. Lawless, an Irishman who had fought with Napoleon and who was disliked by attorneys and Charless, tried to dissuade

Benton from continuing what would look like vengeance instead of a fight for honor. Lucas himself threw oil on the fire by proposing a ten-foot distance. Gossips said Benton was afraid to fight at that distance.

The conflict ebbed and flowed around potential truces. It was the gossips, seemingly intent on another meeting, who won when Benton refused a last effort from Lucas to settle the matter peaceably.

Benton took Lawless and Dr. Farrar—of the earlier duel—to the island; Lucas took Barton. Friends stood on the St. Louis riverbank awaiting the outcome.

Which was what you would expect. Benton got the first shot off, cutting through Lucas' firing arm and probably deflecting his aim, even as the shot lodged in Lucas' chest. Lucas' shot went wild.

Benton was shaken. He stepped toward Lucas and said, "Charles, it is an unfortunate affair." (van Ravenswaay) He grasped Lucas' hand, then left him to his physicians and friends. Observers on the riverbank saw Benton sitting in the rowboat with his head in his hands and Lucas' body carried to his house.

Charless was putting out the week's *Gazette*, but he surely held it for the news. Along with his praises for young Lucas and anger over the loss, the editor wrote, "Tale bearers this is thy work! Innocent blood lies at thy doors." (van Ravenswaay) Whether the gossips repented or not, the repercussions continued for years. Judge Lucas never missed an opportunity to skewer Benton publicly. And Benton apparently took the whole thing to heart. He wouldn't speak of it—until on his deathbed in 1858, when he told his son-in-law, General John Frémont, that he still regretted the episode.

But that was years later. In 1820, the new state of Missouri had to select its first two US senators, an election carried out, as all senatorial appointments were then, by members of the state legislature. Judge Lucas probably agreed to run just to thwart Benton. Benton got the minimum he needed, twenty-seven votes, and Judge Lucas got sixteen. The big winner, vote-wise, was the older brother of Joshua Barton (the Lucas second), David. As Missouri's first two senators, Thomas Hart Benton and David Barton rarely spoke and never voted in tandem.

That same year, Joshua Barton fought a duel with the late Edward Hempstead's younger brother, Thomas, known to be something of a hothead. We don't know the cause, but we know that both men missed and called the matter settled. It was probably a relief as well to Hempstead's second, Thomas Hart Benton. Joshua Barton was elected to the state legislature that year. He resigned to become Missouri's first secretary of state, and he later resigned that post to become St. Louis' first US district attorney.

But the feuds were not over, and Joshua Barton, having made two wrenching trips there, was not through with Bloody Island.

THEY CALLED IT
BLOODY ISLAND

The Benton-Lucas duels sealed it. The annoying towhead just off St. Louis' wharves was commonly called Bloody Island. It had more men to claim.

Joshua Barton, up-and-coming attorney holding state offices, was killed by Thomas Rector. Barton had been second to another young attorney, Charles Lucas. *Missouri Historical Society Collection*

THE SECOND BECOMES A PRINCIPAL

In 1823, Joshua Barton was the US district attorney for St. Louis and his brother, David, was Senator Barton. As senator, David opposed the reappointment of William Rector of St. Louis as surveyor general for Illinois, Arkansas, and Missouri, an appointment then on the desk of President James Monroe. David's opposite number, Senator Thomas Hart Benton, supported Rector. The Bartons had evidence that Rector had given family and friends contracts worth three dollars a mile to do the surveying. Those non-surveyors then sublet the jobs to real surveyors for as little as forty cents a mile, pocketing the difference.

While William Rector was in D.C. to plead his case, back home Joshua Barton wrote a letter reiterating the details of corruption to the editor of the *Missouri Republican*, the new name of the *Gazette*. William's brother, Thomas Rector, furiously issued a challenge to Joshua Barton to meet him on Bloody Island.

Some say Thomas Rector fired early. Whatever the case, Joshua Barton died on the ground where he had held his friend Charles Lucas.

The Rectors were a large family, and many were gathered across the river to watch for a signal from Thomas, which, of course, they quickly got. Rumor said the cheering Rectors held a victor's dinner that evening and boasted that the wine was Barton's blood.

The cry went up from Judge Lucas, from Barton's law partner and state Attorney General Edward Bates, and, of course, from Senator David Barton, who blamed the "junto." Meanwhile, even the support of Thomas Hart

Benton was not enough to keep William Rector in office. President Monroe withdrew the reappointment. One historian says, "the Rectors lost caste." (Scharf) William Rector never managed another public office, and Thomas died two years later, in a brawl by some reports. Public opinion had turned against the family and possibly against dueling. Unfortunately, that didn't stop the mayhem.

THE DUAL
DUEL FATALITIES

The next duel had its start in national politics, surprisingly an extension of the fight over a bank.

Alexander Hamilton had proposed what we call a central bank—think today's Federal Reserve—in 1791. Thomas Jefferson opposed it as too elite, and his followers let the bank's charter lapse in 1811. By 1816, the second Bank of the United States was chartered and headed by a man named Nicholas Biddle. That bank was opposed by another big-name president, Andrew Jackson, and his erstwhile enemy, Senator Thomas Hart Benton.

The political fight raged across the country as well as in Congress. In St. Louis, Nicholas Biddle's brother, Major Thomas Biddle, argued for the bank's rechartering. Thomas, a distinguished veteran of the War of 1812, was serving as army paymaster at Jefferson Barracks in St. Louis. He was handsome and gallant and married to a daughter of the St. Louis elite. Possibly, he had a mean streak.

Biddle exchanged fiery letters in the newspapers with Congressman Spencer Pettis. Pettis represented the Boonslick area of the state, between St. Louis and Kansas City along the Missouri River, and was a protégé of— you can guess it—Thomas Hart Benton. Pettis joined Benton in the 1830 election by crusading, in typically belligerent Pettis-Benton-Jackson fashion, against Nicholas Biddle and the bank.

In the *St. Louis Beacon*, Major Biddle called Pettis "a dish of skimmed milk." In the *St. Louis Times*, Pettis, running again for Congress, questioned the major's manhood. (Steward) That was too much for the major, apparently. When he heard that Pettis was holed up in the City Hotel in St. Louis with a "bilious" attack, Biddle found Pettis' room and beat the younger man with a cowhide whip. Pettis wanted to challenge Biddle to a duel, but Senator Benton urged his protégé to hold off, saying there wasn't enough time to field another candidate before the election. And the sympathy vote may have helped. Pettis took a large majority.

By the summer of 1831, with Pettis safely elected to Congress and having made harshly critical speeches there, the two were back at it. Pettis issued his challenge to Biddle in St. Louis. He surely couldn't have predicted the reply.

The story goes that Biddle was nearsighted and so, as the challenged man, set the distance at five feet. That meant each man would turn and fire, probably with their pistols overlapping: a suicide pact, in effect. Under the usual understanding, Pettis could have refused such insanity without loss of honor. Many have speculated that Biddle thought he would do so. But Pettis, perhaps to Biddle's surprise, agreed.

On August 26, 1831, they followed the usual routine, rowing out to Bloody Island with their seconds and surgeons. They turned and fired on the appropriate count and gave each other mortal wounds. Biddle's shot passed through Pettis' body, and Pettis died the next day. Among the men who showed up before Pettis died to pay his respects was Senator Benton. Pettis' shot had lodged in Biddle's stomach. The major died two days later.

The funerals were well-attended—including military honors for Biddle at Jefferson Barracks. The populace seemed to think the duel would surely be the last, laying to rest the city's bloody history. They were almost right.

A SLAVERY-DEBATE DUEL

But as the country pitched toward civil war in 1856, one last personal battle loomed.

Thomas Caute Reynolds was the US district attorney for St. Louis. He was an anti-Benton Democrat and a dedicated slavery man. He succumbed to exchanging barbs in the newspapers in the 1850s with one of Benton's chief supporters, Benjamin Gratz Brown.

Known as Gratz, he and Benton were not anti-slavery on humanitarian or moral grounds. They feared that if Missouri followed the Southern Democrat model, it would share the South's economic stagnation. The North's growth was fueled in part by immigrants, who would hesitate to settle where they had to compete with slave labor. Benton's position led to his defeat in 1850—after thirty years in the US Senate. Benton's anti-slavery (if not pro-Black) stance had cost him in the heavily Southern-leaning state legislature. Benton founded a new newspaper, the *Missouri Democrat*, in 1850, and by 1852, lawyer Gratz Brown was its editor. Brown was elected to the Missouri General Assembly in 1852 and 1854—where he once challenged a future governor to a duel. The man declined.

Benjamin "Gratz" Brown limped for the rest of his illustrious career, including a term as Missouri governor, because of the bullet he took in his duel with "Confederacy Governor" Thomas Reynolds. *Missouri Historical Society Collection*

After the insults started flying in 1856, Reynolds challenged Brown to a duel, but this time nearsightedness came to the rescue. Brown had the choice of weapons and chose rifles at eighty paces. Reynolds couldn't see well enough to agree to those terms and backed down.

The next year, with insults growing in intensity and Reynolds running for Congress, Brown charged Reynolds of not honoring the first challenge. Reynolds said it was Brown who was the coward. Brown challenged; Reynolds accepted.

This time, they were apparently close enough, at twenty paces, for Reynolds to see. He shot Brown in the leg. Brown missed and Reynolds walked away unharmed. Reynolds lost his congressional race; Brown limped for the rest of his life. Each continued notable political careers.

The Brown-Reynolds duel was the last big Bloody Island event. Aside from the fact that legal challenges were safer, another reason for the decline of dueling soon became obvious. Men were about to start dying for an important reason: the Civil War.

For the record, Brown veered toward Republicanism and served a standard two-year term as governor of Missouri beginning in 1870, during which time he fought off the more embittered Republicans and secured a ruling whereby former Confederates could gain amnesty.

Meanwhile, Thomas Reynolds had an even more fantastical career. He was lieutenant governor of Missouri in 1861 and was pushing hard for Missouri to join the Confederacy. When the state failed to do so, he fled to help maintain a Confederate Missouri government in exile, becoming governor of that nebulous entity in 1862. When he left in 1861, he took the Missouri State Seal with him, to bolster his claim of legitimacy, perhaps. After the war, he joined other rebels in retreating to Mexico. He came back to Missouri in 1868, returned the state seal, and was elected to the state legislature, a thing made possible by Gratz Brown's support of amnesty for former enemies.

A HISTORICAL NOTE: DID ABE LINCOLN DUEL HERE?

Occasionally, we see references to President Abraham Lincoln fighting a duel on Bloody Island, but that seems incorrect. It was more likely on a similar towhead called Sunflower Island, off Alton, Illinois. Alton lies across the Mississippi from its confluence with the Missouri River and today is in the St. Louis metro area. In 1842, Alton was a ways off. And the duel never quite materialized.

Lincoln—with assistance from his future wife, Mary Todd—had satirized in the papers one James Shields, who was the Illinois state auditor. The conflict built, Shields issued the challenge, and Lincoln accepted, specifying broadswords as the weapons. Shields was five foot, nine inches tall; Lincoln was six foot four and had an incredible reach with a sword.

On September 22, 1842, the men took a ferry—Sunflower Island boasted not only a happier name but more convenient transport—to the island. As they readied themselves, Lincoln is said to have taken a sword, reached his long arm overhead, and severed a twig from a tree branch, a reach impossible for any of the men in the party. That included Shields' second, who reportedly called his principal a little whippersnapper and threatened to turn him over his knee if he didn't call off the event. Lincoln said, rightly or wrongly, that he hadn't authored the particular note that Shields' challenge referred to, and Shields backed down amid mutual apologies.

NEWSPAPERS GET
ALL THE HEADLINES

In October of 1882, honor once again led to death. But not on the now-subsumed island. Instead, honor was satisfied in the newsroom of one of the city's battling newspapers.

Twenty years after men chose which side of the Civil War divide to occupy, those decisions structured their lives and the society they moved in. Not an urgent problem in most cities in the country, the split nature of St. Louis society left the city ripe for misunderstanding and mischief. Add to that the fact that many men carried pistols as a matter of habit.

And newspapers, of course, still anchored everyday life, activity, and talk. Talk about politics. Talk about each other. Everyone knew the editors of each paper, what stories they might run, what snide comments lurked

Alonzo Slayback, former Confederate colonel, attorney, initiator of Veiled Prophet fun, and the man who didn't survive his visit to the Post-Dispatch newsroom. *Missouri Historical Society Collection*

on page two. When you shook a paper open, the editor's personality greeted you. Maybe made you smile. Maybe annoyed you. Maybe infuriated you to the point of attack.

Four big dailies dominated the St. Louis scene in 1882, reminiscent of battles past. To understand the events of October 1882, we need a scorecard of players and teams.

First of all—literally first if you trace its roots back to the *Gazette*— there was the *Republican*. During the Civil War, the *Republican* was anti-abolitionist but came down in the center, seeking compromise with slavery to preserve the union.

After the war, the secessionist papers had largely disappeared, and those Confederate patriots who remained likely contented themselves with reading the *Republican*, as did the more conservative, old-money folks. As party politics went, it was Democratic. Confusing as that seems—and it will get worse a few lines below—recall that there was no Republican Party when the paper was named. In fact, the *Republican* was a Whig paper when the Whigs held power. The publisher/editor was William Hyde, known as a Bourbon Democrat, friendly to Southern interests.

The Republican Party was the more liberal, as we would use that word, being the party of Abraham Lincoln and the emancipation of slaves. Just to keep you on your toes, the faithfully Republican Party paper in St. Louis was the *Globe-Democrat*. It was an up-and-coming paper with a feisty editor named Joseph "Little Mack" McCullagh.

McCullagh was only nineteen years old in 1861 when he became a Civil War correspondent and gained a national reputation for aggressive reporting. His political wisdom and biting wit enlivened St. Louis for years. On what was likely a slow news day, Little Mack took on the *Republican*'s boast that it was the oldest paper in the city, dating from 1808. The *Republican* "flaunts its antiquity as proof of its sagacity, but age and experience are not always guarantees of merit." It would be appropriate, Mack said, for the *Republican* to add "B.C." to the 1808, because "the Psalms of David were published in it as original matter and it had the letter list when the Apostles were writing to each other." (Clayton)

Meanwhile, another of the leading papers was a German-language "rag," slang for newsprint and newspapers. The *Westliche Post*'s owners/editors included the first German American US senator from Missouri, Carl Schurz (later secretary of the interior) and Emil Preetorius, whose long run helped propel the *Western Post* into one of the most successful national German-language papers. It comes into our story here because in 1868, Schurz and Preetorius hired an eccentric, young, German-speaking Hungarian named Joseph Pulitzer.

THE ORIGINAL-JOSEPH PULITZER

The man whose bequests would fund the prestigious Pulitzer Prizes came to America for the bounty he could receive. During the Civil War, Union agents scoured Europe for recruits. Pulitzer, from a well-educated family, speaking German, Hungarian, and French—but not English—saw opportunity. But as he neared Boston and realized the bounty would go largely to the recruiters, he literally jumped ship and joined a Union cavalry unit, collecting the entire bounty of $200 for himself. The unit was largely German, so his limited English wasn't a problem.

It was more of a problem when he reached St. Louis in 1865, although he managed to impress almost everyone he met, some favorably, some not. Pulitzer ran through jobs from mule hostler to warden of Arsenal Island during a cholera outbreak to waiter, a job he lost when he spilled a tray of beer on a customer. Nevertheless, Preetorius was one of the German elites favorably impressed and took the chance on the twenty-one-year-old.

Pulitzer never hesitated to take a political stance as a reporter or to venture into politics himself. Not content with digging up dirt on politicians in

Joseph Pulitzer, founder of the *St. Louis Post-Dispatch*, reinventor of the *New York World*, originator of Pulitzer Prizes, and unique individual. *Missouri Historical Society Collection*

52

Jefferson City for the *Westliche Post,* Pulitzer found himself running for state office in 1869. Nominated for a seat no one thought a Republican could win, Pulitzer responded with his usual energy and took the election—even though he was technically three years too young to hold the seat. (Pulitzer later became a Democrat in New York City, as the parties shifted focus.)

The freshman—in every sense of the word—delegate immediately made a splash. The *Westliche Post* was running editorials about the St. Louis County Court, charging that the county supervisor of registration was being improperly given the contract for a new poorhouse. Pulitzer promoted a bill to repopulate the county court. That led the supervisor in question, a Captain Edward Augustine, to board a train for Jefferson City, determined to put the youngster in his place.

The story goes that Pulitzer and Augustine met in a Jefferson City hotel, and Augustine called Pulitzer a liar. Pulitzer suggested that Augustine reconsider his language. Augustine agreed and called Pulitzer a "damned liar."

Pulitzer headed to his room and came back with a revolver. Augustine upped the ante, pulling out that favorite St. Louis insult, one that had begun duels back in the day: Augustine called Pulitzer a "puppy." Literally in his face. Pulitzer was close enough with the pistol that Augustine grabbed it. The shot hit Augustine in the leg. Thanks to the intervention of new friends, Pulitzer faced only fines on an assault with intent to kill charge. And he managed to get Augustine's contract annulled.

Back in St. Louis, Pulitzer picked up a financial interest in the *Westliche Post.* But he wanted to remake the paper

John Cockerill, crusading managing editor of Pulitzer's *Post-Dispatch,* and the man who dispatched Slayback in the 1882 confrontation. *Missouri Historical Society Collection*

in a more aggressive image than Preetorius could stomach. So, the owners bought him out for $30,000. It was more than enough for Pulitzer to buy a bankrupt newspaper, the St. Louis *Dispatch.* The only thing the *Dispatch* had going for it was its Associated Press franchise. The owner of another new start-up, the *Post*, saw possibility, and the two papers consolidated as the *Post-Dispatch* in 1878. It was a chance for Pulitzer to create the paper he wanted, one that identified with neither party, one that would go after frauds and shams, a paper that would oppose the rich and support the average guy along with municipal improvements to benefit him.

Predictably, the *Post-Dispatch* was a magnet for controversy. Pulitzer is said to have been physically assaulted by Hyde of the *Republican*, but most of the sparring was in the editorial columns. Insults between the *Post-Dispatch* and the *Globe-Democrat* grew even more interesting when Pulitzer hired as managing editor John Cockerill. Cockerill had worked for Mack McCullagh in Cincinnati years before, and the two were equally masters of the nasty—and snidely humorous— editorial comment. Cockerill was from Ohio; like McCullagh, he identified with the Union.

Joseph "Mack" McCullagh, managing editor of the *St. Louis Globe-Democrat*, master of solid news and withering wit. *Missouri Historical Society Collection*

In general, the *Republican* under Hyde went after both the *Post-Dispatch* and the *Globe-Democrat* on almost any topic. The latter two papers exchanged witty snipes but saved their venom for the *Republican*, Cockerill (and Pulitzer) from a self-appointed moral vantage point, McCullagh from a dedication to covering as much news as possible as impartially as possible. All this sarcasm and name-calling was about to turn deadly in 1882.

ARMED-AND-DANGEROUS NEWSPAPERMEN

The *Republican* supported attorney Colonel James O. Broadhead in his run for Congress. Cockerill at the *Post-Dispatch* opposed him. In typical *Post-Dispatch* fashion, Cockerill touted a scandal. The paper said Broadhead had taken a $10,000 retainer from the city of St. Louis to represent it in a lawsuit against the Laclede Gas Company. Broadhead then switched sides and defended the utility. The whole affair was ten years old—but potentially criminal.

Broadhead wasn't just any attorney. He was known as the "dean" of the St. Louis bar and had served as the first national president of the American Bar Association. His complicated political stance suggests the difficult position of a split city in a border state during the war. Broadhead was a Virginian from Charlottesville, related to Patrick Henry and Dolley Madison. He believed in the institution of slavery and once said, "every damned Abolitionist in the country should be hung." (Ross) But Broadhead believed even more strongly in the preservation of the Union. In 1861, he was secretary of the Committee of Safety that gave Captain (later General) Nathaniel Lyon the go-ahead to attack Camp Jackson (chapter 9). For some months during the war, he was Provost Marshal General over several midwestern states for the Union and was said to be on good personal terms with President Lincoln. Small wonder the *Republican* supported him.

Broadhead supporters naturally resented the *Post-Dispatch* bringing up the utility lawsuit. Broadhead himself never responded to the attack, but his law partner, Colonel Alonzo Slayback, was particularly vocal. (Civil War colonels were thick on the ground in St. Louis. Even Cockerill was a colonel, but he rarely used the designation.)

Slayback was another interesting character. He was popular across St. Louis society—even the *Post-Dispatch* claimed to respect him following the event about to unfold. He had fought for the Confederacy and had spent time in New Orleans. He and his brother Charles (a Confederate general) created a St. Louis legend in 1878 when they bought costumes and props from the New Orleans Mardi Gras and talked the St. Louis elite into supporting an elaborate piece of boosterism, the annual society affair honoring the Veiled Prophet.

AN ASIDE ON A TRULY
UNUSUAL CITY EVENT

An aside on the Veiled Prophet phenomenon: The idea nominally was to provide a parade that would draw visitors to St. Louis after the harvest in October. A secret society of the St. Louis elite each year chose (chooses) a (male) member to be the prophet. The only identity revealed by the society was the first prophet, John G. Priest. According to the wonderfully wrought words of the society, Priest was a leader of the Mysterious Organization of the Veiled Prophets when it was formed in "10,842 B.C., some 294 years before the creation of the world." (Kirschten) More immediately and more importantly, Priest, a police commissioner, had led many of his fellow elite in violently putting down a strike the year before. (In fact, some see the Veiled Prophet as a political statement regarding the balance of power in the city. See chapter 18.)

While folks from the rural countryside may have enjoyed the parade, only the city elite attended the ball. At some point, the ball also became the occasion for a debutante event. In 1878, the first Belle of the Ball was Susie Slayback, Alonzo's daughter. Ironically, she wrote for the *Post-Dispatch* later in life.

As you might imagine, elites at a ball, especially one ruled over by an unnamed, masked man in sometimes-white robes, has disturbed a number of St. Louisans. In the late 1960s and 1970s, the celebration came under attack. A demonstrator once managed to infiltrate the ball, attack the dais, and unmask the prophet—who turned out to be an executive from the Monsanto company. So, actually, two prophets have been revealed. Since 1992, the event has morphed into Fair St. Louis, a Fourth of July celebration offered by a group that includes community outreach—and still hosts a ball.

AND BACK TO OUR
DEADLY TALE . . .

Specifically, let's go back to the Elks Club in 1882. Cockerill was big into the Elks, donating money for a huge statue of an elk for the nine-teenth-century location. Other members included Alonzo Slayback and General William Tecumseh Sherman. In late September, Slayback was lecturing his fellow Elks about Cockerill's attempts to "blackmail" Broadhead. In front of a crowd celebrating Broadhead's primary victory, Slayback vowed that, "If I am ever attacked in that paper in the way that my partner has been, I will go around to that office and kill the man who assails me." Cockerill, it turns out, was there and overheard; he managed to get Slayback to join him in the club's library, where Cockerill took exception to the blackmailing claim. Slayback backed down, saying that the word blackmailing "escaped me in heat"—although he had used it frequently in public. (Murder by Gaslight) The two parted peacefully, if not happily.

Slayback talked to General Sherman as well, the former Confederate officer seeking advice from one of the Union's most famous warriors. Slayback asked what Sherman knew about Cockerill, and the general is supposed to have said that he knew Cockerill's father as a "fighter" and advised, "I'm sure the son is a fighter, too." (Kirschten) Slayback would soon have reason to find out.

On October 13, the *Post-Dispatch* printed a short note saying that Slayback had attacked the paper the night before in a Democratic committee meeting. The paper also published a "card" from the year before. A "card" was a paid notice in which one gentleman could attack another in public, presumably without the need for a dueling challenge. This particular card had been published by another attorney, John Glover, who had had a confrontation with Slayback during a divorce trial. You can guess it: Slayback called Glover a puppy, among other insults. Glover was more direct. In the note, he accused Slayback of cowardice because he only issued his insults in courtrooms and such and then allowed the attacks to "vaporize."

It was an interesting tactic by Cockerill, to dredge up the card from the previous November but not to call Slayback a coward himself. Slayback read it as a direct insult from Cockerill. We have what happened next from the *Post-Dispatch*'s pages the following day.

About five o'clock that afternoon, Slayback asked his friend, another attorney by the name of W. H. Clopton, to accompany him to the *Post-Dispatch* office, where Slayback intended to confront Cockerill over the re-publishing of Glover's card. Clopton may or may not have been the best second; he had whipped a fellow attorney with a cowhide about a week before. Everyone agreed that Slayback burst into Cockerill's office without knocking, Clopton on his heels. Everyone agreed that Slayback said, "Well, I am here, sir." In the office with Cockerill, discussing advertising, was the paper's business manager, John McGuffin, and press foreman, Victor Cole.

From that point on, Clopton's version of events differs from what McGuffin and Cole had to say. The two *Post-Dispatch* men said Slayback pulled back his coat and drew a gun. They said Cockerill repeatedly told Slayback to stop and to back off, but they agreed that Cockerill picked up his own gun, which was on the table in front of him. Slayback said something along of the lines of "Is that for me?" and Cockerill replied that he would use it only in self-defense. Clopton also said Cockerill picked up the gun but denied that Slayback even had a gun. He believed Slayback was removing his coat preparatory to hitting Cockerill. Slayback and Clopton advanced on Cockerill, who was backed into a corner. One shot was fired. By Cockerill. The bullet took Slayback in the chest, but he may have stayed on his feet for a minute or two.

McGuffin closed in. He said he took the pistol from Slayback, who was apparently about to collapse, and put the pistol's barrel to Clopton's head to get him to back off Cockerill. Clopton turned to Slayback and helped ease the man to the floor. Cockerill rushed to help as well. But Slayback died within minutes.

It didn't take much longer than that for word to spread. A doctor arrived; the mortuary people arrived. Cockerill went home to change bloodstained clothes and then turned himself in to police, pleading self-defense. Someone called Joseph Pulitzer, who was in New York City at the time, to give him the news. The *Post-Dispatch* had already hit the streets for the day, but its editors began putting together the columns of explanation that would fill its pages the next day.

The *Republican* went wild with its denunciation of the *Post-Dispatch*, demanding Cockerill's head for murder, bemoaning the family's loss and the city's loss of a long-standing and beloved citizen. Slayback left a wife and six children, with Susie Slayback the eldest. The funeral drew thousands to its procession.

Cockerill expressed remorse, noted his friendship with Slayback, and insisted he'd acted in self-defense. A friend of Cockerill wrote that he suspected Clopton was behind the event, Clopton clearly being less popular than Slayback.

It was Clopton's word against McGuffin's and Cole's about whether Slayback had a gun. A pawnbroker is said to have identified the gun McGuffin said he took from Slayback's hand as one he had sold to Slayback earlier in the year. The *Globe-Democrat* weighed in with many words, including a surprisingly modern-sounding diatribe against men carrying guns: It was uncivilized, according to Mack McCullagh.

McCullagh, of course, also took on the *Republican*, which he said seemed determined to try the case in its pages. Within a couple of days, McCullagh wrote, "The evidence is all in, according to this high authority, and the summing up is done in two badly-written paragraphs in yesterday's issue, composed in equal parts of personal malice and distorted facts." Little Mack waxed eloquent on the tragedy. "We do not believe in trial by newspaper . . . and least of all in a condemnation in which personal spite against the living is arrayed in the false garb of sympathy for the dead."

In the end, a grand jury did the deciding, not the *Republican*, and returned no charges against Cockerill. By that time, though, the *Post-Dispatch* was taking a financial hit from withdrawn advertising. Crowds stormed the paper's building, threatening to burn it down.

Joseph Pulitzer, who was busy revitalizing the *New York World*, moved Cockerill to New York to help manage that endeavor. The *World* became a bigger, maybe brasher, version of the *Post-Dispatch* and made journalism history. Later in the decade, Cockerill famously hired Nellie Bly, the early female reporter who made a trip around the globe that contributed to the *World*'s fame. Cockerill switched to a rival paper in the 1890s and became a foreign correspondent, dying of a stroke in 1896 in Cairo, Egypt. His body was brought back to St. Louis' Bellefontaine Cemetery to lie in the Elks section.

Broadhead was elected to Congress, served one term, worked in the Grover Cleveland administration, and became minister to Switzerland. He was also buried in Bellefontaine after his death in 1898.

A society woman in St. Louis had written to her brother in the midst of the shooting debate, saying that if the affair "closes the career of that scurrilous sheet it will be a life well spent." (Krewson) But the *Post-Dispatch* persevered and regained its circulation. The *Republican*'s successor, the *St. Louis Republic*, gave up the ghost in the nineteen-teens. For years, St. Louisans read the *Globe-Democrat* in the morning and the *Post-Dispatch* in the evening. That ended with the shuttering of the morning paper in the 1980s. The *Post-Dispatch* remained in the Pulitzer family as the one surviving St. Louis daily until 2005; the chain Lee Enterprises took over at that point.

SLAVERY AND
IMMIGRANTS AND WAR

Early nineteenth-century St. Louis was not only a melting pot of French, Spanish, and Americans from the colonial era. It was a melting pot of immigrants, including large German and Irish populations. It was also a melting pot of Native American slaves, Black slaves, freed local slaves, suing-to-be-free Black women, and freed mulattos who worked the docks.

We'll see here stories sampling the statuses of slaves. And, then we'll move on to the names that moved the country closer to civil war: Lovejoy and Lawless, Francis McIntosh, and Dred Scott.

By the 1850s, St. Louis was seething with battles between nativist and immigrants and between free and slave forces. All of that would stir the toxic brew of war that only a border state could support.

DESPERATELY
SEEKING FREEDOM

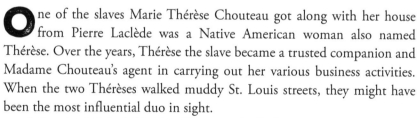

One of the slaves Marie Thérèse Chouteau got along with her house from Pierre Laclède was a Native American woman also named Thérèse. Over the years, Thérèse the slave became a trusted companion and Madame Chouteau's agent in carrying out her various business activities. When the two Thérèses walked muddy St. Louis streets, they might have been the most influential duo in sight.

At her death, Marie Thérèse Chouteau freed Thérèse, leaving her money; flour, which functioned as money in currency-strapped St. Louis; and a cow and calf. Madame Chouteau most definitely did not free the African American slaves who had worked her land and maintained her home.

Slave stories were almost all dismal, but some played out better than others.

Jean Pierre Chouteau Sr., son of Pierre Laclède and Marie Thérèse Chouteau, and cruel slave master. *Missouri Historical Society Collection*

JEANETTE AND ESTHER AND HANNAH–OF WHOM WE KNOW TRAGICALLY LITTLE

Jeanette Forchet is an example of the varying status that Blacks and Native Americans had in St. Louis. She was known as a free Black woman, but the word "free" carries qualifications.

She and her first husband, Gregory, got one of the original grants of a house lot on Church Street and a lot in the common farmlands from Pierre Laclède in 1765. That means their house stood on one of the valuable pieces of land in the center of the city. Gregory blacksmithed and Jeanette may have taken in washing and practiced folk medicine—along with farming their lot. The couple had two sons and two daughters there, but Gregory died in 1770.

Jeanette married another free Black, named Valentin, also a blacksmith. But he was a trapper as well and died in 1789 on a hunting trip. He left behind a debt to a wealthy French merchant. Jeanette had to mortgage the house and some personal property to make the payment.

By that time, two children had died and one son was in New Orleans. That left Jeanette and her daughter Susanna to pay off the mortgage, which they managed to do within eight years. When Jeanette died in 1803, she left the house free and clear to Susanna. It was valuable property, later subdivided and sold to the benefit of Susanna's descendants. Susanna's daughter married Antoine Labbadie, a wealthy free Black man.

This sounds like a success story, and it is, as far as it goes. But it's notable for what Jeanette and her family couldn't do: leave what was then a small town without permission from the authorities. When Valentin went on his fatal fur-trapping expedition, he had to have gotten permission from the Spanish governor's office.

And, if it sounds like the family lived orderly lives, the fact was, they had to do so. "Free Black" would have meant they were manumitted slaves, freed by some owner along the way—easier to manage on the frontier than in the South. But manumitted slaves could be re-enslaved for any minor infraction of the law. And judging by stories of early St. Louis, infractions of the law were common enough.

Finally, there were the subtle social distinctions. Marie Thérèse Chouteau carried the title "Veuve," French for widow. It was a title that implied the social standing of a woman who now controlled the remaining family wealth. Jeanette Forchet could not be called "Veuve Forchet," because she was Black. Subtle. But a powerful reminder of social status in a small community.

Esther was a Black woman who became free, but her story is more disturbing because it involves Jacques Clamorgan, and most stories of Jacques Clamorgan are disturbing, if colorful. Clamorgan had Welsh ancestors who had landed in the West Indies, where Clamorgan was born. His fast talking financed the Missouri Company's early explorations of the upper Missouri River. It was a success in terms of mapping the territory but a financial disaster. Clamorgan always had another plan up his sleeve, though, and seemed able to convince Spanish authorities of its worth. The Chouteaus and their influential in-laws never accepted Clamorgan, in part because of his flamboyance and dubious business dealings, but also because he lived with mulatto women he didn't bother to marry.

One of those women was named Esther; Clamorgan had obtained her in payment for a debt owed him. For whatever reason, Esther presented a more suitable face to the community than Clamorgan's other women. She took on the duties of a proper colonial wife. In turn, Clamorgan purchased Esther's daughter, Sally, who came to live with them.

When Clamorgan got worried about one of his risky financial ventures—which was likely most of them—he came up with a plan. If Esther were a free Black woman, she could own property, as Jeanette Forchet did. So Clamorgan freed Esther and transferred some of his property deeds to her, reasoning that that would protect them from creditors. In the bargain, he also signed Sally over to her mother.

Esther promptly began to treat the property as her own and resisted Clamorgan's control. In fact, she left him when he became even more abusive. The Spanish administration backed her land claim and her freedom. And the Americans would have done so in 1804 if they were sure that the claims had been in place for ten years, which they had been. But Clamorgan is said to have done what was necessary at the recorder's office to sign the deeds back to himself, forging Esther's name. Esther was unaware of this piece of fraud for a while; when she found out, she battled not only Clamorgan's actions but also what she considered fraud on the part of her white attorney.

Esther is said to have spent the rest of her life fighting Clamorgan and his heirs in court. She managed to keep a house at Third and Poplar and a large tract of land. That property, along with long-pending lawsuits, she left to her grandchildren.

Not an ideal outcome, but for St. Louis Blacks—and especially for Black women—the courts were the only answer.

Hannah, the only name we have, was a Black slave. We know that she was married and had "a number" of children. She may have belonged at one time to a family in Washington, D.C. By 1834, however, she and her husband had the misfortune to belong to one Major William Harney.

Harney, later General Harney, could be a character in a number of scandals. He was known in the army for courage and incompetence and cruelty. Active in the Native American conflicts in the upper Midwest, he had a child with a Winnebago woman named Ke-sho-ko, Mary Caroline Harney, born around 1830. Stories of Harney at that time include him beating one of the camp's hunting dogs that took an unfortunate shortcut across a vegetable garden. (Harney did more damage to the vegetables chasing the animal.)

Another time, Harney severely flogged a civilian who had sold liquor to a soldier. Later, in St. Louis, he beat an auctioneer who had the audacity to suggest that a picture of President Andrew Jackson wasn't worth much.

In January of 1833, Harney had been transferred to St. Louis and married Mary Mullanphy, daughter of Irish immigrant and St. Louis' first millionaire, John Mullanphy. In 1834, the Harneys accused Hannah of hiding a set of keys. Hannah claimed no knowledge of the missing keys, which triggered Major Harney's fury. According to a published report, Harney tied Hannah up for three days, returning each day to whip her, until she died. The coroner's jury, which held an inquest at the house, ruled that it was impossible to say whether the damage had been done by a whip or a hot iron because her flesh was so badly lacerated.

At some point during the torture, Harney suspected Hannah's husband of telling neighbors what was happening. So, Harney took to torturing the husband as well. But the man escaped. According to a St. Louisan writing to a friend in New York, the husband ran into the Mississippi and drowned himself. "The man was a pious and very industrious slave, perhaps not surpassed by any in this place," according to the letter writer. (Weld)

The jury heard testimony from a physician and witnesses and found that Hannah "came to her death by wounds inflicted by William S. Harney." A grand jury indicted Harney for Hannah's death, but Harney didn't stay around to face justice. He fled to D.C., returning when he thought Judge Luke Lawless, of whom you can read more below, would be likely to move the case from St. Louis, where Harney's reputation for violence was palpable. Lawless did that, and a judge in Union, Missouri, acquitted Harney in March of 1835.

Harney's military career took him west, where he was known to be equally cruel in fighting Native Americans. He was back in St. Louis in 1860, in command of the Department of the West, just in time to get involved in the little matter of Camp Jackson and the St. Louis Arsenal. That was the military encounter that kept Missouri out of the Confederacy; see chapter 9 for details.

THE SCYPIONS V. CHOUTEAU

This multigenerational story starts with legalities in 1805—although we could really trace it back to the founding days of St. Louis when a pioneer named Joseph Tayon moved with his family and slaves across the river from Illinois Territory. One of those slaves was Marie Jean Scypion, the daughter of a Black slave we know only as Scypion and a Native American mother captured during a fight between tribes and sold into slavery.

When the Spanish took over the former French territory, they issued an edict prohibiting Indian slavery. They may have been stunned by the fierce French reaction, and, in fact, relented to the extent of insisting that owners of Native American slaves could continue their ownership but couldn't transfer those people—usually women—to another owner. In the lawsuits the Scypions would pursue, until a final decision in 1838, they always based their claims on their Native American heritage.

Marie Jean was a force to be reckoned with by all accounts. She was a cook and housekeeper but got out and around enough that there were folks in St. Louis who doubted her slave status. She had three daughters while working for the Tayons, and Spanish rules or no, saw the two older girls given to two of Tayon's daughters. Her youngest daughter stayed with her mother and the Tayon family.

That turned out to be unfortunate because, when his wife died, Joseph Tayon took his slaves and moved into Pierre (Sr.) Chouteau's large home. (That relationship centered on the Tayons having raised the orphaned Pelagie Kiersereau, Pierre Sr.'s first wife.) The unfortunate part was the temperament of Pierre Sr. While both he and his half brother Auguste were known to be cruel slave masters, Pierre Sr. had more of a temper.

In 1799, Joseph Tayon up and decided to sell Marie Jean, now aged, and all three of her daughters. But, of course, the Tayon daughters refused to release the Scypion daughters. The lieutenant governor of the region said that the women couldn't be sold because of their Native American heritage. We can imagine the renewed uproar in French Creole households, and, in fact, Auguste Chouteau is said to have approached one of the Tayon daughters to suggest that she keep the matter private. She responded by testifying in court that Auguste Chouteau's own Native American slaves weren't seeking their freedom because Chouteau whipped them when they suggested they might do so.

The Tayon sisters managed to keep the Scypion sisters, and one of them took in the ill Marie Jean, where the elderly woman died in 1802. A Tayon brother took possession of the third Scypion daughter and the children she now had.

The Scypion sisters filed for freedom in the new American system in 1805. The judges hearing the case were J. B. C. Lucas and Rufus Easton— both opponents, you might recall—of the junto that included the Chouteaus. Considering affidavits from the Tayon daughters saying the two women were free Indians who lived voluntarily with the families, the judges freed the women. This is one of the incidents that led to the hard feelings between the junto and anti-junto parties and led to Charles Lucas' dueling death.

The sisters' freedom didn't last long because Tayon and Chouteau continued the legal maneuvering, including a jury trial in 1806—one in which St. Louis whites testified because "persons of color" couldn't testify against a white person in court. Pierre Chouteau got his brother-in-law onto the jury, and the expected happened. The jury ruled against the Scypions. Soon after the verdict, Joseph Tayon sold the Scypion girls and their children to Pierre Chouteau for $1,142.

You would think the legal battles would have ended there. In fact, it is not obvious how Marie Jean's descendants managed to communicate with each other, any more than she had been able to communicate with her enslaved daughters. But a new law in Missouri gave the family hope and communicate they did.

In 1824, the Missouri General Assembly passed a law saying that slaves who claimed to be held illegally could sue for their freedom "as poor persons." That meant the court would provide free legal counsel, guarantee their right to communicate with that counsel, and order that the "poor persons" not be mistreated or removed from the jurisdiction while the case was pending.

The Scypions' new suit bounced back and forth between the St. Louis Circuit Court and the Missouri Supreme Court. One of the sisters' appointed counsels, Hamilton Gamble, went on to serve as a chief justice of the Missouri high court and as governor. Pierre Chouteau responded by hiring Luke Lawless and Henry Geyer. Lawless was famously racist, as we will see. Geyer would go on to argue before the US Supreme Court against freedom for St. Louisans Dred and Harriet Scott.

And it wasn't just the freedom issue at stake. Pierre Chouteau had reacted so violently against one of the Scypion sisters—now a grandmother—that she sued him in court. One day in April 1825, she claimed, he had beaten her and put her in confinement for a month. She and her attorneys charged him with trespass and assault and battery and sought $500 in damages. A judge required a surety bond from Chouteau to make sure he allowed the woman and her family to see their attorney during the proceedings. It must have been tense in the Chouteau household, because Lawless and Geyer managed to delay the trial. Then they got a favorable verdict that hinged on controversial instructions from the judge.

The Scypions again waited, in bondage, for favorable legal help. They didn't get it until 1834 when a new member of the Missouri Supreme Court helped rule that the judge's instructions were faulty. Thirty years after Marie Jean Scypion had sued for her freedom, a trial took place in 1836 in Herculaneum, a town about halfway south to Ste. Genevieve, on a change of venue. By now, it was Joseph Tayon's son, seventy-three years old, who was testifying, and the estate of one of the Tayon daughters that was a defendant.

The jury freed every "poor person of color" involved. It also found for the Scypion sister in her suit against Pierre Chouteau but granted her only a penny of the $500 she had sought. Appeals went on for another two years, but the verdicts stood. Another of the daughters didn't live to see the final victories, but Marie Jean Scypion would have been proud of all her daughters, who never gave up their fight.

NAMES THAT DEFINE US

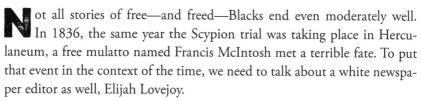

Not all stories of free—and freed—Blacks end even moderately well. In 1836, the same year the Scypion trial was taking place in Herculaneum, a free mulatto named Francis McIntosh met a terrible fate. To put that event in the context of the time, we need to talk about a white newspaper editor as well, Elijah Lovejoy.

And then there is the St. Louis story familiar from history books: Dred and Harriet Scott sued for their freedom in the city; by the time the case went to the Supreme Court, it helped trigger the Civil War.

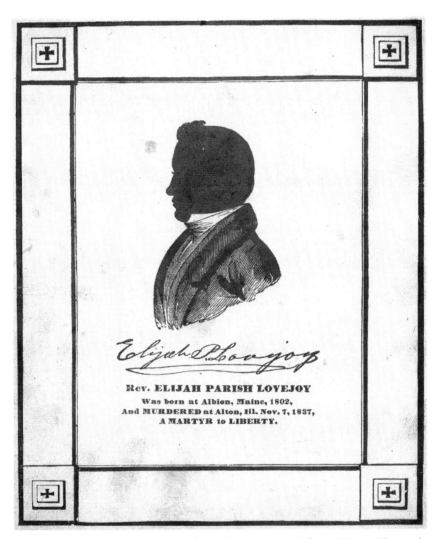

Memorial card for Elijah Lovejoy, proclaiming him a Martyr to Liberty. *Missouri Historical Society Collection*

AN IRONIC OPPOSITION OF NAMES: LOVEJOY VERSUS LAWLESS

Elijah Lovejoy came from Maine, as did many Easterners who fancied that the West was where the battle over the nation's future would be fought—the East having hardened into its own versions of good and evil. Certainly, the West was being built by aggressive young men. From a religious family and college-educated, Lovejoy began editing the *St. Louis Times* when he was twenty-seven years old. The paper allied with relatively liberal causes, opposed Andrew Jackson, and supported the Missouri Compromise—of which more below. The men Lovejoy associated with in St. Louis hadn't yet gotten to the point of calling themselves abolitionists, but they were looking for ways for the United States to move gradually beyond slavery. Some of them favored helping slaves return to homelands in Africa.

A group of these men said they would finance a Presbyterian newspaper if Lovejoy would edit it. They didn't have to ask twice.

Lovejoy printed his first edition of the *St. Louis Observer* in November 1833 and began a crusade on several fronts. He railed against the use of tobacco and liquor and the worship practices of the Roman Catholic Church. Over the next several years, he became the area's loudest abolitionist voice, managing to infuriate both the pro-slavery faction and the moderate, gradual-abandonment-of-slavery folks.

For Lovejoy, the issues mattered in their own right, but freedom of the press mattered as well. He contended that he had the right to express himself regardless if the Catholic Church was really evil. Or if slavery was really evil.

That stance got him in trouble with two groups. One was the vigilante committees who sought out insurrectionist ideas; a mass meeting of such men in late 1835 condemned Lovejoy's writing. Maybe worse, the men who had asked him to edit the paper—men who touted the gradual route—abandoned him.

And then there was Luke Lawless, Thomas Hart Benton's second back in 1817. By now, he was Judge Lawless—one of the most ironic names in St. Louis annals. For one thing, freedom of the press irritated him, probably because newspapers routinely criticized his conduct on the bench. In March of 1836, the *Missouri Republican*, a long way from being a gadfly like the *Observer*, had called Lawless out for his, uh, lawless approach to the law. He filed suit asking for $10,000 in damages. (That's more than a quarter million in current dollars.) The *Republican* argued that its editorial couldn't be libel because it was true. It took the jury five minutes to agree. Sixteen members of the St. Louis bar asked that Lawless not be reappointed, but the governor did so anyway—leaving Lawless on the bench for the upcoming showdown.

Lovejoy had choice words for Judge Lawless, but more for slavery. "It presses like a nightmare on the body politic," he said, implying something dire for the large majority of St. Louisans who supported slavery. "The time is coming when we will be tried by fire," he wrote. "As surely as there is a thunderbolt in Heaven and strength in God's right hand to launch it, so surely will it strike the authors of this cruel oppression." (Tabscott)

It's not hard to understand that each time a slavery-related incident erupted, there were threats to destroy the *Observer* office and to attack Lovejoy himself. The most violent of those events flared into history on April 28, 1836.

Francis McIntosh, of Pittsburgh, Pennsylvania, was a free mulatto working as a cook on a steamboat docked on the St. Louis wharf. On the afternoon of the twenty-eighth, he was arrested by a deputy constable named Mull for helping two of the boat's deckhands escape capture. A magistrate ordered McIntosh to jail to await trial, and Mull had the job of escorting him there. A deputy sheriff named Hammond appeared to assist Mull. When McIntosh asked what the sentence would be for such a crime, Hammond threw out a harsh number. Some have reported it as five years. Another source says Hammond told McIntosh he would be hanged.

McIntosh drew a knife and attacked. He stabbed Mull in the side and Hammond in the neck. Hammond was dead within a few steps, and Mull collapsed not long after, but enough men were nearby to chase down McIntosh. They got him to the jail, where a Sheriff Brotherton locked him up—but he had to know trouble was brewing outside. A crowd followed the body of Hammond as it was carried to his home and saw the distress of his wife and children. Others carried Mull from the scene, assuming he would die as well. (We don't know that he did.) And then the crowd turned its attention to the jail. And became a mob.

Brotherton didn't hold out long, given that his family lived in the building housing the jail. After he left through a back door, the mob broke down the jail door. They pulled McIntosh from the jail and dragged him four blocks west to what was then open land at Tenth and Market Streets. If there was a discussion about hanging versus burning, supporters of burning won the day.

McIntosh was chained to a black locust tree, and boys sprinted about collecting wood scraps and shavings. The fire was lit, some say by Hammond's fourteen-year-old son.

There were those who objected. Joseph Charless Jr., son of the *Gazette* publisher, had a friend hoist him on his shoulders, the better to be heard as he begged the mob to stop. Another young man, an Easterner apparently appalled that stories of the West were true, begged someone to shoot McIntosh—as McIntosh was asking as well. A city alderman countered the calls for mercy, threatening to shoot anyone who attempted to free or shoot McIntosh.

Witnesses said it took about twenty minutes for McIntosh to die. Even at the time, St. Louisans knew it would take years for the story to die. The *Missouri Republican* the next day pleaded with the city to keep the matter quiet.

Elijah Lovejoy was out of town at the time, but he found the spot the next day and promptly wrote, "We stood and gazed on the blackened and mutilated body of McIntosh." Admitting that there was provocation for the violence, he nevertheless asserted, "When constitutional law and order are at stake, when the question lies between justice regularly administered or the wild vengeance of a mob, there is but one side on which to rally. We must stand by the law or all is lost." (Tabscott)

The law was about to be tested. The men who had led the attack were readily identified, and an inquest was called in May, with Judge Luke Lawless presiding. In his closing remarks, Lawless attacked the *Observer* as "the source of all unrest and its editor as the sanctimonious extremist who had incited McIntosh to violence"—even though Lovejoy hadn't been in town that day and it is unlikely McIntosh knew of the young editor. Lawless went on to say that the jury might find against a small number of individuals, but that, "if the destruction was the act of the multitude . . . seized upon and impelled by that mysterious, almost electric frenzy . . . then I say, act not at all, for the case transcends your jurisdiction." (Tabscott) The jury apparently decided on the side of frenzy and issued no indictments.

Lovejoy's special edition the next day was eloquent. He even went so far as to say, "Better that the office of *The Observer* be scattered to the four winds, that the editor be chained to the same tree as McIntosh and share his fate, than that the doctrines promulgated by Judge Lawless become prevalent in the community." (Tabscott) In fact, he went further, chalking up Lawless' twisted logic—that abolitionists were responsible for the Black man's death—to Lawless' Irish ancestry and Catholicism. "Lawless is a Papist," Lovejoy wrote, "and in his Charge we see the cloven foot of Jesuitism, peeping out." (van Ravenswaay)

In the same issue, Lovejoy announced that he was leaving St. Louis, that he would move the *Observer* across the river to Alton, Illinois, which, if not friendly to abolitionists was at least in a free state, not a slave state. Actually, the town of Alton was divided on the issue. Many citizens were pro-slavery, but the town hosted a stop on the Underground Railroad.

Lovejoy barely made it out of St. Louis. One of Lawless' mobs, perhaps in a frenzy over the anti-slavery remarks if not the Papist ones, broke into the *Observer* office and thoroughly vandalized it. When Lovejoy got his family's possessions down to the wharves, a mob attacked and dumped everything in the Mississippi.

Lovejoy managed to get his press crated and moved upriver. But it arrived on a Sunday, so workers left it sitting on the riverbank. It was torn apart by an Illinois mob and thrown in the river. Lovejoy seemed to dial his rhetoric down a bit, and the city bought him a new press.

But soon enough, Lovejoy found a way to irritate Illinois. In March of 1837, the national economy plunged. Unrest and vagrancy followed the economic collapse in St. Louis. In Alton, Lovejoy suggested that the financial panic was heaven-sent. The *Missouri Republican* suggested that Alton should expel all the anti-slavery types in the name of harmony.

In August, a mob broke into the *Observer* office and destroyed the press. The Alton mayor tried and failed to stop the men but promised to protect the new press that would arrive in September. The mayor ended up watching a mob obliterate that press the evening it was delivered—the third press Lovejoy had lost, if you're keeping count.

In October, Lovejoy was in St. Charles, on the west side of St. Louis, where his mother-in-law was tending to his ill and pregnant wife. Her name was Celia Ann French, and the couple, married in 1835, had a young son, who was present. When two men ran in and seized Lovejoy, Celia Lovejoy went on the attack, and the intruders fled the house but joined others in the yard. Elijah's friends convinced him to slip away, and he did, making it back across the river to Alton.

In November, matters came to a head when the fourth press arrived and was stored temporarily in a warehouse on the river. Soon enough, a crowd of armed men surrounded the warehouse and demanded to have the machine. Lovejoy, the owners of the warehouse, and supporters were armed as well. The mayor went inside under a white flag and tried negotiating for some time, but Lovejoy held fast.

Soon alarm bells were sounding, men with ladders were climbing on the roof to set it afire, and a gunfight ensued. When things quieted for a moment, Lovejoy stepped outside. He was shot five times but managed to run back into the warehouse, where he died. The other defenders ran away; the mob threw the press out a window and tossed shattered parts in the river. Just to make sure.

As in St. Louis, the Alton mob was made up of well-recognized prominent citizens. Among the eleven charged in Alton—and acquitted, of course—were a prominent merchant, two physicians, and a future mayor.

If anyone in the country had missed the story of Francis McIntosh, they now heard the story of the abolition movement's first martyr. National, and particularly Northern, watchers condemned the actions and the legal proceedings. The defense in the Alton case provided the counterargument: The citizens of the two locales valued "good order" over freedom of the press and the rights of Blacks.

Lovejoy was buried on his thirty-fifth birthday in an unmarked grave in Alton. His body was later recovered and interred in Alton's City Cemetery, marked by a 110-foot-tall monument. Someone even dredged the last press out of the river, and part of it is on display in Alton. In the years since, the journalism profession has honored Lovejoy for his stand on press freedom, but in 1837, the man he inspired most was not a journalist. It is said that John Brown, on hearing of Lovejoy's death, dedicated himself to the elimination of slavery. It was a course that led to Harpers Ferry and war.

DRED–AND DON'T FORGET HARRIET–SCOTT

By 1818, Missouri was seeking statehood—as a slave state. That would have upset the balance between slave and free states in the Senate, where Henry Clay proposed a Compromise. One of many compromises brokered in Congress over the years, this one was important enough to get a capital "C." Commonly called the Missouri Compromise, it might well have been named the Missouri-Maine Compromise. The state of Maine was carved out of Massachusetts territory and entered as a free state to balance Missouri's entrance as a slave state. But the legislation went beyond that. It ordered that there could be no more slave states west and north of Missouri in the Louisiana Purchase territory.

Southern interests said every new state should be able to choose its status; growing abolition sentiment in the North opposed slavery anywhere. The Compromise held for about thirty years. The final nail in its coffin was a slave freedom case that originated in St. Louis.

In the 1830s, a family named Blow brought a slave named Sam from Virginia when they made the journey west. The father of the family died in 1832. One of his daughters married Joseph Charless Jr., the son of the *Gazette* editor and the man who tried to stop the McIntosh burning. Charless became executor for the Blow estate and saw to the education of the younger sons, including twelve-year-old Taylor Blow. In the financial arrangements that followed, Sam was sold to Dr. John Emerson, an army surgeon stationed at Jefferson Barracks in St. Louis.

Dred and Harriet Scott were the subjects of lawsuits that went from St. Louis to the Supreme Court, where the ruling that they must remain slaves helped trigger the Civil War. *Missouri Historical Society Collection*

Dr. Emerson took Sam with him as a valet, first to an assignment in Illinois and later to a post, Fort Snelling, in what is now Minnesota. Several major events in Sam's life came out of the Minnesota stint. At least one historian claims that Sam became "Great Scott" because of the teasing of Fort Snelling soldiers after a visit by General Winfield Scott, another Virginian. Great Scott, one of the general's nicknames and then the slave's nickname, morphed into Dred Scott by the time Sam/Dred and Dr. Emerson returned to St. Louis.

Also, at Fort Snelling, Sam/Dred met a slave woman named Harriet. When he announced he wanted to marry her, a civil ceremony was performed. That was unusual, and the ceremony was used later to imply that her owner intended to free Harriet. One way or the other, she accompanied the men back to St. Louis. On the trip, a daughter was born, specifically on a steamboat headed down the Mississippi. Arguments broke out years later on whether the boat had passed the Iowa/Missouri state line at the time. It made the difference in whether the daughter was born in a free state or a slave state. A second daughter was born a couple of years later in St. Louis.

It gets complicated here, but when Dr. Emerson died, Mrs. Emerson headed east. She left Dred and Harriet working for wages in St. Louis and gave agency of them to her brother John Sandford. It is believed that Dred Scott sought out the Blow family, and they suggested he and Harriet sue for their freedom. The Scotts had lived in free states for some time, and the argument had worked for many others.

But 1846 was not 1824. Pro-slavery rallies filled the streets in St. Louis near what is now called the Old Courthouse but was then brand new. The Missouri Supreme Court that had overseen the freeing of a good number of St. Louis slaves, such as the Scypion sisters, had hardened in its opinion. The case argued in the Old Courthouse granted the two, and therefore their daughters, freedom, but the state Supreme Court reversed the decision.

As most students learn in school, the case of Dred and Harriet Scott went to the US Supreme Court, likely as a test case. There were grounds on which the case could have been ignored or decided by precedent, but the SCOTUS had an agenda as well. The nation waited for this one decision in particular, and when the decision in *Dred Scott v. Sandford* was announced, it became the prelude to war. In 1857, the court's majority ruled that the Missouri Compromise was unconstitutional because it violated the right to hold property under the Fifth Amendment in the Bill of Rights. The nation's highest court had announced that slaves were property, regardless of where they lived. And the Civil War became inevitable.

Back home in St. Louis, irony intervened. Because John Sandford had died within weeks of the Supreme Court decision, the Scotts supposedly answered to Irene Emerson. But she had remarried to, of all people, a physician and abolitionist named Chaffee who had just been elected to Congress as a Republican. He tried to cover up his wife's involvement in the Scott case, but word got out. Because Chaffee was a resident of Massachusetts, he couldn't free a slave in Missouri. Finally, someone remembered the Blow family.

The Blow family, led now by the grown Taylor Blow, managed to buy the Scott family and promptly freed them. Dred died a year later, but Harriet worked as a laundress, survived the upsets of the war, and listed herself in the City Directory until 1870, by which time she had apparently passed away. Her descendants lived in St. Louis well into the twentieth century.

In a tragic footnote, Joseph Charless Jr., the husband of Charlotte Blow, the son of the *Gazette* editor, a co-founder of Washington University, and the man who tried to turn the mob from burning McIntosh, was shot and killed on Market Street in 1859, by a man he had had to testify against in a lawsuit. Ironically, city authorities had to call out the military to keep a mob from lynching the killer—who was later hanged legally. In a sad but hopeful footnote, Charlotte Blow Charless started a home for aged and poor women who no longer had families. Today it is the Charless Home for senior living in Carondelet.

IMMIGRANT WARS

The news media are in wild competition, each one staking out a defiant point on the political spectrum. The breaking news asks questions that arouse citizens' passions. How secure are the ballot boxes? When will the streets be safe from rioters? How are the police reacting and whose police are they, really? What about all these immigrants in our midst? Are they going to try to *vote*?

True today. True in the two decades leading up to the Civil War. St. Louis put its particular stamp on these events.

The National Guards (not the official military bodies of today) were one of the volunteer militia groups in pre-Civil War St. Louis, noted for their attention to uniforms and sociability . . . until they were called to dangerous service in the nativist attacks of the 1850s. *Missouri Historical Society Collection*

THE GERMANS AND
THE IRISH ARRIVE

Immigrants to the city after it became American property in 1804 were largely just that: American. These newcomers probably were united only in their inability to speak French. The people who made their way from the Northeast—such as Elijah Lovejoy—were more likely to dislike slavery and drinking alcohol. The flood of folks from Southern and border states—Kentucky, Tennessee, the Carolinas, and Virginia—almost uniformly supported slavery if not booze.

But by the 1840s, those Americans, many not far from their own English immigration status but considering themselves "natives," saw a new menace. Waves of immigration from Ireland and Germany changed the face of St. Louis. The Irish were fleeing social injustices and unrest and, of course, the potato famine of the late 1840s. A failed Irish rebellion in 1848 added another cohort. The Germans came in two waves, the first in search of economic advantage beginning in the late 1830s. Many were Roman Catholic or Lutheran. The second wave included the intellectual elite and laborers who had failed in their attempt to overthrow the Prussian and Austrian monarchies in 1848. Many were Protestants—or freethinkers.

The census of 1850 revealed what irritable "Americans" sensed: 43 percent of the city's population was born in Ireland or Germany. If you added in children born to those immigrants after their arrival in St. Louis, they were the majority.

The Germans made a huge impression almost immediately, setting up schools that taught in German and beer gardens that not only quenched thirsts but offered family-friendly entertainments. Many settled to the south of the business district in the area now called Soulard. Others located north and west of downtown. Their Turner halls were the equivalents of modern gyms, emphasizing physical health, plus offering a heavy dose of socializing and culture. Although the Germans split along religious lines, they were more united in their opposition to slavery. The Turner halls began to be associated with political and labor movements as well as German culture.

We associate the Irish with Boston, but a large number of Irish arrived in New Orleans over this time period. Many made their way up the Mississippi and stayed in St. Louis to work the steamboats and the levee. Some lived in the slums near the levee in buildings known as Battle Row. Others settled in the Kerry Patch, the neighborhood around St. Patrick's Church at Sixth and Biddle, just north of the business blocks. Almost all were Roman Catholic.

Roman Catholicism itself was under attack in the 1840s and 1850s: Churches and St. Louis University, a Jesuit school that had been in the city since 1818, were in danger at various times.

EVERYDAY VIOLENCE

It's easier to understand conditions for immigrants if we acknowledge the violence of the era. It's tempting to say St. Louis was a frontier outpost and therefore its citizens were prone to fighting. But the record shows that hoodlums were not a feature of the colonial/frontier era. Prior to 1804 and the American takeover, St. Louis was a relatively easygoing place. By 1840, the frontier had moved west, and the growing city reeled from the debaucheries of riverboat crews, the rivalries between volunteer firefighting companies, and even the political brawls of leading citizens.

The duels of the early part of the century seem tame—or at least gentlemanly—compared to such incidents as the fight in 1849 between Frank Blair Jr., an attorney and Thomas Hart Benton's lieutenant in the city, and Loren Pickering, editor of the *St. Louis Union*. Blair actually did challenge Pickering to a duel, which Pickering responded to in print with sarcasm, suggesting a running battle through downtown with bowie knives. When they met shortly thereafter on the street, they went at it with umbrellas. That was inconclusive, as you might imagine. Pickering set aside the bowie knife idea as well. A few days later he was waiting for Blair as the lawyer left the courthouse. Pickering fired three shots from a distance of ten feet and missed. Blair—note here that he had been armed in the courthouse—fired back and missed as well.

Pickering was charged with assault but acquitted, possibly because the city would have had fewer lawyers, editors, politicians, industrialists, and doctors if such actions put the elite behind bars. There are also reports of a doctor killing a judge, of a school board member taking after a citizen in a public meeting, and of a killing in a judge's office. And then there was

Ferdinand Kennett, industrialist, president of the Bank of Missouri, and brother of a future mayor and congressman, beating up the pastor of the Centenary Methodist Church.

Ten volunteer fire companies responded to alarms in the 1940s and 1950s. These were grand organizations that at first competed on the brilliance of their uniforms. But as the years wore on, they out-and-out fought each other. The teenagers who made up the "hose companies" of each group were notorious for destroying property near the brothels around Third and Almond Streets in 1850. It appears they knew they couldn't get into serious trouble if they harassed the transients, the free Blacks, and the laboring Irish who lived and partied in the area. There are reports of the adult men in the companies fighting over fire plugs and cutting other companies' fire hoses.

In 1849, after a major fire destroyed a large section of downtown, a smaller fire led to a riot that took on nativist overtones. Steamboats were prone to fires, all on their own, and when one burst into flames along the crowded riverfront, the flames had good tinder for spreading. Several fire companies turned out for the devastation occurring in July of 1849, in full view of the slums of Battle Row, which overlooked the wharf.

An Irish heckler among the onlookers issued an insult that drew the companies to respond. The resulting fistfight grew into a rock-throwing contest. Hopefully, the fire was contained, because the companies chased the outnumbered Irish into a saloon—politely known as a coffeehouse. The proprietor, one J. O'Brien, apparently kept arms, because the Irish workers used them to shoot at and repel the fire companies. Other Irish dockworkers and general laborers joined the fight; several hundred men who simply didn't like the Irish joined the firefighters.

The sitting mayor organized his small police force and together they arrested the men they considered to be the ringleaders. That left the Irish badly outnumbered. The nativist mob proceeded to destroy O'Brien's place, several other "coffeehouses," and a boardinghouse near St. Patrick's Church. A young priest named Father John Henry garnered acclaim for facing down the mob as it approached his parish.

At St. Louis University, the priest of St. Francis Xavier, the college church, walked up and down the street in front of the mob, reading psalms.

Rumor had it that the basement of the church was full of armed Irishmen, waiting for an attack. Not so. The arms were in the basement of another medical college, not the oft-besieged one at the St. Louis University. But the mob decided to desist just in case.

Meanwhile, the mob found a weapon of its own. By evening, it had a six-inch howitzer loaded with scrap iron trained on the boardinghouses of Battle Row. Police finally managed to commandeer it.

When the city finally beat back the fire companies' political clout in 1857 and established a paid department, there were reports of former volunteers arriving at fire scenes individually to throw insults and stones at the city's paid firefighters, cut hoses, and stab the horses that pulled the fire wagons.

ENTER THE KNOW-NOTHINGS. AND A CADAVER

Americans' belligerence toward immigrants more recently arrived than themselves, plus a fascination with secret organizations, led to a national movement and a short-lived political party. As early as the 1840s, xenophobes in New York City created the Order of the Star-Spangled Banner. Members had to pledge to oppose Roman Catholics at every turn, vote only for native-born politicians, advocate to raise the time requirement for naturalization to twenty-one years, and, most importantly, disavow any knowledge of the order. If asked about the club, a member was to say, "I know nothing." If a member needed to know when the next meeting was, he asked another member, "Have you seen Sam?" The movement spread across the country and one of its publications, *The Mystery*, carried the legend, "Published nowhere, sold everywhere, edited by Nobody and Know-Nothing."

When the nativists wanted to be active in politics, they couldn't be quite so secretive, so they created a new political entity, the American Party—sometimes called the Native American Party just to confuse modern readers. That party added new planks to the club's foundation: restricting liquor sales (because immigrants were known to be heavy drinkers—this alone would have kept German Protestants in St. Louis from active membership), requiring public school teachers to be Protestant and read daily from a Protestant Bible, and limiting immigration from Catholic countries. The pushback against Catholics had to do with a fear that the Pope, Pious IX at the time, would order clergy (who would order parishioners) to oppose democracy.

The Know-Nothings became a force in St. Louis politics in part because the old parties were breaking up on the shoals of the slavery question. Democrats in Missouri were split into two camps based on whether one supported Thomas Hart Benton. Anti-slavery Whigs veered off toward the new party in town, the Republicans. But whoever was in St. Louis' city hall, nativism was running strong.

In 1844, three thousand rioters took up a stance outside St. Louis University because of a bizarre incident. The Jesuit university included a medical school and routinely used cadavers in classes. On a February Sunday, boys were playing ball on the commons near the school when, predictably, their ball flew into a fenced area. The boys went in after it and, in their searching, came upon an opening into a vault. What they saw must have soured them on digging for the ball. The vault contained parts of a discarded cadaver. The boys rushed out to tell their parents and others.

What started as a protest against dissection of human cadavers took on anti-Catholic overtones. Bricks and rocks were thrown and windows shattered. Of course, Irish and Germans were drawn to the scene and talked out of a clash by an anti-nativist judge, Bryan Mullanphy—from the Mullanphy family of Irish-commoners-become-elite philanthropists.

The mob seemed to disperse, but a few men went to the vault/pit and brought out bones and body fragments. That caused the mob to re-form, and this time there was no talking them back. They broke in, destroying labs and specimens. An observer said they "left nothing of the institution save only the bare walls and roof." (Scharf)

Much of the other nativist violence centered on the real issue: voting.

ELECTION DAY RIOTS

In the 1840s, nativist violence combined with questionable election settings in deadly ways. First of all, the city, state, and national elections were held in April, August, and November, respectively, so election fever boiled for six months out of the year. Offices for mayor and city officials were on the ballot every spring. There were no voter registration procedures, so judges at the polls decided a man's legality to vote. Polling places were crowded because their number couldn't keep up with the ballooning population. There were no distancing regulations as there are today: supporters of any candidate could harass a voter right up to the ballot box. And there was no prohibition against the sale of liquor; in fact, election day was an excellent excuse to drink.

In the April 1844 election, fighting broke out between the supporters of opposing candidates in the Fifth Ward, which was heavily Irish. The fighting got worse in the evening. One man identified as a well-known citizen was not involved in the actual fisticuffs, but he was shot and killed when someone fired from a tavern. The mob tore the tavern apart.

On Monday, April 5, 1852, men (only native and naturalized white men, of course) went to the ballot boxes to vote for mayor and city offices. The First Ward, at the time, covered a large but less densely populated area on the south side of the city. It included the neighborhood known today as Soulard, including the Soulard Market, where voting took place. At the time, the many Germans in the area voted Democratic. Soon enough, many would turn to the emerging Republican party. But the contestants in 1852 were Luther Kennett, running for his third term on the Whig ticket, and John How, on the Democratic ticket.

Kennett, who would later beat out Thomas Hart Benton for a seat in Congress, was known for walking a fine line on the nativist issue. He had old-line French Catholic supporters, and he tried to appeal to the Irish by touting his remote Celtic ancestry. But he privately favored Know-Nothing partisans. The *Democrat* newspaper opposed him. Its editor, Gratz Brown (of the last duel on Bloody Island) said Kennett "changed his forefathers so often there is no telling how long he will remain an American."

Between the newspapers' continual flinging of insults and very real political differences, tempers flared at Soulard Market. Word spread across the city that Germans were trying to keep Whigs from voting. It got physical. As mayors did, Luther Kennett appeared to try to calm the belligerents, which only made matters worse. A Democratic city official had better luck until crowds from other wards moved in during the afternoon. Stones were thrown and shots fired from houses. Beer houses were destroyed, even as the voting continued. Soulard Market-house was riddled with bullets.

At the tavern of a Mr. Neumeyer at Park and Seventh, one Joseph Stevens, a young member of one of the fire companies, broke in a piece of the door. A gun barrel appeared in the opening, someone fired, and Stevens fell dead. The men behind him pushed into the building, first destroying its contents and then setting it on fire.

By evening, the nativists had gotten two brass six-pounders, presumably from the federal armory, and installed them at the corner of Park and Carondelet. From there they could sweep Second Street, which was crowded with German residents and protestors. Marshal Phelps arrived to talk everyone down. Meanwhile, other demonstrators moved to the German *Anzeiger des Westens* newspaper office at Third and Chestnut. Kennett wisely didn't appear, but he sent out two of the volunteer militia groups, the Riflemen and the St. Louis Grays. The well-respected groups drew up in two lines in front of the office and remained until the mob gave up. The toll for the day was one dead, eight to ten seriously wounded, and another two-dozen injured.

It was a dress rehearsal for the big election in August 1854. This one pitted the mayor from the 1952 riots, Luther Kennett, against Thomas Hart Benton, who was now running for Congress and a return to Washington.

The newspapers were still at it. The *Anzeiger des Westens* was supporting religious freedom and the rights of immigrant groups to their traditional customs—often read as the right to drink at beer gardens on Sunday afternoons. The *Republican* attacked the German paper, saying, "The American people will not stand innovations upon their rights, their principals, their institutions." The *Democrat* was more specific. It charged that the judge who issued naturalization papers had gone into slow motion. Fewer immigrants naturalized presumably meant fewer people who would vote for the Democratic ticket. Kennett's Whig/Know-Nothing supporters responded that the polls needed to be protected from the illegally voting immigrants Democrats might encourage and called for volunteer poll-watchers. The *Republican* claimed it had lists of unnaturalized immigrants it was going to offer to election judges. On top of that, there had been sporadic and mysterious fires across the city. Street corners were the sites of preliminary clashes over the weekend.

And it was August in St. Louis. Before air-conditioning.

On Monday morning, the seventh, the violence again started with the Irish in the Fifth Ward, where an election judge decided to spend an inordinate amount of time reviewing each set of naturalization papers. The volunteer poll-watchers called for by the Know-Nothing coalition were sufficient to constitute a mob that warily watched the line of Irish voters back up due to the delay. More and more men were turned away from voting. Fights broke out. A boy was stabbed, presumably by an Irishman.

The man with the knife fled into the nearby Irish neighborhood. The nativist mob followed, throwing objects at Irish establishments along the way. Gunfire erupted from upper-floor windows. The nativists turned and headed back toward the levee and engaged a defensive line of dockhands. By now two men were dead. The levee was a source of weapons, though, and the mob got hold of sufficient axes to return to attacking Irish houses and saloons. The attack spread west to St. Louis University—this time simply because it was Catholic, no cadavers necessary. And predictably, the Germans came under fire as well with a mob outside the *Anzeiger des Westens*.

Mayor How had sixty-three policemen, and they managed to make some difference. But the mayor was forced to call out the volunteer militia to make a real difference, particularly in defense of the university and the newspaper office. These militia groups were more military versions of the fire companies. In addition to being social clubs, many included veterans from the Mexican War. The most often noted were the St. Louis Grays, who claimed various professional men and businessmen. There were also the National Guards (not the official body); the elitist Continental Rangers; the Pioneer Corps, which recruited Germans; and the Washington Guards, which recruited Irish—who would fire on their brethren over the days of riot. At least five hundred men turned out from the militia clubs to battle crowds that numbered up to five thousand across the city.

By Tuesday, the eighth, the university was under siege again because it was rumored to have storehoused arms for Catholics. Students prayed for the school, and the militia defended it. The mob actually fired back at the militia, a sign that the respect usually given those groups was waning. Both the Grays and Continentals had men wounded.

By Wednesday morning, with sporadic violence still flaring, Major How called a citizens' meeting. Kennett attended, representing Know-Nothing forces. James H. Lucas, financier, and son of J. B. C. Lucas (and therefore brother of Charles, who died on Bloody Island at the hand of Benton), was fresh from an elite businessmen's meeting held at the Merchants' Exchange. Lucas offered resolutions from that group, including closing saloons early and banning street corner congregating, and two more surprising resolutions. One was to disband the regular police force—all sixty-three of them. They would be temporarily replaced by a seven-hundred-man volunteer force to be led by Major Meriwether Lewis Clark, son of William Clark, named for his father's fellow explorer.

Either because of the efficiency of the patrols Clark organized or because men were tired or because a heavy rain opened up, the mobs gradually went home. The result of the disorder had been at least ten dead—many claimed it was more than that—and Irish homes and shops demolished in at least a three-square-block area. And there was the one other result of the statewide election. Kennett defeated Benton, in part because Democrats split over the slavery question. (Benton had been forced from the US Senate by the state legislature because he supported anti-slavery movements.)

St. Louis regained some semblance of law and order, which lasted until the slavery question broke into hostilities in 1861. Immigrants again were at the forefront of that fight, but now they fought each other.

The Germans and the Irish had united in their hostility to the Know-Nothings and nativists in general. Certainly, both groups defended their traditions, including the right to drink alcohol whenever they chose. But beyond that, the two groups had different views of slavery. The Irish feared that a large contingent of freed Black men would be rivals for the jobs that had drawn the Irish to the country in the first place. The Germans thought that freedom was what they had fought for back home, and they extended that vision of freedom to Blacks. They also feared that being associated with an agrarian Southern economy would harm the city's reputation for business and industry with Northern trading partners. The two groups were about to put their money where their mouths were, as the saying goes.

THE BIG WAR

The fateful election of 1860, when Abraham Lincoln was voted into office, and 1861, the winter of his inauguration, were as crazy in St. Louis as anywhere else in the country. Maybe crazier.

St. Louis, seemingly removed from regions we associate with the Civil War, was regarded as critical for each side. If the city joined the Confederacy, the money and guns sitting in the St. Louis sub-treasury and its arsenal could make the difference. St. Louis would have been the largest and most industrialized city in the Confederacy. The solid Unionists, on the other hand, needed the city as a bulwark to protect the upper Mississippi and trade across the continent.

Missouri had entered the union as a slave state, but it actually had relatively few slaves. And St. Louis' commercial standing depended on the North and West, not the South. No one could predict where the city and the state would fall. At first, the middle ground—stay in the Union but allow

A pin worn by a member of Blair's St. Louis Wide Awake chapter in support of Lincoln in the 1860 election. *Missouri Historical Society Collection*

slavery where it currently existed—seemed to be favored across the state, but as compromise became an increasingly dirty word, most of the state seemed to be leaning toward secession. Everywhere but in St. Louis. There every group, including the Irish and the Germans, the pro-Union, the pro-South, had a few tricks up their sleeves.

ARMED CITIZENS AND THEN–CAMP JACKSON

It was a St. Louis newspaper, the *Republican* (which wasn't partisan Republican, you'll recall), that urged Claiborne Jackson and Thomas Reynolds to run for governor and lieutenant governor, respectively, as moderate Democrats. They won, and as soon as they took their oaths of office, they made their true allegiance clear. In his inaugural address, Jackson insisted that Missouri's interests should lead her to stand by the South. Reynolds told his fellow St. Louisans the same.

The main man for the strong Unionists was Frank Blair, a politician with national connections (rising above his umbrella duel). As Blair went around speaking, he was met with the kind of violence we've noted. So, he decided St. Louis should have a chapter of Wide-Awakes—not coffee addicts, but young and youngish men who were rallying to the Union cause. Wearing distinctive caps and capes, some three hundred Wide-Awakes, German almost to a man, accompanied Blair everywhere. They carried lighted lamps on sturdy poles and were ready to use them as weapons. The camphene that fueled the flames was probably more of a deterrent than the poles themselves.

On the face of it, the Wide-Awakes might look like any other social-club-posing-as-militia. But they were much more. They were keenly aware of what might be coming. One story has them putting on an art exhibition as a benefit. The three-day event was so elaborate that plaster casts of sculptures were shipped from New York City. St. Louis folks from all persuasions attended, possibly glad for a break from the politics, and the event raised a goodly sum of money. But the public-spiritedness was an illusion. Some of the crates labeled plaster actually contained muskets, provided by Unionists in New York City.

In another incident, a number of the Wide-Awakes were probably in the crowd of the two-thousand young men who gathered for the traditional New Year's Eve Day slave auction on the courthouse steps. Seven slaves, property of people who had died during the previous year, were up for sale, When the auctioneer called for the first bid, the crowd was ready. They shouted, "Three dollars!" and kept up the chant for twenty minutes. The auctioneer laughed off that low offer at first. But his next request for a bid was met with cries of "Four dollars!"—which they kept up for another agonizingly long time. And so it went. The auctioneer never managed to get them above eight dollars and gave up after two hours. The slaves went back to jail, perhaps to stay there until emancipation. That New Year's Day exercise was said to be the last slave auction held in St. Louis.

Meanwhile, the pro-secessionists in the city set up their own militia, the Minute Men. Probably not as homogeneously Irish as the Wide-Awakes were German, the group still drew a large number of Irish citizens. Their role was to spy on Blair and counter the Wide-Awakes—renamed the Home Guard by 1861. The Minute Men seem to have been less effective than the Home Guard on several fronts, including on a critical day when they tried to lure the Home Guard into a confrontation.

March 4, 1861. In Washington D.C., Abraham Lincoln swore his oath to protect the Constitution. In St. Louis, the Minute Men hoped to stir up backlash against the Home Guard by drawing them into battle. The Minute Men used as their headquarters an old mansion once owned by Bartholomew Berthold and his wife, Pelagie,

Captain (later General) Nathaniel Lyon led Union-sympathizing militiamen in a successful offense against Confederate-leaning militia in 1861, keeping guns and money and the state of Missouri from falling into rebel hands. *Missouri Historical Society Collection*

Pierre Chouteau's only daughter. They had decorated it, and several other sites around town, with an unusual new flag meant to represent the Confederacy—not that the Confederacy had its own flag yet. The Union men tore down every rebel flag they could find and advanced on the Minute Men's headquarters to do the same. The secessionists were armed with hand grenades, but the police and city administration would likely side with them if the Union men attacked. Which they didn't. After a tense time, Blair talked them into dispersing, leaving the Minute Men with their hand grenades and no excuse for authorities to banish the Home Guard.

Everyone knew the real issue was the arsenal. Its sixty-thousand muskets numbered more than half the arms possessed by the states of the Confederacy at that point in time. The officer in command of the Department of the West was now-General William S. Harney, the man charged with and acquitted of murder in the death of his slave Hannah (in chapter 6). Harney was in charge of the arsenal and worked to keep his command neutral—apparently convincing himself that Governor Jackson wasn't angling to get the guns and join the Confederacy. Blair kept complaining to Washington until, at just the right moment, he got the secretary of war to recall Harney to Washington to explain what was going on. That left the fiery Union man Blair favored, then-Captain Nathaniel Lyon, to oversee the arsenal. And Lyon had a sleeve full of tricks as well, military and otherwise—including acting before General Harney could get back to St. Louis.

Given the news that Confederates fired on Fort Sumter in South Carolina, Lyon knew he needed reinforcements. Instead of marching his men into the arsenal, he arranged to have Germans from one of the Turner halls casually wander into the arsenal beginning at about four a.m. one morning. Once inside, they formed up to do guard duty. Word that the arsenal was defended spread, and no attack came.

A few nights later, after the governor of Illinois requested some ten thousand of the muskets, Lyon wasn't sure he could put down the expected secessionist riot if and when the guns were seen being moved to a free state. Instead, a newly formed Union regiment escorted streetcars filled with decoys along Fifth Street. While the secessionists stopped the cars and went through the contents, double the number of requested muskets plus other arms were loaded onto an unlighted steamboat. The vessel moved so quietly and slowly upriver that the secessionists manning a makeshift battery on the north side of St. Louis missed it. Soon enough the arms were on railcars and headed for Springfield, Illinois. What was left in the arsenal was enough for Lyon's men in the coming conflict.

Secessionist governor Claiborne Jackson had hopes for the state militia, which traditionally held its annual muster on grounds just inside the city limits and would do so in May 1861 under the command of General Daniel Frost. The event was usually big on marching and parading, but this year was different. The Minute Men responded, of course, true to their secessionist leanings. Some of the other traditional militia members were not so sure and didn't report.

Governor Jackson asked the Confederacy for big guns to attack the arsenal's defenders. Two of the leaders of the Minute Men headed south to pick up heavy artillery that the Confederates had taken from the federal arsenal in Baton Rouge, Louisiana. Taking a page from the Wide-Awakes' tactics, the disassembled guns were carried in crates labeled "Tamaroa Marble." That was sufficient to get the guns and the men past inspection, and they arrived to unload their bounty on the night of May 8. Lyon got word from German deckhands shortly thereafter. General Frost hoped to install the guns on high ground above the arsenal. But Lyon had his men waiting when Frost's men arrived there, so Frost had to take the unboxed guns back to his campground, the muster grounds housing less than nine hundred men.

Lyon was about to have a busy day. Camp Jackson was spread out, and Lyon needed to know specifics. Because of the usual social air of the encampment, spectators came out in carriages to survey the scene, maybe see someone they knew on parade. Lyon is said to have borrowed and donned a black gown and a heavy veil from Blair's nearly blind mother-in-law. The Unionist captain hid two pistols under the skirts, chatted with his companions, noted the layout and streets labeled "Jeff Davis" and "Beauregard," and had what he needed for the next day.

The morning of the 10th, Lyon marched six thousand men to four positions around the camp. (An observer named Ulysses Grant, then restarting his military career in Illinois, was in St. Louis that day and wished men well as they left the arsenal.) At Camp Jackson, Frost protested that he was just on routine encampment and had no thoughts of attacking the arsenal. The truth was the guns from Baton Rouge hadn't been unpacked yet. Lyon demanded surrender and got it. Not that he likely heard about it for a while.

Lyon was awaiting Frost's response when he passed too closely behind a horse that kicked him in the gut. He fell to the ground and lost consciousness. In the critical time it took him to recover, his men apparently were at a loss. Because about then things began to go really wrong.

Word spread across the city and crowds gathered, including women and children, men and ministers. Had Lyon's men been able to march the militiamen who were now prisoners directly back to the arsenal—where a recently emptied storeroom awaited—violence might have been avoided. Frost and his militia were being marched between lines of Lyons' men, and the shouts from proponents of both sides rang out. Lyon regained consciousness from his injury, but possibly because of it, the lines of captives came to a halt, in front of the gathered crowd, for at least two hours.

Some of the crowd threw rocks, some shouted, "Damn the Dutch," although there were very few taunts for the "American" Union troops. Surely as concerned as any of the onlookers, future General William Tecumseh Sherman was there with his son. "Cump" Sherman, as St. Louis' friends might have called him, wrote later that a man he assumed to be drunk tried to push through the ranks and was shoved back by a soldier. When the drunk regained his feet, he pulled out a pistol and fired. A Captain Blandowski was hit and was possibly the one who gave the order to fire back. Firing broke out from the crowd and from the troops as well. Sherman pushed his son Willie to the ground and fell on top of him.

By the time the shooting stopped and the troops moved on toward the arsenal, twenty-eight people were dead and many more wounded. Some of the dead were children. It didn't take long for the pro-slavery folks to decide who to blame. Clearly, it was the German Americans. One secessionist announced a plan: "Burn all the breweries and declare Lager Beer to be a contraband of war. By this means the Dutch will all die in a week." (van Ravenswaay) The unrest, including shootings and deaths, continued for two days. Some secessionists fled.

The city of St. Louis was saved for the Union. Lyon, by then General Lyon, died shortly after in a battle in southern Missouri. Blair managed to get Harney removed from his command; by 1863, Harney was forced to retire. Governor Jackson and his lieutenant governor, Thomas Reynolds, who had battled Gratz Brown in the last duel, fled the state but purported to represent it in absentia for the Confederacy. Reynolds returned in 1868 from a flight to Mexico with the Missouri State Seal he had taken in 1861. Sherman went on to be one of the most respected Union generals, working for another spectator that day, Ulysses Grant.

Residents in a Southern city, say Richmond or Atlanta, could assume that their neighbors shared their beliefs. Residents in New York City or Philadelphia or Boston could do the same. But in St. Louis, the war was fought daily in relationships between neighbors. Martial law was imposed; fines were demanded of secessionists; prisons on Gratiot and Myrtle Streets filled with Confederate soldiers and women deemed to be Confederate spies. St. Louis became known not as a battle site but as a place that took in the suffering from both sides and offered the whole country aid on the battlefields and on the hospital ships anchored in the Mississippi.

As for the immigrant populations, the Irish merged into the mainstream. Irish names will surface in later chapters, particularly in labor and literary endeavors. Germans built on their prominence in fighting for the Union to move into civic authority. A number of German American mayors will cross the stage. But the German lifestyle had just more than another fifty years of vibrancy. The anti-German sentiments that arose from World War I would mean the end of the German press and German traditions like the Turner halls and beer gardens.

The horrible civil war ended, leaving scars in St. Louis as elsewhere. In fits and starts, life returned to a new normal.

CRIMES AGAINST NATURE

When it comes to environmental concerns—including disasters—the good old days weren't so good. St. Louis saw waves of cholera epidemics in the nineteenth century and then the 1918 influenza pandemic hit. Both remind us of the 2020 COVID-19 pandemic, but with a social twist. Not only were poorer people more often victims, but foreigners, immigrants, and people of color were blamed for causing the deaths.

When the tornado of 1896 struck, it destroyed much of an immigrant neighborhood, requiring less help from the city, apparently, than the light destruction located in a rich, native neighborhood. Then another tornado in 1927 took aim at Black neighborhoods.

Meanwhile, civic improvements aimed at building good streets, removing waste, and battling the pervasive smoke took on class overtones. Streets were better and nuisance industries less prevalent where rich folks lived.

ACTS OF GOD: "IN THE GRAVEYARDS THE SAD STORY IS TOLD"

Cholera was a widespread and feared disease in the 1800s. Older generations sometimes laid its devastation at the feet of an angry God. But by the mid-1800s, the rapid spread of the disease was as often blamed on the poor. Immigrants pouring into the city from New Orleans and other points south were quarantined, but the incidence among dockhands spread first to the poorer population living closest to the river and then to the general population.

The tornado of 1896 devastated a swath of the south St. Louis German neighborhoods. *Missouri Historical Society Collection*

We know now that cholera is caused by bacteria that flourish in dirty water. Doctors in nineteenth-century St. Louis didn't know about the bacteria—and had no antibiotics in any case—but they did suspect bad water, of which St. Louis had plenty.

St. Louis is built on limestone bluffs, and limestone is subject to erosion (over many, many years) as water drains through it, creating caves below ground and sinkholes above ground. Early St. Louisans thought the sinkholes and caves would serve as natural sewers. It took several decades to realize that the caves didn't connect to the Mississippi.

Meanwhile, as citizens put more garbage, more animal carcasses, more human waste into what looked like natural garbage pits, the passages beneath the city became masses of pollution.

The city authorized the first waterworks in 1832. The idea was to pump water from the big river to a reservoir. Theoretically, the water would sit in the reservoir long enough for the hefty sediment from the Mississippi to settle, and then the relatively clear water at the top would be pumped out through iron and lead pipes. But the city grew so fast that the supply of what we would consider decent drinking water was never enough. Sediment never had time to settle, so the water always recalled its Mississippi origins as near gruel.

And when disease came in the form of cholera, dirty water made all the difference. Residents blamed the "vapors" rising from stagnant water in the sinkholes and in the ill-drained streets. The least well-drained streets, of course, were where the poor and recent immigrants lived. Not only did those people die in larger numbers, but wealthier citizens accused the poor of causing and spreading the illnesses.

Cholera moves fast, attacking the small intestines and causing vomiting and diarrhea. Its victims usually died of dehydration. And, once someone got cholera, the cure was predictably nasty.

In 1849, every doctor had a different notion of how to treat the disease, and in some cases, the doctors changed treatments every week or so after watching patients die. One remedy was a mix of asafoetida, opium, and black pepper. (Asafoetida is a gum from an herbal root, popular from the Middle Ages when people wore it in bags to ward off disease. That probably worked by promoting social distancing since asafoetida's sulfur content led to it being called stinking gum.) This mixture was administered every half hour or so until the patient recovered or died. Other doctors used remedies containing mercury. Whatever the doctors' limitations, they can't be blamed for not trying. Several prominent physicians died, including Dr. Bernard Farrar, Benton's second from the deadly duel with Charles Lucas.

Citizens reported conditions we would find familiar. Courts closed because jurors and witnesses refused to attend. Businesses closed. Public schools closed and were converted into temporary hospitals. No one wanted to go outside their homes. Although—a crowd did gather at one point to demand that city officials do something or resign.

The worse the home conditions were, the more likely cholera would strike. One difference between cholera and the viral infections of the twenty-first century is the toll on children. On the day the *Republican* reported the death of Dr. Farrar, it also said the previous day had seen 160 burials, 123 of them for children. The death toll reached its peak in July of 1849 with the oft-quoted toll of 145 in one day and 722 in one week.

Another famous name died as well. Pierre Chouteau Sr., Marie Thérèse and Pierre Laclède's surviving child, died at age ninety-one. When the city cemeteries were overwhelmed, land at Stephen Hempstead's farm was donated for what became the city's premier burying ground, Bellefontaine Cemetery.

Then, as now, it was hard to separate out why people died. The total toll for 1849 ranges from 4,500 to close to 7,000. The latter figure would be at least 10 percent of the city's population, a much higher per capita figure than any other city in the country.

Bad as tainted water was in 1849, no water was worse. As if that year wouldn't go down in history because of disease, the city's major fire struck on May 17. A steamer caught fire on the wharf. When firemen cut the flaming boat loose from its moorings, hoping it would drift away from the other boats thick along the wharf, it simply jammed into the next boat in line. A whole dock-worth of steamships, with their volatile fuels and cargos, went up in flames. Cargo sitting on the wharf caught as well, and the flames spread to buildings several blocks west.

Water pressure to fight the flames began to diminish, and access to water in the Mississippi was blocked by the flaming boats. By the time firemen managed to haul water from other sources, and destroy and dynamite buildings, some fifteen city blocks had burned.

So, 1849 was a pretty bad year. Nearly seventy years later, an even more dramatic onslaught of illness would replace it in the history books.

THE KANSAS FLU OF 1918

The influenza outbreak of 1918 was an international event, of course. And the story in St. Louis is less scandalous than most, although it's hard to put the words "success story" and "three-thousand dead" in the same sentence.

The people most maligned in the story may actually be the Spanish—because "Spanish flu" was the name widely used at the time. Apparently, the Spanish didn't manage the spin well. There is credible evidence that it should be the Kansas flu, having shown up in a sparsely populated southwest Kansas county and then spreading to a densely populated army facility farther east (near the current Fort Riley/Junction City area). The county was Haskell, which lies southwest of Dodge City; the army facility was the Camp Funston cantonment, a training camp for the men the United States was urgently recruiting to fight World War I.

A physician in Haskell County was so alarmed by the outbreak that he reported "influenza of a severe type" to *Public Health Reports*. It would be the first written report of the pandemic. (Barry)

The United States had only joined the war in April of 1917 and required months to enlist and train soldiers at what were called "cantonments," of which Camp Funston was the second largest in the country. Fifty thousand recruits trained there over the course of the war. In the very cold winter of 1917–1918, the camp was badly overcrowded and men huddled together around stoves. Men from all over the Midwest, including Haskell County, trained there in the early months of 1918, and several thousand were ill with the flu by March. The 89th Division deployed from Funston to France that spring.

It is quite possible, according to historian John M. Barry, that this particular virus strain moved with American soldiers to the fighters in Europe, and to neutral Spain, and came back with soldiers and military to the United States. Viruses, busy mutating no doubt, don't publish their travel itineraries, and it takes significant detective work to trace them. By the time this virus began frightening civilian populations, folks in St. Louis saw it coming *from* the East Coast, not traveling from their own region *to* the East and across the ocean.

The good news was St. Louis had time to prepare. The better news was that St. Louis had a city health commissioner described as "clear-headed, effective, and forceful." (McKinsey, McKinsey, and Enriquez) A German American and son of a Civil War surgeon, Dr. Maximilian Carl von Starkloff succeeded to the extent he did because of his personal determination but also because he usually had the support—which wavered occasionally—of Mayor Henry Kiel.

Starkloff knew St. Louis was home, still, to Jefferson Barracks, where some two-hundred thousand enlisted men passed during the war. The first flu cases were reported there on October 1 of 1918 and grew to eight-hundred cases within a week. Red Cross nurses arrived and saved the day.

With a hundred civilians sick as well, Starkloff got permission to begin sweeping closures. A week after the first soldier showed symptoms at Jefferson Barracks, theaters, movie houses, fraternal lodges, library reading rooms, and pool halls were closed and public gatherings banned. Hours were cut back for department stores, and factories introduced staggered work schedules so streetcars wouldn't be as crowded. The next day, schools closed, and church services were banned for the coming Sunday.

Public schools not only sent school nurses to help hospitals, but asked teachers to volunteer as well. Police went on watch for cases in their districts, and Red Cross efforts spread across the city. That group coordinated volunteer drivers and their autos to serve as makeshift ambulances as well as ferry nurses to homes where citizens quarantined. Some private hospitals turned away patients, but City Hospital on Lafayette Avenue took in everyone it could manage. Papers ran articles on making flu masks.

The predictable backlash ensued. Some high school sports teams managed to play, albeit without fans. Businessmen complained loudly to the mayor, and bootleg businesses in almost everything sprang up. Archbishop John Glennon's arguments to keep Catholic churches open fell on deaf ears, and he had to allow Catholics to miss weekly masses. Not all priests got the message: One Father Frederick Holweck drew a police officer visit after someone reported two hundred parishioners in the St. Francis de Sales church. He claimed ignorance; they must have come in through the windows, he said. In the face of such incredible misunderstanding, police didn't press charges.

And accounts differ on this one, but it seems saloons stayed open. Either the order didn't include them or police ignored the violations.

Early in the period of closure, even the federal government objected because some of the factories were producing war goods. But that objection faded on November 11, the first Armistice Day. The shooting war in Europe was over, although the medical one continued. St. Louisans celebrated outdoors.

In the end, St. Louis had 31,693 reported cases, with 2,883 deaths. (There were almost surely more among people who couldn't get to a doctor or a hospital.) It was the lowest toll among the nation's ten largest cities, although smaller Midwestern cities such as Minneapolis had better records. Among the forty-nine cities with population more than 100,000, St. Louis ranked thirty-second in deaths. Less vigilant folks in Kansas City ranked seventeenth. Chicago had a worse record than St. Louis, and in hindsight, we might note that the worst was over when the two big Midwest cities started trading boasts about their death rates.

TORNADOS EXPOSE THE UGLY FACE OF PRETTY POLITICS

I n St. Louis, a deadly tornado laid bare more than the insides of homes; it exposed the fault lines of political bossism.

Tornados can be judged not only by the intensity of their winds, but also by how long they're on the ground, by the path they leave. A tornado that settles in to cut a two-mile by three-mile swath is serious business. The twister that hit St. Louis at 5:00 p.m. on May 27, 1896, bounced off a well-to-do West End neighborhood to settle in on the south side and devastate five square miles. From there it proceeded to tear through steamboats docked on the river. It challenged the tornado-proof Eads Bridge and twisted on across the river to kill almost as many people in East St. Louis.

The bridge lived up to its designer's claims, although approaches were damaged. The West End sustained relatively light damage, none of it deadly. But on the south, German, side of St. Louis and in East St. Louis, homes and businesses were flattened, utility poles and wires were scrambled, and the death tolls rose.

In St. Louis, collapsing factories caused many of the deaths, along with the flattening of smaller businesses and apartments. Electricity was lost immediately due to downed lines, and escaping gas ignited fires that were luckily extinguished by a driving rain. It is unlikely fire crews could have negotiated streets filled with debris.

St. Louis' businessmen, the ones not checking on neighbors in the Central West End, met in the Merchants' Exchange (on 'Change, as the phrase went) the next morning to start subscription drives, sectioning off the city as to which group would help where. The Provident Association, of long-standing and relatively deep pockets, would help the Central West End deal with its light injuries; the South Broadway Merchants' Association, new and made up of men dealing with the destruction of their own businesses, would help the devastated south side.

This scheme was approved by the mayor, Cyrus Walbridge, forcing him into a defensive mode. He asserted that St. Louis could take care of its own and suggested that cities across the country volunteering to send aid, send it instead to East St. Louis. Which they did. Meanwhile, the Missouri city's aid was small, and the private groups raising money largely used it to aid the Central West End. Even the independent, reform-talking Civic Federation group, led by the Rev. W. W. Boyd of the "fashionable" Second Baptist Church, favored the richer neighborhood.

Power wasn't restored to the German neighborhood for months, repairs moving slowly. The district's lovely Lafayette Square would take much longer to regrow trees—although the statue of the toga-clad Thomas Hart Benton survived. With up to six hundred applicants a day still requesting aid, the Merchants Exchange closed the South Broadway relief office early in June. Even after German residents protested and hung Wallbridge in effigy, he lectured them: "Self-help is the best help possible in such a situation." (Rogers)

The City Council appropriated $100,000 for repairs on June 5. The Merchants' Exchange allocated most of it to repairs on city hall and the Merchants' Exchange building. Twenty-thousand dollars of the appropriation went to Democratic boss Ed Butler's garbage company to clear streets, but nothing happened on that score. Meanwhile, the Reverend Boyd declared success.

The enraged south siders would support neither Walbridge nor Boyd's reform group. Instead, they helped elect German Republican Henry Ziegenheim, a rough speaker (who boasted about his bad English) and a former city collector charged with costing the city more than a million dollars by failing to collect dram shop license fees, much to the benefit of German taverns. In the end, Ziegenheim did little as mayor to help the German community. His corruption was noticeable, and he offered his most famous line in 1900 when a lighting contract fell though, leaving much of the city dark: "We got a moon yet, ain't it?" (Rogers) Ziegenheim's corrupt administration caught the attention of journalist Lincoln Steffens a few years later. (See Steffens' claims in chapter 20.)

Meanwhile, to everyone's amazement, East St. Louis, the much smaller city on the Illinois side, organized a massive cleanup and aid campaign. If anything, the tornado was even more destructive when it crossed the river; the death toll was 137 in St. Louis compared to 118 in East St. Louis, a town one-seventh the size of its Missouri sister. With the outside help St. Louis had rejected as a matter of pride and with superior internal organization, East St. Louis was essentially back on its feet the next month.

In late September of 1927, another F4 (nasty) tornado tore through St. Louis. It avoided the German Soulard neighborhood but ripped across streets in the central corridor. North of the Mill Creek Valley, it found Blacks who had moved up and out from the Valley slums of the early century. Some of the most well-off Blacks lived on Enright, West Belle, and Finney. From those homes, the tornado struck the neighborhood commonly called the Ville (short for Elleardsville and a topic for the final chapter), home to a growing Black middle class.

Several churches, hotels, and mortuaries were destroyed. A building collapsed at West Belle Elementary, killing a young girl, and numerous houses were flattened. Up to thirty Blacks died, a third of the toll for the second worst tornado in the city's history. In the gusty rain, residents of the Ville mobilized private autos to get the injured to the only Black hospital in town—City Hospital #2 in Mill Creek Valley, a facility described as "unfit for the inhabitants of the Zoo." (Hurley, Jones, and Murray)

In the days that followed, the city's Black newspaper, *The St. Louis Argus*, led fundraising. A group of high-profile Black leaders formed a relief committee to advise residents who were beset by swindling insurance companies, repair shops, and lawyers. The response of the community was rapid and effective. (Technology had improved since 1896; the city used a radio station, KMOX, to help call out employees and volunteers.) But threats came quickly as well.

The city called out police, six hundred National Guard members, and one thousand soldiers from Jefferson Barracks to prevent looting. What might have been a helpful presence in devastated white neighborhoods was ominous in Black ones. The armed white men were ordered by the police chief to "make a coroner's case out of everyone you catch looting." And the tornado had struck only months after a local legal aid society had issued a warning that "police officers are recklessly shooting and killing negro people upon the scantiest pretext of resisting arrest." (Hurley, Jones, and Murray) Before the storm, St. Louis had fifteen hundred police, six of whom were Black. During the emergency, the city looked to hire another five hundred police, none of them Black.

Just as the 1896 tornado led German residents to question their political loyalties, the 1927 tornado marked a turning point in Black support of Republican officeholders. The party of Lincoln was failing them, and in the 1930s they supported a Democratic mayor whose first move was to build a Black hospital in the Ville.

ACTS OF MAN: RAISING A STINK ABOUT RAISING A STINK

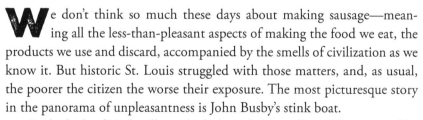

We don't think so much these days about making sausage—meaning all the less-than-pleasant aspects of making the food we eat, the products we use and discard, accompanied by the smells of civilization as we know it. But historic St. Louis struggled with those matters, and, as usual, the poorer the citizen the worse their exposure. The most picturesque story in the panorama of unpleasantness is John Busby's stink boat.

Busby had political pull, particularly with Mayor Joseph Brown, and he used it to get the city contract for picking up dead animals. Once his crews

A man balances on a cable, giving us a sense of the size of the Mill Creek Sewer under construction. *Missouri Historical Society Collection*

collected carcasses, the Busby plant in the Cheltenham neighborhood went to work boiling down remains in open vats for the valuable by-products. The protests and lawsuits from the overwhelmed Cheltenham residents finally forced the City Council to buy a steamboat for Busby in 1871. He was to take it out into the river before his company began its rendering operations.

What seemed like a creative solution failed because Busby wouldn't move the boat away from its docking. His workers proceeded to boil down carcasses at the foot of Barton Street. The smell, described as "villainous," rolled up into the German immigrant neighborhood as far as fifteen blocks from the river. Bad enough in winter, the stink forced residents in summer to retreat inside and close the windows. In the heat of mid-July 1873, a German-immigrant mob threatened to cut the boat loose but was stopped by police.

Next, Mayor Brown found a plot of land for Busby on Arsenal Island—also called Quarantine Island when needed. The island lies even with the more southern St. Louis neighborhoods but closer to the Illinois side. So, Brown and Busby's solution worked for St. Louis. It didn't work so well for folks in Illinois, but then, they didn't vote or form mobs in Missouri.

We have better processes and use fewer animal remains, but those weren't options in the 1800s. To force a nuisance to move meant initiating legal actions, and that wasn't always an option for poorer residents. Besides, if the man who owned the polluting company had wealth and political pull, it wasn't a given that the courts would rule against him.

The nuisance industries had to be somewhere. By 1880, the Board of Health was making its political and economic calculations and planning a campaign to concentrate the worst offenders somewhere in the city. Moving outside the city limits was rejected because then the city would have no control whatsoever. A shift in the wind could raise a severe stink.

So, where to put the nuisance industries? Who to inconvenience—if not sicken?

To their relief, the German-immigrant neighborhoods to the south of downtown were saved by the prevailing winds. Because those winds came from the south, you couldn't put stench there because it would blow into downtown, where too many important people worked and the property values were high. How about west, away from downtown? That wouldn't do. The rich were moving west to get away from nuisances, which included undesirable industries and undesirable neighbors.

That left north of downtown and the unfortunate Lowell community. By a campaign of enforcing standards and generally harassing offenders, the board succeeded in moving much, although not all, of the stench to the Lowell area. The area's citizens thought they had hope when they convinced the city that the two heavily polluted streams flowing through the neighborhood were entering the Mississippi above the city's waterworks, threatening the entire city's water supply. But city engineers had an answer for that: They diverted the waste with a sewer that emptied below the waterworks. The industries stayed.

Not all nuisance industries would move, though. Some stayed in nicer neighborhoods. The solution was finally for the rich to move even farther west. And they did. Because they could. Even the West End wasn't far enough out for some, who moved beyond the city into St. Louis County.

One society gentleman complained of the waste. Fine homes were built, only to be abandoned. "Those who have the means move continually, leaving behind what they cannot endure." He estimated that each generation was "forced" to move three times. (Primm)

And then there was the ultimate relocation of nuisances. Across the Mississippi. The city of East St. Louis, Illinois, was founded in 1861. Historian Walter Johnson calls the early city "a municipal shell of unbridled capitalist extraction and unchecked governmental corruption." While St. Louis, Missouri, may have answered to its elite in positioning nuisances, it at least had nuisance laws on the book and enforced some of them. East St. Louis was where a company went if it didn't want to deal with such laws at all. Once the railroad and streetcars could cross the Mississippi on the Eads Bridge, completed in 1874, workers from St. Louis could, if desperate enough, find work on the Illinois side. And goods could pass freely between the two cities. It was a great solution—if you could live on the Missouri side.

STREETS AND SEWERS—AND SEWER GAS

Building streets was a St. Louis obsession in the years surrounding the Civil War. The popular notion was that the city needed to grow and, in order to grow, it needed streets pushing beyond downtown. But which direction from downtown? Where the rich and influential lived, of course. What was less important, in particular, were usable streets on the south side, home to German immigrant residents, not to mention sinkholes and caverns.

Not that any street in the city was always usable. The city, like other American urban sites, used macadam. Crews packed and leveled dirt and then put a foot of limestone gravel over the dirt. Aside from the ecological damage to the limestone bluffs beside the Mississippi, limestone was a poor choice. Traffic broke it down to dust. And that was before it rained. Men complained about wading rivers of mud. Women in long skirts had even more laundry to contend with.

Most disturbing, the city was divided. Mill Creek, which Auguste Chouteau had dammed for his pond and which had become hopelessly polluted, was by now a dry valley running east and west across the city. Where a bucolic stream had once flowed, rows of steel rail divided the more established land to the north from the immigrant neighborhoods to the south. At one point, only two paved streets (roughly today's Seventh Street and Fifth Street/Broadway) crossed the divide. So, the south side was not only distinguished by its immigrant population but also by its isolation. And its unpaved streets.

By 1880, the city reversed itself. Maybe so many paved streets to maintain weren't a good thing. By 1900, it was clear that streets within a mile-wide strip conveniently containing major business interests and homes of the elite would get the attention.

Alongside street construction, the city worried about sewers—for good reason. Early settlers may have thought the sinkholes and caverns *were* sewers, but in fact the geology of sinkholes *required* sewers. It was easy to look around in St. Louis and say that wastewaters could be channeled to roll east down to the Mississippi River. But once engineers tried to put those channels underground, they found rows of ridges, underground limestone formations, that ran *parallel* to the Mississippi. Not only might sinkholes (filled with garbage of various disgusting descriptions) drain into an underground chamber and be trapped there, but providing an opening to the river meant drilling through the ridges. That meant money, and St. Louis never had enough, never could pay men to dig underground trenches fast enough to keep up with the demands of industrial growth and new housing.

It almost goes without saying that most of the sewer-building activity took place from the Mill Creek Valley north and west. Residents on the German south side, stuck with most of the sinkholes anyway, coped. Meanwhile, the problem on the north side of Mill Creek Valley was often due to the very business community that continually asked for more services—and opposed the taxes to pay for them.

One of the main sewer lines to the Mississippi was in fact the Mill Creek Sewer, taking advantage of the depressed floor of the old stream. It took years to cut through the ridges to first extend it to the Mississippi, and then to extend it back west to keep up with growth. When construction on the Mill Creek Sewer couldn't keep up, exclusive new western subdivisions built smaller lines that emptied into the dwindling Mill Creek itself or the River des Peres.

As a matter of fact, the poor River des Peres became so polluted that the city basically drove it underground—although a small stream flows on top of it today. In 1919, the Muny Opera in Forest Park offered its inaugural productions, and the River/Sewer des Peres overflowed nearby, chasing the cast and the audience from the venue one evening. A 1923 bond issue provided the funds to bury the river/sewer underground.

Laterals connected to the main Mill Creek line. But the laterals often got clogged, due to the nonchalance with which industries used the sewers. Some factories directed boiling water and steam into the sewer laterals, which threatened their structure. Slaughterhouses and the like forced carcasses into their sewers. Households added garbage and ashes from fireplaces and coal-burning stoves. Sewers were never meant to handle these things, of course, and the result was formations that hardened like concrete, backing up the storm runoff as well as sewage.

Still, after thirty years of digging, the Mill Creek Sewer finally ran from the foot of Chouteau Avenue to Vandeventer and Market by 1890 and functioned most of the time. Like most sewers, it was not a major topic of thought or conversation until a July day in 1892 when events conspired to put it on newspaper front pages in St. Louis and around the country.

On a Friday, July 22, city firefighters had battled what could have been a disastrous blaze. It broke out at an oil company at Twelfth (now Tucker) and Gratiot Streets in a barrel warehouse. The firemen faced two problems: Flames could spread to the oil storage tanks and burning oil from barrels in the warehouse was leaking into the streets. A bag company, a chemical works, a carriage plant, a brewery, and a foundry were all in harm's way. Water directed on the flaming building eventually quelled that threat, and the fire chief directed his men to take care of the leaking, burning oil by washing it into the Mill Creek Sewer.

It is estimated that on any normal day, that latter action would have been the right one because the now-flameless oil would have washed into the Mississippi in less than an hour. But that didn't work on July 22. The Mississippi was flooding, onto the St. Louis levee, and, most critically, above the level of the sewer outlets. Sewage laced with oil began to back up in the system. Gas fumes escaped through manholes sufficiently to alert some citizens. One man claimed after the fact that the smell led him to contact a sewer commissioner—who did nothing.

And, of course, the fumes escaping were nothing compared to the fumes and gases building up in the sewer. We can picture the Mill Creek Sewer as an enormous cut-stone chamber with an arched top and a floor twenty-feet wide. The top of the sewer arch was exposed in some of the older buildings, including a building at Fourth Street and Chouteau Avenue. In fact, the top of the sewer was the floor of the basement for the building that housed a saloon on its first floor and tenements above. A medical doctor and an extended family with two children lived upstairs. Because the building was in the older part of the city, it wasn't required to have a stack to vent sewer gas up to roof level. A house drain in the basement led directly to the big sewer below.

At 4:25 on the afternoon of July 26, the residents of the tenement were at home, and there were as yet only three or four men in the bar along with the bartender and the owner. A bit later and crews and travelers from the Iron Mountain Railroad depot across the street might have crowded the bar. The owner had apparently just been in the basement to fetch some of the liquor he stored there. He had carried a lit candle.

An eyewitness said he was slowing his horse and vehicle nearby, waiting for a freight train to pass when he heard thunder rumble and what felt like an earthquake begin. The first puff of smoke was white, but it was followed by a green hazy gas. "The sun looked green," he said, and he began to vomit from the smell.

The explosion that accompanied the gas sent stones from the sewer, bricks from the buildings, manhole grates and nearby macadam from the streets, and metal and broken ties from the Iron Mountain rails into the air. And then streaming down. A gash a thousand feet long and twenty feet deep lay along Chouteau Avenue—while the sewage continued to flow fitfully and wash over the debris in the Mill Creek Sewer. The sewer gas would slow residents and firefighters for hours.

Luckily, a firehouse was only two blocks away, and a fire crew was on the scene almost immediately looking for people buried in the rubble. It wasn't an easy job. The sewer gas is said to have acted like chloroform on the men, leaving them stumbling. Potential survivors had to deal with the gas as well. One man, believed to have been a bar patron, was dropped or washed into a depression partially filled with debris and sewage. He couldn't manage to climb out, due to injuries and the gas, and firefighters struggled, finally tying a rope around him and dragging him out. Another man was trapped under a fallen beam, and firefighters managed to lift it sufficiently to pull him to safety. Three of the men in the saloon, the owner, the bartender, and one other patron, were found dead, buried under the mass of debris.

Upstairs, the father and two children, and the doctor survived with minor injuries. An elderly woman, a member of the family, had been sitting on the back porch on a second floor. She was thrown to the alley fifty feet away and died of her injuries. Reports of an earthquake spread, but as word about what really happened got out, citizens hurried to the site. By Sunday, entire families were free to come witness the destruction. It took months to repair.

As with so many other blemishes and underlaying problems in St. Louis, the city went into high gear fixing the place up for the 1904 World's Fair. If any of the millions of visitors expected to attend would see a blemish, it got fixed. If the city needed clean water, not only for visitors to drink but for the water displays at the fair, it got clean water at last. With weeks to go before the fair opened, the city managed to put the right chemical (calcium carbonate) in the water at the Chain of Rocks plant, located on the Mississippi at the extreme northern edge of the city—above the sewer outlets. Taps emitted the cleanest water the city had ever seen, and the cascades and fountains at the fair sparkled. (Historian Primm wrote that "Dark brown waterfalls [had] haunted the dreams of the [fair] directors.")

Like many American cities of the day, the city hadn't managed clean air yet. That problem would take more years to fix, and part of that was laid at the feet of the city's poor: They argued they couldn't afford cleaner fuels like oil and continued to burn the cheap Illinois soft coal. It wasn't until the late 1930s and early 1940s that the US Weather Bureau reported an improvement in the visibility of benchmarks buildings. And another report "brightened."

For years, the Missouri Botanical Garden compared the hours of sunshine at the garden itself on Shaw Boulevard, southeast of Forest Park, and at its arboretum, located thirty-five miles away. It took a 1940 ordinance regulating households, businesses, and railroads to pull the garden's sunlight hours close to the arboretum's hours of good sun.

JUST HAVIN'
SOME FUN

When all is said and done, the reputation of St. Louis boils down to beer and baseball, ragtime and the 1904 World's Fair. Luckily, all those items are both storied and scandalous.

"WE APPEND THE SCORE": BEER AND BASEBALL

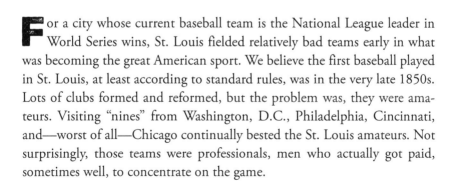

For a city whose current baseball team is the National League leader in World Series wins, St. Louis fielded relatively bad teams early in what was becoming the great American sport. We believe the first baseball played in St. Louis, at least according to standard rules, was in the very late 1850s. Lots of clubs formed and reformed, but the problem was, they were amateurs. Visiting "nines" from Washington, D.C., Philadelphia, Cincinnati, and—worst of all—Chicago continually bested the St. Louis amateurs. Not surprisingly, those teams were professionals, men who actually got paid, sometimes well, to concentrate on the game.

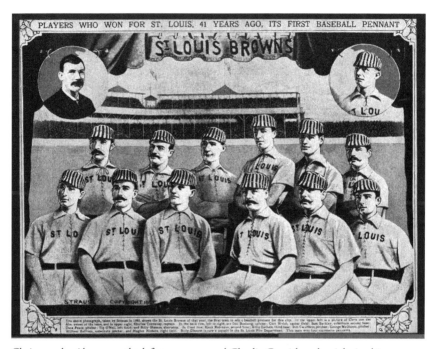

Chris von der Ahe graces the left top corner and Charlie Comiskey the right in this team photo, which should properly say St. Louis Brown Stockings to avoid confusion with the twentieth-century Browns of the American Association. Curt Welch is second from left in the back row; Bill Gleason is on the extreme right in that row; Arlie Latham is second from left on the first row. *Missouri Historical Society Collection*

Turning to old-line money, boosters focused on J. B. C. Lucas II, son of Judge Lucas, brother of deceased Charles Lucas (from chapter 3's duel), who led them in raising $20,000 to start a professional St. Louis team in 1874. With that, baseball became a business in St. Louis, one that would see ups and downs and more than its share of characters. And, one in which beer became not just a moneymaker but a cause célèbre. In the years leading up to the twentieth century, the game became a spectacle as well, occasioning the city's newspapers to comment on the crowd and the festivities. At the end of one such story, the old *Republican* noted, "We append the score." (Lampe)

LET THE GOOD TIMES ROLL

O n St. Louis' north side, in the second German-immigrant neighborhood that centered around Vandeventer and Grand, an entrepreneur-
ial saloon owner was puzzled.

Immigrant Christian von der Ahe knew nothing about baseball. He
wondered why his Golden Lion Saloon sometimes cleared out for three
hours at a time and then refilled with happy, thirsty patrons. A man named
Ned Cuthbert became a regular appearing after the crowd had settled in,
talking about "the game" they'd just watched. Ned Cuthbert, it turned out,
was manager of a nearby baseball team and, soon enough, he was talking to
von der Ahe about baseball.

Cuthbert described the beginnings of fame. The year after its founding, 1875, the newly named St. Louis Brown Stockings invited the Chicago
White Stockings into town to see how this notion of professional players
would pan out. Over the course of three days, the St. Louis nine beat the
Chicago club in both games played. The Lucases were happy; General William Tecumseh Sherman, who had worked for the Lucases before the war
and who sat in the press box for one of the games, was presumably happy.
The crowds were large and ecstatic.

One of a dizzying number of countrywide professional "leagues" was
formed in 1876, and St. Louis joined. But scandal struck the team in the
1877 season. In his quest for professional players, Lucas had signed four
members of the Louisville team who had thrown games the year before they
joined the Brown Stockings. The players admitted it in 1877; they were all

banned for life from playing the game. Lucas was accused of knowing about their deeds when he signed them. It was the end of Lucas' baseball career, as well, and the end of the Brown Stockings' tenure in the new league.

That meant the team went back to quasi-amateur status, although it continued to play, to win, and, in one brilliant move, to pick up a player named Charlie Comiskey. Crowds got larger. Cuthbert just happened to mention to Chris von der Ahe an intriguing possibility: von der Ahe selling his beer directly to customers at the ballpark. Von der Ahe saw dollar signs.

But there was a problem. Al and William Spink currently owned the team. And, the Spinks were drys. Prohibitionists. No beer was allowed at Brown Stockings games. Von der Ahe knew the way around that: He jumped in and bought the Browns for $1,800. He leased the ballpark on Grand Avenue and, most importantly, hired men who could carry steins of cold beer up and down the steps to sell to thirsty fans. Those fans who didn't want to sit in the stands could watch the game in a bit more comfort, if distantly, from one of von der Ahe's properties, a two-story house outside the right-field fence that he converted to a beer garden.

It all sounds so obvious to us today. But drinking beer, or any other form of alcohol, was a dividing line in American society, and St. Louis wasn't exempt. The Spinks were willing to sell to a "wet," but there were powerful men in the early baseball world who would hold out for a "clean" game.

William Hulbert, who had established the National League in 1876, had standards: no beer at games, no games on Sundays, no gambling on games, no lower-class fans. No Sunday games meant working-class families couldn't attend, given that they put in six-day workweeks. Plus, the exorbitant National League admission fee of 50 cents was about half a worker's daily wage. Hulbert and his partner, Al Spalding, promoted baseball as a game for middle- and upper-class fans.

A note on names is helpful. Hulbert and Spalding were owners of the Chicago White Stockings, early rivals of the St. Louis Brown Stockings, as well as leaders of the National League. Spalding had been a star pitcher for the team. He was also co-owner of a business that sold sporting goods; he was credited with using a glove when he pitched and making the glove popular. (We know the Spalding company today for all sorts of sports equipment, of course. The company brags that Spalding also produced the first football in 1887, the first basketball in 1894, the first volleyball in 1895, and the first liquid-center golf ball in 1930.) Al Spalding gets credit for initiating the idea of a spring training camp (in Hot Springs, Arkansas), and he argued throughout his career against women and Blacks playing the game. When competition grew most fierce, he perfected the strategy of raiding other teams for the best players.

Team names seem like a plot to confuse us. As the realignment of teams and leagues would play out, the early-dominant Boston *Red Stockings* would become the Boston Braves (and then the Milwaukee Braves and then the Atlanta Braves). The Boston *Red Sox* was a new team that joined the new American League when it started up in 1901. The Chicago *White Stockings* would morph into the Chicago Cubs. The Chicago *White Sox* also formed in 1901 to help found the American League. The St. Louis *Brown Stockings* would don red stockings by 1900 and be called the Cardinals. And, a new team called the St. Louis *Browns* joined the American League in 1902, having moved from Milwaukee, where they were called the Brewers.

But we get ahead of ourselves. In 1881, other National League teams were unhappy with Hulbert and Spalding's vision, and in 1882, they formed the American Association—just in time for von der Ahe to enroll the St. Louis Brown Stockings. One of the association's first rules allowed for beer. Sunday games and 25 cent admissions followed. The National League might cater to upper-class attendees who also belonged to temperance organizations and were largely old-line English. The new American Association appealed to working-class families from immigrant backgrounds, particularly the Germans and Irish, once again united in St. Louis against nativist drys.

And those fans went to games to see two things: increasingly good baseball and the spectacle that was Chris von der Ahe. Not a distinguished-looking man by any assessment, von der Ahe nevertheless dressed the part. He wore a top hat and frock coat to lead the team in a parade to each game. His matching greyhounds accompanied him. Over the years, the northwest side of St. Louis became a playground as von der Ahe added fireworks and lawn bowling and horse races to the venue. And more saloons on neighboring corners. Von der Ahe at one point hired an all-female band to entertain before games. Noting women's attractions to first-baseman Charlie Comiskey, the owner arranged discount tickets for ladies along the first base line.

He advertised in ethnic newspaper that baseball was the all-American game in an attempt to recruit immigrant fans who wanted to appear more native. And he promoted the beauty of the open field in a crowded urban environment—although the dusty infield would lack bucolic beauty for modern fans. Von der Ahe's nickname in the press became "der boss president," and reporters didn't fail to record his broken English in praise of himself and his business.

In fact, the baseball might have been better sooner if von der Ahe could have kept his hands off the management. Because von der Ahe considered himself the brains behind the business, he thought he had the brains for the game as well. He famously ordered the team to "hit all balls to right field," after a game had been won with a right-field hit. He liked to say he had the "biggest diamond in baseball," only to be reminded that all baseball infields were the same size by then. Most seriously, he sent continual memos to managers and fined players when he saw a play he didn't like. We can imagine the irritation of players who had to live in von der Ahe's apartments and were ordered to drink only at his pubs.

Having run through three managers and with little to show in the standings by the end of the 1884 season, von der Ahe appointed his talented first baseman, Charlie Comiskey, to be player-manager of the team. The combination of der boss president and the most aggressive player in the game led to four successive championships—and legends.

We talk today about benches clearing as a rough day at the ballpark. That is nothing compared to the day-to-day roughness and even violence in a ballpark where Charlie Comiskey played. He was a brilliant baseball strategist off the field, almost cerebral. But on the field, he combined excellent play with something close to hooliganism. He could have taught Ty Cobb. In addition to managing, Comiskey was also a base coach when he wasn't on the bases himself.

He continually argued with umpires. He terrorized second basemen when he was running and would "accidentally" block the other team's runners from his position at first base. Comiskey's shortstop, Bill Gleason, did the same on the other side of the field. When Comiskey was functioning as a base coach, Gleason was often doing the same at the other corner. Except that neither stayed anywhere near first or third bases. They would close in on the opposing catcher, "comment on his breeding, personal habits, [and] skill as a receiver, or rather lack of it . . ." (Golenbock quoting the Louisville manager) That habit was so offensive, and so damaging to opposing catchers' performances, that the association insisted on coaching boxes starting in 1887.

Comiskey gave free rein to the biggest mouth in the game, third baseman Arlie Latham. It is said that, once upon a time, players were relatively silent during a game, rarely calling out encouragement to their fellows or insults to their opponents. Latham changed that. He would start his running commentary on the sins of the opposing team with the first pitch and could keep it up for at least nine innings. Wildly popular in St. Louis, he may have been the acrobatic forerunner of 1980s shortstop Ozzie Smith. Smith famously did a forward somersault as he approached his position to open a game. Latham was known to perform during a game. Naturally, it was against the Chicago White Stocking that we have a description of Latham somersaulting over the first baseman, who was bending to retrieve Latham's bunt. Latham not only avoided the tag, but he reached first safely, talking, of course, jibing at the Chicago player, superstar Cap Anson.

The Brown Stockings' most vulgar voice was center fielder Curt Welch. Welch was fast, a good batter, and an expert at getting hit to get on base. He literally started a riot in Baltimore because of the way he crashed into the second baseman on a steal attempt. Von der Ahe had to bail him out of jail.

We should also note Comiskey's contributions to the game. A driving perfectionist with a great memory, he could remember a batter's tendencies and advise his battery on pitch selection. He may have been the first to have outfielders shift based on his memory of opponents' hitting. He certainly was the first to play his own position the modern way, positioning himself well to the right of a vacant first base bag and letting the pitcher cover first on grounders.

Most importantly, Comiskey could deal with Chris von der Ahe, at least for a while. It must have been hard at times. In 1885, the St. Louis team played the White Stockings in an early version of the World Series. Von der Ahe and Spalding called them exhibition games, with the team winning the best of seven to split a $1,000 purse. It was a crazy series by our standards. The first game, in Chicago, was called a tie because of darkness. The second game in St. Louis featured fans storming the field; police had to rescue umpire Dave Sullivan and escort Chicago players off the field. Later in the evening, from his hotel, Sullivan declared the game a forfeit to Chicago. Comiskey refused to abide by the statement, but the teams continued to play. St. Louis won two games at home, and Chicago won "exhibitions" in Pittsburgh and Cincinnati.

The series sat at 3-2-Chicago with a tie and included the controversial forfeit that would give the series to Chicago. At that point, Cap Anson, the Chicago captain, announced that they chose not to claim the forfeit, that they wanted to play the deciding game. So, they did. To Anson's dismay, Chicago had to put their pitcher from the previous game on the mound because the announced starter was late to the park and likely drunk when he got there. The Brown Stockings took the game and therefore the series—if you didn't count the forfeit.

But even in victory, von der Ahe was back to seeing dollar signs. To the dismay of the team and fans, he announced that the forfeit should count as such and that the series was a tie. That meant he got to keep the $1,000. Von der Ahe would fail to pay players in the post season several more times, usually by citing poor results in exhibition games.

In 1886, the championship again pitted the Chicago team against the St. Louis team. Almost any day of the games would have generated outraged headlines in the twenty-first century. On the second day in St. Louis, Chicago's odd play led reporters to ask about the possibility of hippodroming—throwing the game. The evidence grew with the next game, in which Cap Anson started his shortstop as pitcher and then substituted his second baseman in relief.

The next game was also played in St. Louis, and in this one, Arlie Latham led off the controversy. Coming to the plate with men on, Latham might be expected to bunt, being an expert bunter. That led the Chicago catcher to examine Latham's bat. What he saw made him complain loudly that one side was flat. Apparently, Latham had planed away one side of the wood to lessen the chances of fouling off his bunt. The umpire ordered Latham to get a new bat, and the crowd was supremely unhappy.

And then it started to rain. Comiskey called for a delay. Cap Anson of Chicago got in the umpire's face arguing that there was no need to stop the game. That was too much for the crowd that was still roaring about Latham's bat, and they surged onto the field. By the time the police got control and the fans returned to the stands, the rain had stopped. Latham returned to the plate, and a Chicago outfielder decided to shift closer to the left field line, knowing Latham's usual hitting and possibly reasoning that Latham wouldn't bunt without his flat-sided bat.

Latham loudly informed both base runners he'd bring them in, to the crowd's delight, and hit a liner to the spot the left fielder had vacated. By the time the fielder ran the ball down, Latham had a triple and the two men on base had indeed scored, tying the game.

The next controversy, with the game by now in extra innings, involved the irascible Curt Welch promptly stepping in front of a pitch and being waved to first. Of course, Chicago's Anson again protested, and the umpire agreed, calling Welch back to the plate. As it turned out, it made no difference. Welch singled. A few plays later, he was at third. When he started to steal home, the Chicago pitcher, trying to make the pitch as easy to catch as possible, instead threw high. Welch scored, on a slide when he could have waltzed across standing, and Charlie Comiskey, coaching at third, ran along beside him. Comiskey is said to have caught the karooming ball himself before the Chicago catcher could get to it, pocketing it as a souvenir.

In the 1887 season, the team was even better, although there was the incident where von der Ahe got arrested. A municipal judge had ruled against Sunday games, based on the state's blue laws. On a Sunday in June 1887, in front of a capacity crowd of ten thousand, mounted St. Louis police rode into the stadium and arrested der boss president. Von der Ahe was bailed out and got back to the park while the crowd waited. But von der Ahe canceled the game so his players wouldn't get arrested as well. The religious lobby was shortly thereafter disappointed when von der Ahe's lawyers convinced the judge that baseball was recreation, not work, so it could proceed on Sundays.

THE GOOD OLD DAYS ALWAYS END

I t was already the good old days in St. Louis, although not for long.

After St. Louis' 1887 championship, von der Ahe began to trade away players, often the ones who complained the most about his interference. By 1892, Charlie Comiskey left. Even moving to the new ballpark at Vandeventer Avenue and Natural Bridge Road didn't help. The team turned in a losing record, and the slide began.

In 1895, von der Ahe's wife left him; their son, who had helped with baseball operations, joined her in an infidelity suit. Von der Ahe responded by marrying one of the women named in the suit—which prompted a second woman named in the suit to sue him for breach of promise. Apparently, he had promised to marry that woman, his former housekeeper.

In 1897, the team, at one point managed by von der Ahe himself because he couldn't keep a manager, went 29-102. The league wanted to drop the Brown Stockings from its membership, largely to get rid of von der Ahe.

In 1898, the relatively new Sportsman's Park was swept by flames during the second game of the season. Faced with declining fortunes and the national economic woes that started in 1893, von der Ahe had skimped on insurance. People burned or trampled in the fire sued; von der Ahe had lost a saloon, business records, gate cash, and personal possessions in the fire. Rebuilding a smaller stadium was a financial burden von der Ahe could ill afford.

Matters worsened that year. Back in 1891, von der Ahe had had a former player named Mark Baldwin arrested for trying to bribe a St. Louis player to switch to the Pittsburgh team. (This may have been common; one story says that's why the Pittsburgh team picked up the nickname "pirates.") Von der Ahe was in Pittsburgh for a game in 1898 when he was arrested because Baldwin had charged him with false arrest. The president of the Pittsburgh team, W. A. Nimick, posted bail, but von der Ahe responded by fleeing home to St. Louis.

Nimick proceeded to hire two detectives, who lured von der Ahe to a meeting in St. Louis, essentially abducted him, and managed to keep him quiet on what must have been a long train ride to Pittsburgh, where von der Ahe finally faced the charges.

Nimick also encouraged the other National League owners to take the St. Louis franchise away from von der Ahe in 1899. Despite legal challenges, the team was auctioned off on the notorious steps of the Old Courthouse to two baseball men from Cleveland, Frank and Stanley Robison. One of their first actions was to change the uniforms, a step toward changing the team's image. The brown stockings became red, and a sports reporter for the *Republic* nicknamed the players the Cardinals.

Von der Ahe returned to bar tending and poverty. When he died in 1913 of cirrhosis of the liver, someone located the grand statue he'd had made of himself years before. It stands over his grave in Bellefontaine Cemetery.

The new Cardinals never had great success under the Robisons, but one noteworthy event occurred. Frank Robison had stepped aside in 1905, and Stanley Robison died in 1911. Ownership of the team went to Frank's daughter, Stanley's niece, Helene Britton, making her the first woman to own a major league baseball team. (The next female owner of a current major league club was Grace Comiskey, Charlie's daughter-in-law, who inherited the Chicago White Sox at her husband's death in 1939.)

When Mrs. Britton decided to sell the underperforming club—following years in which other National League owners suggested she should sell just because she was female—she made the deal with a management group that pulled Branch Rickey in as vice president and general manager. Rickey had been with the St. Louis Browns, by now of the American League, for years. Rickey, of course, is known for establishing the farm system, for hiring Jackie Robinson as the first Black to play major league ball years later in Brooklyn, and for starting a St. Louis institution, the Knothole Gang. Named for the tradition of young boys looking through knotholes in the fence, Rickey's "gang" of poor St. Louis youth got free tickets from stockholders that allowed the boys to attend games—on condition that they not skip school to do so. It is speculated that the program helped shift the loyalty of St. Louis fans from the Browns to the Cardinals.

AS COLORFUL AS A CARDINAL

Over the years, St. Louis has seen a good number of controversial players. Dizzy Dean, Leo Durocher, Pepper Martin, from the 1940s Gashouse Gang era, were controversial in various ways. Rogers Hornsby stands out along those lines.

Hornsby was a fixture on the Cardinals by the time he helped the team win the World Series in 1926. He drifted among other teams and returned to the Cardinals in 1933, only to be picked up by the Browns in a management change that year. (Historian Golenbock says that the Browns' purchase that year involved nine hundred stockholders, which was "almost as many owners as fans.")

Hornsby had always been known to gamble, but it became obvious in the mid- to late-1930s. He was said to send the clubhouse boy across the street to a saloon, where the lad would place bets for Hornsby on horse races and ball games. The boy would return while a game was in progress to give Hornsby, a player-manager by this time, the results. Finally, the new management hired Pinkerton detectives to get the goods on Hornsby and fired him in 1937. Even a .358 career batting average didn't make up for the gambling problem.

Chris von der Ahe would have at least appreciated the publicity. He would also have appreciated the ownership of the Cardinals many years later in the person of Augustus "Gussie" Busch. Gussie's company, Anheuser-Busch, was fourth in national sales of beer in 1947. In 1953, Busch bought the Cardinals. A few public comments to the contrary, Busch intended the purchase solely to boost sales. He may have understood the game better than von der Ahe, but Gussie thought it "dull" because there was too much standing around.

He proceeded to fix up old Sportsman's Park and rename it Busch Stadium (having been talked out of naming it Budweiser Stadium). He changed all the advertising to trumpet Busch beer. He trotted Clydesdales pulling a beer wagon around the stadium on special occasions. He encouraged broadcaster Harry Caray—long before Caray ended up with the Chicago Cubs—in Caray's highly successful efforts to sell beer. (When Gussie Busch and Harry Caray broke up the relationship in 1969, Caray said it was because of rumors that he was having an affair with Busch's daughter-in-law, something no one ever confirmed.) And equally in the mode of von der Ahe, Gussie Busch believed he could run the team as well as the baseball men. The Cardinals had some success under Busch's interference, notably in the 1960s, but didn't entirely escape his meddling until the 1980s, not long before Busch's death.

SCANDAL AND GLORY AT THE PIANO: THE RAGGED HEART OF RAGTIME

He was a polite, reserved Black man. Had anyone on the train spoken to him, they would have been struck by his lack of a traditional Southern Black accent—although he was born the son of a freed slave in northeast Texas—by his "refined speech," a white newspaperman called it. He was Scott Joplin, the anointed King of Ragtime.

Joplin might have been visiting friends and former music instructors in Sedalia, Missouri, off toward Kansas City, on any given day between 1901 and 1907. He might well have ridden the Katy (Missouri, Kansas, and Texas) rail or the MoPac (Missouri Pacific) into St. Louis to get back home to one of the modest apartments he rented in those years. As he pulled into the grandest of America's rail terminals, he had to be struck by the contrast between its elegance and the surrounding shabbiness, a reminder of the contrast between the praise he got and the revilement, between his ambitious musical dreams and the reality of ragtime.

Scott Joplin, King of Ragtime and St. Louis resident during his highly creative years. State *Historical Society of Missouri Collection*

SCANDAL AT THE KEYBOARD AND ACROSS THE BOARD

If you had asked St. Louis residents for an example of something "scandalous" in the first decade of the twentieth century, "ragtime" would have been the answer as often as not. There were a few positive voices: Alfred Ernst, distinguished director of the St. Louis Choral Symphony Society, called Joplin "an extraordinary genius."

Joplin dreamed of rag operas and rag ballets but as often as not found himself listening to his own compositions played in bars and brothels.

His train would have lined up three or four blocks south of Market Street. Then the puffing engine would back the cars under the elegant glass and tin train shed—a marvel in its own right.

Before the Gateway Arch served to identify St. Louis, there was Union Station, a medieval castle towering over the surrounding mass of peasants and pilgrims. The biggest terminal in the country when it was finished in 1894, the station was faced with huge squares of limestone and sturdy arches and adorned with statuary and marble and gleaming tiles. Its clock tower rose 230 feet above track level.

Once off the crowded car, Joplin would push his way through the busy Midway. Multiple rail lines put hundreds of trains into the station daily; in the ragtime era, one hundred thousand people could be counted passing through the Midway in any given twenty-four hours. Joplin likely stayed on the main floor, crossing out onto Market through the stylish porte cochere that shielded folk using carriages or the new autos from the weather. Had he ventured up a floor, he could have taken in the Grand Hall, with its sixty-five-foot-high barreled ceiling, stained-glass window, and elaborate carvings.

But, of course, the elegance was something Joplin aspired to, not something he routinely enjoyed.

Many African Americans lived in the shadow of Union Station. In the first years of the twentieth century, "Mill Creek Valley" or "Chestnut Valley" was the loose designation for a fourteen- by nine-block area ranging on either side of the main thoroughfare of Market Street, starting about a mile east of the Mississippi. It was the primary abode of some poor whites as well as struggling African Americans pouring into the city from the South. The houses were aging and ramshackle. Shabby businesses on Market and Chestnut served tourists as well as locals who used the saloons and brothels.

The tourist business—in everything from trinkets to sex—flourished because, in the midst of squalor, stately Union Station provided steady trade. The station was a true terminal. Trains didn't simply slow to pick up or discharge passengers and then continue on their way. All passengers, those headed on to nearby towns or across the country, disembarked, dealt with their baggage, and had to await another train.

Almost as soon as the station was completed, the neighborhood around it opened for the business of entertaining passengers with time on their hands. Upper-class passengers might use the hotel inside the station or indulge in one of the first chain restaurants: Fred Harvey's fine restaurants dominated train stations across the country. But many other passengers headed to the derelict buildings in the surrounding blocks to eat, sleep, get a photo taken, buy tobacco or beer, or enjoy the services at brothels. Depending on the time of day, some might have stopped to listen to genuine ragtime, played by the greats.

The neighborhood had a reputation for bars and brothels, music, and mayhem. Ballads of the "murder-legend" genre were fed by actual events. One of the most famous roughly reflects an event in 1899. One night, a young black woman named Frankie Baker waited up for her lover, Allen Britt, to come home to a boardinghouse on Targee Street, three and a half blocks east of Union Station. According to what may be legend, he had been performing in a cakewalk contest—a cakewalk being a strutting dance performed to ragtime. Problem was that Allen was obviously dancing with another woman when the pair won the contest. Frankie had cause, she said, to believe Allen was cheating on her—"done her wrong" as song lyrics had it—and the two argued. However the confrontation went down, she shot Allen in the abdomen, claiming self-defense. He died four days later.

Legend—again—has it that a song was written about the event the next day, assuming Allen's demise. The song, as well as public opinion, police, and courts, debated Frankie's status as wronged woman or vicious murderer. By the time Scott Joplin was living in St. Louis, a new version had been put to music and—perhaps for the rhyme or rhythm of the thing—Allen's name had changed to Johnny.

Several versions of the lyrics, and hence the story of Frankie and Johnny, exist. Some of us may remember country-great Jimmie Rodger's version.

Frankie and Johnny were sweethearts oh Lordy how they did love
Swore to be true to each other true as the stars above
He was her man he was doing her wrong

In that version, Frankie is condemned to die for murder. However, the real Frankie Baker was acquitted. She complained, on the other hand, that she couldn't get away from the song and sued to block its spread. She died, possibly in a mental hospital, in 1952.

We can easily believe she couldn't get away and that the song lived on after her. The list of performers who have sung it in one version or another spans music styles and generations. Imagine the story told from these perspectives: Johnny Cash, Bob Dylan, Sammy Davis Jr. (with Cyd Charisse dancing Frankie's role), Van Morrison, Dinah Shore, or Stevie Wonder, among many others. The story was the basis for movies in 1936 (Helen Morgan and Chester Morris), in 1966 (Donna Douglas and Elvis Presley), and in 1991 (Michelle Pfeiffer and Al Pacino).

Most importantly, the ballad of Frankie and Johnny set a mood for the Mill Creek Valley. The Valley was dangerous. It rang with ragtime and vice.

For that matter, Blacks also owned, frequented, and played music a few blocks north in the neighborhood called "Deep Morgan." Morgan Street, now renamed Delmar, supported another deadly legend celebrated in song. In 1895, on Christmas Day, a pimp named Lee "Stagolee" Shelton shot and killed Black ward boss Billy Lyons in a saloon at Eleventh and Morgan. At dispute were the men's hats. Shelton had crushed the crown of Lyons' bowler, and Lyons had responded by grabbing Shelton's Stetson.

Mississippi John Hurt recorded the Stagolee event in 1928. Duke Ellington, Woody Guthrie, Bob Dylan, and the Grateful Dead would follow up.

Scott Joplin at one point lived in Deep Morgan, at the boardinghouse that now survives as the Scott Joplin House State Historical Site on Delmar Boulevard. But, just arriving in the city by train, he most likely would have crossed Market Street into the Mill Creek Valley and the heart of both controversy and creativity.

RAGGED RHYTHMS

We hear a tinny piano rocking with the distinctive "ragged" rhythm today and the message is "old." Maybe we think nostalgic, maybe quaint, certainly difficult to play. But hardly controversial.

Music historians say ragtime combined with Cuban habanera elements to form jazz by 1920, possibly leading to rock in the 1950s. But between 1892 and 1917, ragtime was the hot new thing, embraced by the restless young, blasted by the more conservative—and unmistakably identified with its African American "sports."

Ragtime was hailed in some circles as the first truly American music, with Joplin's creations at the center of it all. At one point, Ernst, the symbol of elevated music in St. Louis, wanted to take Joplin to Europe to meet "serious" composers. The trip never happened, but a few European musicians, including Claude Debussy and Antonín Dvořák, picked up ragtime as a motif for their compositions. Certainly, Scott's works such as the "Maple Leaf Rag," "The Entertainer," "The Cascades," and many more, sold to white musicians across the country and garnered praise for the composer who clearly had good musical training and a great ear.

But many more people panned and berated the music and its practitioners. Ragtime ruined young people's taste for good music, the milder reviewers said. More worried critics called ragtime "virulent poison," its syncopated rhythms damaging the brains of America's youth. The most agitated claimed that America was "falling prey to the collective soul of the negro," charging that ragtime "is symbolic of the primitive morality and perceptible moral limitations of the negro type." (Berlin)

But it wasn't just white Americans who uttered vicious words. Across town, the middle-class African Americans in the Ville and along Enright and West Belle were alarmed. They likely agreed with a Black writer who insisted that the association of ragtime with African Americans was a "libelous insult" and that "the typical Negro would blush to own acquaintance with the vicious trash put forth under Ethiopian titles." (Berlin)

So, Scott Joplin, the man who wanted his music to be accepted by serious musicians and white society, took all this in and still had little choice but to compose ragtime in a city slum. The distance between the Mill Creek Valley and the St. Louis Symphony Hall was much greater than a map of 1905 St. Louis would indicate.

Given his options, Joplin might well have turned west coming out of Union Station to visit his friend Tom Turpin.

If the dismay and disdain so many people felt for ragtime had a face in St. Louis, Tom Turpin's was as good as anyone's.

While ragtime was played across the country, its heartbeat was in St. Louis. The city in the middle of it all drew the best ragtime composers and players to the seedy Valley, to its saloons and brothels, and to Turpin's towering figure.

Turpin is celebrated today, as then, as the first African American to publish a ragtime piece, his *Harlem Rag*, written in 1892 and published in 1897. The small collection of his other published rags contains excellent examples of his style, solid and professional—though often judged as easier to play than Joplin's more sophisticated works.

But that is only one factor that made Turpin larger than life. Reading between the lines, we can intuit that Turpin's talent, energy, and expansive personality didn't just fit the mold of a ragtimer; he defined one.

Tom held court at various entertainment venues his family owned in the Mill Creek Valley. The one we know most about is Tom's Rosebud Café, located a couple of blocks west of Union Station on Market. The Rosebud was the epicenter of all that St. Louisans found scandalous.

Tom promoted it as the headquarters for colored professionals and sports. It had pool halls, dining rooms—Tom sometimes listed himself as a cook in the City Directory—and downstairs entertainment spaces.

"Furnished apartments for gentlemen" were upstairs. Some sources suggest the upstairs functioned for assignations as well as living quarters. The establishment was certainly in the red-light district. A business card for the Rosebud has survived showing Turpin in a sporting pose.

A self-taught piano virtuoso, Tom stood at least six feet and weighed perhaps three hundred pounds. Contemporaries wondered how his beefy fingers could fit the slender ivory keys or move so fast across them. One of his favorite pastimes was "cutting contests," in which the young Black sports competed in virtuosity and improvisation.

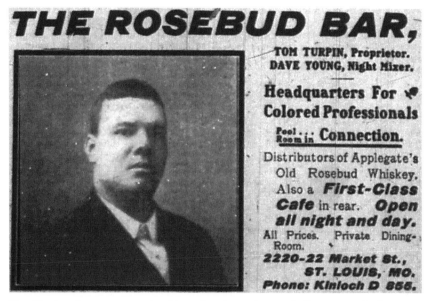

Tom Turpin, piano maestro and emblem of ragtime culture to St. Louisans in the first decades of the twentieth century, from an ad for his Rosebud Bar in 1905 in the *St. Louis Palladium. Missouri Historical Society Collection*

Amazingly, Turpin didn't always win. Among his particular protégés were Sam Patterson, Joe Jordan, and Louis Chauvin.

Patterson went on to lead the famous Clef's Club in New York City in the 1920s and played with Joe Jordan in the orchestra of the WPA (the depression-era Works Progress Administration) in the 1930s. Sam was a particular friend of Scott Joplin.

Joe Jordan's specialty was Black musical theater, although we have a report of him winning at least one of Turpin's contests. He wrote piano rags as well and was known for a song featured by Fanny Brice in the Ziegfeld Follies.

Regarded by some as the outstanding pianist even in a circle that included Tom Turpin, Louis Chauvin was Patterson's boyhood friend. Chauvin's improvisational playing was brilliant, and he composed as well. But he was considered undisciplined; he couldn't read music and declined to learn. Patterson and Joplin each notated at least one published piece for him.

Perhaps the poorest actual pianist in the Valley was Scott Joplin. The sports took delight in playing his pieces far better than he did. The kindest thing said of his piano performances in the early 1900s was "technically indifferent." He had put in his time with quartets back in Sedalia and apparently sang better than he played piano by Valley standards. Patterson himself noted that Joplin never played well, but that he was widely respected for his composition.

It is said Joplin took lessons so he could perform "Sunflower Slow Drag," one of his more famous compositions. His most precise biographer wonders if his deficiency at the keys in the first decade of the 1900s was an early sign of the illness that would kill him in 1917. Admittedly, Joplin's playing was lauded in other locales, even in the years to follow. But that playing didn't cut it in the Mill Creek Valley.

So, Joplin and Turpin, Patterson, Jordan, and Chauvin, and others in their orbit built an art form of syncopated music in the heart of a red-light district. We know that Joplin played in several brothels, providing the entertainment "downstairs," and the others likely did so as well. Maybe the scandalous trappings of the music made it all the more daring for white teenagers who bought the sheet music and sweated over the difficult rhythms. In that sense, the image paid off, at least for the sheet music publishers.

We should report another of the musicians not so closely associated with Joplin but musically tied to St. Louis for the ages. W. C. Handy at one point was a vagrant who favored a vacant lot on Deep Morgan, a block from the

Stagolee/Lyons saloon. He later wrote about the need to avoid police, who had no patience for such behavior. By that time, he was famous for his "St. Louis Blues," which marked the revamping of ragtime to a new form.

We also remember the Turpins for more than ragtime. Tom and his father and brother Charlie, a talented guitarist, did indeed operate saloons and entertainment venues in the Valley for years. But they also left their political mark on the city.

Charlie made history as the first African American officeholder in Missouri when he was elected constable for the Valley township in 1910. He wasn't seated until after an election challenge, but his ultimate victory resonated through the city.

Later in the 1910s, the Turpins erected first a tent and then a building named the Booker T. Washington Theater, also on Market close to the station. It held a thousand spectators and brought in such performers as Eubie Blake, Ethel Waters, and Bessie Smith.

Charlie went on to partner with other businessmen and lawyers to form the Citizens Liberty League. That group, sometimes successfully, promoted the political ascent of Blacks in the state.

Undoubtedly, much of the attention Tom, and even Charlie, Turpin enjoy today comes from their association with Scott Joplin during the years he lived in St. Louis. The Rosebud is recreated next door to the Scott Joplin House on Delmar. Photographic portraits of Tom and Charlie grace the walls leading into the "bar."

Whatever chuckles his playing elicited in the Valley, Joplin flourished in the city professionally, publishing a long list of notable works; he also wrote a rag opera lost to history. However, Joplin left St. Louis for New York City in 1907, surely thinking that he could stage his second opera, "Treemonisha," begun in St. Louis, more easily in the Big Apple. He and his wife, Lottie, struggled with that dream for ten years while Joplin's health declined.

There are telling incidents along the way, tales of Joplin's increasing paranoia over people stealing his compositions, tales of his increasing inability to play. We don't know if he knew of Louis Chauvin's death in 1908 in Chicago, most likely of syphilitic sclerosis.

It would have been one more indication of Joplin's fate, perhaps a sad by-product of years of playing ragtime in the only venues where he could play it, establishments rightly connected with prostitution.

In early 1917, Joplin was admitted to mental facilities in New York City. He died on April 1 of that year in the Manhattan State Hospital of dementia paralytica, a condition associated with advanced syphilis.

That same year, in the same city, the Original Dixieland Jazz Band was drawing crowds. In a century in which blues, then jazz, then rock, then rap exploded on the scene, we have adjusted our definition of "scandalous," but one of the scandals of the early twentieth century was surely this: The only places to hear the first true American music played by its creators were bars and brothels like the ones in St. Louis' Mill Creek Valley.

Historian Walter Johnson captured the paradox.

Joplin wrote the soundtrack for desire and dread, for the inflated festivity of the night before and the pounding payback of the morning after, for pleasure rung out of pain, for the hard work that subtended the easy life. For the rumble and the bell of the streetcar that carried the wealthy white men of the West End downtown to Chestnut Valley and Deep Morgan. (Johnson in *The Broken Heart of America*)

MEET ME IN ST. LOUIE, LOUIE, FOR THE NEWEST AND SHABBIEST AT THE WORLD'S FAIR

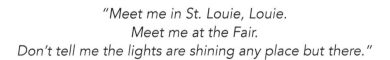

*"Meet me in St. Louie, Louie.
Meet me at the Fair.
Don't tell me the lights are shining any place but there."*

A true meeting of cultures at the fair, a white St. Louis lady teaches a Filipino youth the cakewalk, a dance associated with Black ragtime—which was banned on the fairgrounds. *Missouri Historical Society Collection*

Thanks to a catchy theme song and a still-vibrant movie made in 1944, the 1904 Louisiana Purchase Exposition, commonly known as the St. Louis World's Fair, is an institution that lingers on in American lore. That particular fair, in an era of fairs and expositions, was once considered a seminal event of the new century, drawing millions of attendees who exclaimed over a wealth of new technology, new foods, and new experiences.

Today, we focus on the experiences and are ashamed of a record of racism, imperialism, and profit-seeking that degraded—and perhaps killed—people treated as sideshows. To say those incidents reflected the times is less an excuse than a truism requiring historical explanation. From dying premature babies to living-zoo Filipinos, the fair showcased as much about the visitors as about the exhibits.

Let us set the scene first. Planning for the fair began in 1899, directed by men such as Pierre Chouteau, a great-great-grandson of Marie Thérèse Chouteau and Pierre Laclède, channeling the old aristocracy, and David Francis, St. Louis' new aristocracy—former mayor, former governor, briefly secretary of the interior, and, in the future, US Ambassador to Russia during the Bolshevik Revolution. Along with other businessmen and boosters of the "New" St. Louis, they chose the western end of Forest Park, along with real estate that spilled over Skinker Avenue to include parts of the new Washington University campus and the area near Wydown and DeMun Streets (close to the current campus of Concordia Seminary). One enthusiastic fairgoer and native St. Louisan had initial misgivings, noting that woodmen axed giant monarchs of the forest "such as few cities could boast to possess" to clear the way for some fifteen hundred buildings.

Some of the buildings were as small as huts built by Filipinos who brought their own construction materials. Others were grand, themed palaces, huge square footages to showcase Machinery, Horticulture, and so on. Forty-two American states and sixty-two foreign countries constructed smaller buildings. They all were elaborate and they all were fake, as permanence goes, save one. Art Hill in Forest Park still holds what is now the St. Louis Art Museum. The rest were made of plaster and "staff," a fibrous material; the material could be carved in fantastical detail. It all held until the fair was demolished in December of 1904.

The Pike was the amusement and fast-food zone, stretching for a mile along the north side of the fair's more than twelve hundred acres. Water features, including the wondrous cascades—captured in music by Scott Joplin—and lagoons large enough to host gondola rides lay among the rises and dips of the park.

When it became obvious that the Forest Park site wouldn't be sufficient for the increasingly elaborate plans, the directors talked the board of Washington University into delaying its move to the new campus located off the northwest corner of the park. The 109-acre campus was leased by the fair directors and used, in part, for the concurrent Olympics. The sites used for the Philippine Reservation were also added, to total almost two square miles of fairgrounds.

Mayor Rolla Wells pushed through all sorts of civic improvements, including converting macadam and gravel streets to stone paving. One of those streets was Lindell, the major thoroughfare leading to the grounds. It was gravel when the preparations began and fronted the homes of leading citizens, including Mayor Wells. When the other homeowners balked at paying their share of paving costs, Wells suggested that anyone who was so cheap should move to another street. Lindell got its stone paving.

In addition to the actual exhibits and glorious grounds, some 155 national conventions were scheduled during the fair's six-month run. The Democratic National Convention of 1904 took place in St. Louis, as did the first "international" Olympics held in the United States—of which more below.

The fair was initially financed by the same amount of money Thomas Jefferson had paid Napoleon for the entire Louisiana Purchase: $15 million. Five million each was to come from private subscriptions, the city of St. Louis, and the US Congress. Eventually, it all rolled in—which didn't mean that the fair wouldn't be expected to raise money from admissions. And, in order to do that, the fair would host more than self-congratulatory technology displays.

THE HUMAN ZOO

The visitors' guide to the fair promoted it as "an exhibit of processes, rather than of products"—meaning, apparently, that the fair was a showcase of living exhibits. Certainly, the fair featured not just the output of foreign countries, but the actual people of foreign countries.

The fair's theme was the advancement of civilization during the preceding century. That meant white civilization was setting the standard, showing the way for lesser societies to continue their upward climb. There were certainly Europeans at the fair, showing off their arts and mechanics, evidence of acknowledged civilization, but the exhibits that remain in memory are those of the less civilized—everyone else—trying to catch up.

GERONIMO!

An obvious starting point was the Native American tribes that had been the victims of exploitation of the Louisiana Purchase. Of course, there would be "Indians" at the fair because Wild West shows were a popular entertainment. The Pike offered a cacophony of cowboys and Indians. It also featured a live Eskimo village and a Cliff Dwellers scene of pueblos.

In fact, the head of the Bureau of Indian Affairs objected to Wild West shows as sensationalism that retarded Native American civilization—which is to say, the march toward white civilization. Embracing the fair's "process" preference, the official exhibition featured a two-story Indian School, the vehicle for impressing white Americans of the natives' industrial evolution.

Several hundred Native Americans were recruited, mostly from tribes and reservations to the west and south of the groups Manuel Lisa would have known. The large exhibition building featured contrasts. On one side of a walkway, women wove blankets and baskets, carved pipes, ground corn, and worked beads. Geronimo, on loan from the Apache prison in Ft. Sill, Oklahoma, held court in one section. The fierce, last holdout against American and Mexican aggression occasionally sang or danced and made bows and arrows for sale, along with selling his autograph. He celebrated his seventy-fifth birthday at the fair.

Across the walkway from him, students from Indian schools built impressive furniture, ran the latest printing presses, cooked white food, painted, and blacksmithed. Students, who were rotated into St. Louis from various real Native American schools, took classes in front of visitors, as well as parading, gardening, and showing off literary and musical talents—including two popular band performances a day.

It all added up to an undeniable truth. White America had not just conquered the native tribes; it was leading them peacefully to assimilation and civilization.

Located near the Native American tribes—and sometimes in active competition with them for visitors—were the Pygmies from Africa. They were recruited with bribes and gifts and with their return guaranteed by leaving a hostage. Two American Black men, presumably from the Tuscaloosa, Alabama, area, had accompanied the minister from the Stillman Institute who undertook to procure the "volunteers." One of those American men stayed behind in a village as "a sort of hostage and custodian of the goods held for use as final presents" when the villagers returned. (Gauss)

Like the other ethnic groups on display, the Pygmies learned the value of producing "native" trinkets and artifacts to sell—or asking for donations from photographers. Geronimo may have been the most adept because of his reputation, but all the groups sold objects in order to have some financial benefit. None were paid anything to be there—although recruiters like the minister from Stillman were paid—and the exhibited people used the funds they raised to buy products available at the fair or in St. Louis.

The Pygmies used some of their revenue to buy Western clothing for warmth. The director of the exhibits recorded that "it required constant vigilance and half-cruel constraint to keep them out of close-fitting clothing which would have interfered with the functions normal to their naked skins" as the weather grew colder. (Gauss) And then there were visitors who took it poorly if the Pygmies chose to stay indoors in cold weather. Some threw rocks at the dwelling—as if that would induce the men to come outside.

The Pygmies and others also had to be aware of a special problem: American soldiers. As men shuffled through the nearby military bases, they would visit the fair and seemed to particularly enjoy harassing the human zoo subjects. Their most common ploy was to offer sufficient liquor to induce unfortunate behavior.

The most lasting Pygmy story is that of Ota Benga, the man who had been bought from slavers in the Congo rather than recruited. A popular subject of photographers at the fair because of his sharpened front teeth, Ota Benga returned to the Congo with the other Pygmies only to find virtually none of his tribe left. So, he returned to the United States. By 1906, he found himself on exhibit again—with the monkeys in the Brooklyn Zoo. He managed to rid himself of that chore and eventually found something of an education and a job in Lynchburg, Virginia. He saved money to make the trip back home to Africa but was stymied by the ban on passenger travel in World War I. In 1916, he committed suicide.

Another "native" group was the Ainu from an outlying island in the Japanese archipelago. This group, nine people from four families—including two children—was more of an enigma because they appeared to be "whiter" than any other native group. As a matter of fact, they lived in remote villages and were essentially victims of Japanese colonial policies. Japan needed a presence in the Ainu lands to protect against Russian encroachment and sought to assimilate the Ainu much as the United States had done with its Native Americans. The Japanese government, of course, had given permission for the Ainu to travel to the fair, as much to demonstrate the cultural superiority of the Japanese as for educational purposes.

And finally, the "natives" participated in an athletic competition—or, perhaps we should say, a competition between the head of the Olympics games and the head of the Archeology department. In the weeks leading up to the 1904 Olympics, discussed below, the fair hosted Anthropology Days, in which the archeologists recruited various members of the native groups to compete in quasi-Olympic events. At first, the press was sure that athletic ability was a natural trait of less-civilized people. But, to their surprise, the natives did not always excel. It seems that shot put and standing broad jumps were not the "natural" forte of untrained men not chosen for athletic ability in the first place.

THE NEW IMPERIALISM

Even more popular than the Native American and other "native" exhibits was the Philippine Reservation. For one thing, it was much more extensive, covering forty-seven acres between present-day Skinker Boulevard and Big Bend Road. And it was of recent political interest.

The American annexation of the Philippine Islands during the Spanish-American War six years before had given rise to intense debate. Represented by Missouri's own Samuel Clemens (Mark Twain), opponents argued that a democratic republic couldn't impose its rule on a people who simply were a third party to a minor military effort. Others, led by Theodore Roosevelt, argued that the expanding global presence of the United States necessitated a naval base in the Far East for both military and commercial reasons. On top of which, Roosevelt wanted to free the Filipinos from the chains of barbarism. And, of course, if the United States didn't rise to the occasion, some European power—or even the Japanese—might do so.

The barbarian inhabitants of the island certainly recognized imperialism when they saw it, having been subject to the Spanish version for some time. The resulting resistance introduced the United States to Asian-style guerilla warfare and split the Philippine tribes between those who supported resistance, those who supported the United States, and those who wished to stay out of the affair. The United States was nominally victorious two years before the fair, but resistance continued until 1913. In 1904, therefore, the civilian commission that ruled the islands under the aegis of the War Department was eager to convince the American public of its paternal duty. At the same time, impressing the many Filipinos brought to St. Louis of the worthiness of its new overlords couldn't hurt.

Unlike the paltry sums given the Bureau of Indian Affairs to stage its exhibits (probably not more than $30,000), the Philippine commission received well over a million dollars in 1904 money. The expenditure was deemed worth it to demonstrate the value of American imperialism. Over a hundred buildings, from huts to Manila cathedrals, were reconstructed. Fifteen hundred Filipinos resided in the human zoo—and occasionally ventured out to inspect their new American overlords for themselves.

The commission created a lake to surround an island accessible only by bridges. The main bridge put visitors directly in front of the re-creation of the walled city of Manila, representing the most advanced part of the country. Spanish-Filipino elites lived in the Manila compound, although they were often off making contacts with St. Louis elites. Around the walled city were the villages of the various tribes, arranged according to how civilized they were.

The highest rank went to the Visayans, likely because they were Christian. There also were two tribes of Islamic Moros—described as "fierce Mohammedans" who opposed American forces in Mindanao. The Igorots drew attention for their distinctive dietary habit: They held dog feasts frequently enough to lead to concerns about whose dogs were being roasted. (There is some evidence that the commission directed the Igorots to eat a lot more dog than their usual customs prescribed.) At the low end of the scale were the Negritos. They were considered so low on the social Darwinism scale that they would "soon be extinct." A sign told visitors to see Negritos while they still existed, somewhat similar to signs one can find today at the St. Louis Zoo indicating threatened species. (As it turns out, the Negritos of the Philippines and other southeast Asian locations are still around and, in some case, fighting to preserve their traditional lifestyles.) The least civilized tribes also caught visitors' attention by their dress, or lack thereof. There were continual debates about allowing loin-cloth-only during the warmer months or requiring slightly more coverings.

Meanwhile, there were the Filipino Scouts. Drawn mainly from Visayans and other American allies in the fight for occupation, they were technically responsible for patrols and firefighting. Fair visitors enjoyed them instead for their drills and their bands, with precision performances offered at least daily at six o'clock. In addition, the Scouts were allowed to travel off the fairgrounds and reportedly made a favorable impression on St. Louis' women. One particular incident made the news when visiting schoolteachers toured the fair with off-duty Scouts. The Jefferson Guards, a private police force that patrolled the grounds, weren't having it. Joined by some US Marines who were simply visitors, the Guards and the Scouts had a confrontation described as a riot. The Scouts broke off and made their way back to the reservation, followed by Guard members firing guns in the air and threatening to burn parts of the Philippine island.

Meanwhile, the freedom allowed the Scouts so irritated the Igorots, who were confined to the reservation, that they took to beating drums during Scout drills to prevent the marchers from hearing voice commands.

EXOTIC CHINESE AND CONFOUNDING JAPANESE

The fair's anthropological guru was William McGee. McGee insisted that human progress lies along a continuum from savage to civilized, and he hoped to illustrate that in exhibits of cultures of Pygmies, Ainu, and Native Americans. Like most who claimed to be anthropologists (McGee was self-educated with no academic background or identification), culture scientists, and eugenicists, McGee put the white races, particularly Americans and western Europeans, at the top of the continuum and stated that the yellow races were inferior. That left him with the difficult task of pigeonholing the formidable and ancient cultures of Asia.

More so than any other groups, the delegations from two sovereign nations had something to gain by convincing Americans to view them favorably: the Chinese and the Japanese.

The Chinese delegation apparently wanted two things: for Americans to appreciate aesthetic elements of their culture and for Americans to engage in mutually beneficial economic exchange. On the face of it, the Chinese simply built lovely exhibit spaces. Behind the scenes, the workingmen of the Chinese group faced discrimination, and the elite spent time trying to convince the corresponding St. Louis elite to accept the country if not all the countrymen.

Unlike its interactions with native cultures and even the Japanese, St. Louis had experience with Chinese. A few hundred lived in the city at scattered locations, but they shopped in a small area, called Hop Alley, located

172

on one side of Eighth Street between Market and Walnut. While a few local Chinese mingled in proper St. Louis society, no doubt wearing strictly Western clothing and speaking good English, most Chinese in the city carried the usual reputations as deviants. Many St. Louisans believed the Chinese spent their time in fan tan gambling and smoking opium when they weren't taking jobs from American workingmen or worse: marrying white women.

These prejudices spilled over to the merchants and workers who accompanied the Chinese delegation to the fair. Because of the Chinese Exclusion Act of 1882, some couldn't even get to St. Louis. The ones who did found US customs officials waiting. Those officials assumed that the men would try to remain in the country illegally and thus set up procedures where the Chinese had to report in regularly and detail their activities. Workmen who missed a check-in for more than forty-eight hours were listed as fugitives.

The men and their wives at the head of the delegation had their own issues to deal with. Prince Pu Lun, the Imperial commissioner for the fair, spoke no English, and had, in fact, never been outside China. The press wanted to know if he would make visitors kowtow, eat exotic and unpalatable foods, or offer an opium pipe. Of course, he did none of those things. He shook hands with guests, even female guests, and seemed to enjoy trying American foods, surprising St. Louisans by seeming democratic. The vice commissioner, Wong Kai Kah, was even more popular, having graduated from Yale in 1883 and speaking perfect English. His wife was frequently in the press for the brilliance and variety of her clothing. The most controversial thing the men did was exchange their mandated Chinese robes for Western wear when they were outside the fair's borders.

In hindsight, China was in one of its periods of opening to the outside world and may have been seeking knowledge of Western methods and processes as much as putting on a good show. The presence of the Chinese in St. Louis and the United States may have yielded more for the delegation than it did for fair visitors or anthropologists eager to prove inferiority.

Even more politically motivated were the extensive exhibits of the Japanese. Early in the process, the Japanese government claimed prime land and outlined striking exhibits. The emphasis was on the aesthetics of static art and the living art of the geishas, who performed in musical venues and in the widely watched tea ceremonies. The modern and yet graceful civilization was contrasted with the nine Ainu in their encampment in the human zoo. The Japanese exhibits were acknowledged as the largest and most comprehensive of any foreign nation attending. Ironically, the Japanese were able to take over space from Russia, which withdrew from the fair. And why was that?

In 1904, the Japanese were making headlines as they continued to win battles in their war with the Russia Empire. It wasn't lost on anyone that in the face of war, Russia had withdrawn from the fair; Japan had expanded its presence—and projected serenity. In 1895, Japan had defeated China in a war over Korea. The 1904 fair allowed the Japanese the opportunity to fight what they considered their most important battle: convincing the world that they were a modern, military power, ready to be taken seriously in every measure of civilization.

If the press and fairgoers were uncertain about Chinese civilization, they were even more conflicted about the Japanese. Here was a nation clearly defeating a European power, while displaying artistry, tradition, and modernity. What did that say about white superiority?

NOT ALWAYS AS
FAIR AS HOPED

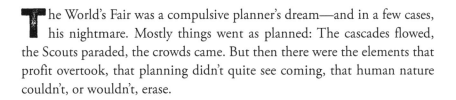

The World's Fair was a compulsive planner's dream—and in a few cases, his nightmare. Mostly things went as planned: The cascades flowed, the Scouts paraded, the crowds came. But then there were the elements that profit overtook, that planning didn't quite see coming, that human nature couldn't, or wouldn't, erase.

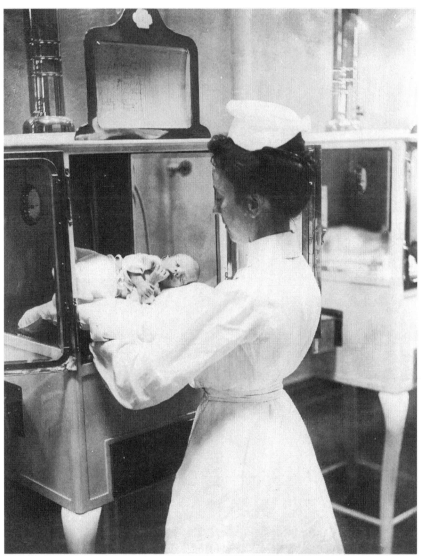

An incredible sideshow on the fair's Pike, a premature baby in an incubator, with nurse.
Missouri Historical Society Collection

PREEMIES IN INCUBATORS AS A SIDESHOW

Major fairs, exhibitions, and permanent amusement parks across the country had featured a new medical device, the incubator, for several years. As hospitals were slow to adopt the new technology because of its high cost and low success rate, incubator proponents took the device directly to the public. It seems there was something going on even more surprising than the technology itself: People would pay to see tiny newborns struggle to survive.

So, naturally, the concessions committee of the fair wanted to include a preemie exhibit. There were concessionaires around the country skilled in doing so, at least one of them a reputable doctor using the exhibits to convince other medical men of the value of the machines.

But the St. Louis committee ignored the reputable providers. They handed the contract to a local promoter who in turn handed it off to a doctor who had no experience with either the incubators or newborns in particular. The resulting disaster should not have surprised anyone.

Fairgoers who crowded to ogle the youngest draws saw very sick babies. The poorly chosen doctor fed the babies cow's milk and cereal, a vitally wrong choice. Flies buzzed about the babies in the St. Louis summer, and the temperatures overheated the incubators as well. (It could have been worse as far as temperatures were concerned; St. Louis had one of its more moderate summers in 1904.) The death toll among the first 43 babies was 39.

The exhibit drew local and national attention of the wrong kind. The St. Louis Humane Society wrote to fair director David Francis insisting that something be done within twenty-four hours of receipt of the letter. One of Francis' employees wrote back, two days later, saying that Francis was unable to take time for an immediate reply.

The doctor who had run many such shows—and who, it should be noted, had contended for the concession—heard about the situation. His letter to the editor of the *New York Evening Journal* labeled what was happening in St. Louis as the "Crime of the Decade." By this time, the St. Louis directors had found another doctor, John Zahorsky, who at least mixed breast milk into the babies' diet, and who had higher standards of cleanliness. He also erected glass partitions between the incubators and the public. The death rate fell, although infants continued to die in the display.

In his final report on the sad exhibit, Zahorsky blamed the deaths on "the catastrophe of hospitalism." Apparently drawing on an early twentieth-century fear of hospitals, Zahorsky charged that germs could spread in institutional settings—as they had at the fair's exhibit—something that didn't happen when patients, including preemies, were taken care of at home. One historian insists that Zahorsky's report gave doctors an excuse to dismiss incubator use, an expensive and labor-intensive technology.

Still, some babies were saved. And there was one local feel-good story. On July 1, 1904, a St. Louis police officer found an abandoned little girl, weighing in at two pounds, eleven ounces. Because the preemie exhibit seemed to offer the child her best chance, she was taken to the Pike. She spent almost two months in an incubator, visited often by the officer and his wife. At the fair's end, they adopted the little girl and named her Frances, after director David Francis.

AN AMERICAN OLYMPICS

Despite the fair's implied claim that America boasted superior civilization, the Europeans were the ones turning up their noses at American claims of superiority on the playing fields of the third international Olympiad. St. Louis had wrested the games away from Chicago, and the nation seemed primed to cheer exemplars of the "strenuous life." But Europeans largely chose not to attend. No one came from either England or France, and only about 60 of 650 athletes were from outside North America. The 1904 Olympics included some national championship games and became largely a competition between athletic clubs from the Midwest and the dominant Eastern power, the New York (City) Athletic Club.

The urge to prove scientific superiority led to a strange marathon. Laid out on dusty hills west of the grounds, the course had to allow for not only the twenty runners but also the automobile that accompanied each, complete with a physician for each runner. Some of the runners had crews that provided specialized support. The ultimate winner, an Englishman living in Massachusetts and running for the United States, was given doses of strychnine and egg whites during the race; the final drink he got was strychnine and brandy. The scientific conclusion was that Thomas Hicks ran "like a well-oiled piece of machinery," but that his mental condition involved hallucinations. (Dyreson) He was too exhausted—or confused—to hold the trophy when he finally won.

As it turned out, survival, let alone winning, wasn't a given. The early autos threw up so much dust that runners would stop, choking, to cough up the debris. A runner from San Francisco suffered a nearly fatal stomach hemorrhage because of the dirt he swallowed. Meanwhile, two more near fatalities were the result of one of the autos rolling down an embankment. One runner was said to have veered off course when he was chased by wild dogs.

The crowd waiting in the new Francis Field on the Washington University campus first cheered the apparent winner, Fred Lorz of New York City. But Lorz fairly soon admitted that he had hitched a ride in his accompanying automobile, explaining why he was in so much better condition than Hicks. The runner-up was a French immigrant running for the Chicago Athletic Club, stoking national pride that top athletes chose the New World over the Old.

Meanwhile, American organizers chastised the Europeans for not attending and at the same time claimed that there were only a couple of athletes in the rest of the world who would have been contenders anyway. The founder of the modern Olympics, Baron Pierre de Coubertin, refused to attend the St. Louis games and noted the Anthropology Days exhibitions, saying, "in no place but America would one have dared to place such events on a program, but to Americans everything is permissible." (Dyreson)

In the end, the United States took 70 gold, 75 silver, and 64 bronze medals, the first time those metals were associated with winning. The nearest competitor was, interestingly, Cuba, with 5 gold, 2 silver, and 3 bronze. Germany was close with 4 gold, 4 silver, and 5 bronze. It was the start of Americans associating medal counts with national superiority.

One true achievement at the games came in the person of George Poage. An African American who had starred in his days at the University of Wisconsin and who represented the Milwaukee Athletic Club, Poage took bronze medals in both the 400- and 200-meter hurdles. He is considered the first Black to enter and win a medal in the modern Olympics—although only by hours. Joseph Stadler, a Black man from Cleveland, took the silver in the standing high jumps the same day Poage won his first medal. Poage has more history in St. Louis, because he stayed in town for ten years, teaching English comp, English lit, and Latin at the notable Sumner High School. (See the final chapter.) Outside the classroom, he advised debate and drama—along with athletics.

Poage and Stadler's successes were a bright spot in the fair experience for African Americans. They had expected much more from the fair and been disappointed repeatedly.

ON BEING BLACK
AT THE FAIR

You would expect a fair dedicated to trumpeting the superiority of white, civilized Americans would have been a turnoff for St. Louis' relatively large Black population. But the community was heartened by the clean-up-before-the-fair campaign that saw new streetlights on dark roads, new pocket playgrounds on vacant slum lots, and new repairs on aging tenements. There was no specific Negro Building as there had been at earlier fairs; instead, the governing committee said it wanted the participation of all citizens, and fair president David Francis out-and-out promised the Black community equal treatment.

Ironically, it was middle-class Blacks who had the highest social hopes for the fair. In some cases, they sought to distance themselves from what they considered the coarser aspects of African American society. When the Board of Lady Managers (yes, there was such a thing) banned ragtime music and dances like the cakewalk from the fair, middle-class Blacks approved. The National Association of Colored Women's Clubs was one of the 155 conventions meeting in the city during the fair; a speaker for that group went out of her way to condemn ragtime and its dances as vulgar.

At the same time, ragtimers wanted an opportunity like the fair to lift the generally bad impression ragtime elicited. (See chapter 13.) That didn't happen. But ragtimers didn't let that stop them from maintaining a presence. Restaurants on the Pike hired such pianists as Louis Chauvin, Alfred Marshall, and Sam Patterson to play. Marshall reported earning $12 a week when unionized musicians officially playing for the fair earned $45.

Still, ragtime composers put out work that sold wildly. There was James Scott's appropriately named "On the Pike"; Tom Turpin's "St. Louis Rag"; Scott Joplin's "Cascades," a memorial to the glorious waterfall that captivated crowds; and W. C. Powell's "Funny Folks," descriptive of foreign visitors.

Many more lower-class African Americans made good livings for a while offering visitors shoeshines, well-made beds, and more. In fact, there was a considerable Black immigration experience, with most of those arriving to seek jobs staying on in the city.

At first, Blacks attended the fair in large numbers and appreciated exhibits on Black achievements in the Missouri State Building. But gradually, complaints about discrimination, particularly at the fresh-water concessions, in restaurants, and on the internal transportation lines, surfaced. A Black cavalry regiment was refused housing. Eventually, the situation became bad enough that the National Association of Colored Women's Clubs decided to boycott the fair. An Emancipation Day event was canceled because Black leaders gave up on participating. Francis issued orders banning discrimination, but one writer advised Blacks attending to carry a knapsack and a canteen.

In the end, a good number of Blacks benefitted economically, as did many working-class whites. But as far as making a difference in white perceptions, the fair failed to live up to expectations. One writer said, "Every people are heartily received at the fair but the Negro." (Lerner)

FAIR/FAST/FOOD

We should point out that there were many fine things to see at the 1904 World's Fair. Attention focused on St. Louis, and the city lived up to the hype. Critics as well as boosters insisted that the city clean up both physically and politically, and it did so to a large extent. At least for the time being.

And we would be remiss if we didn't note the fast food and fun food. A lot of what passes for St. Louis Fair creations weren't, given that hamburgers, hot dogs (in buns designed for the meat!), cotton candy, the ice-cream cone, and iced tea had been around before the fair. (Consumers were familiar enough with hamburger meat to be wary of its contents.) Puffed rice—yes. That was introduced in the Quaker Oats exhibit. And "natural," even "healthful," foods were demonstrated and promoted. But it may be true that a whole new way of eating took off in popularity because of the fair.

As far as the Progress of Man goes, we can acknowledge the pure foods exhibits, agree that the grounds were beautiful and maybe even ingenious, and still sigh over early twentieth-century notions of progress.

THE ROMANCE AND TRAGEDY OF BEER

Adolphus Busch made himself into a nineteenth-century legend. A true prince couldn't have done it better, with the houses, the paternalistic embrace of his subjects, the flourishes of wealth. And then there were the Lemps of the second-place company, a tempestuous and secretive family overcome by the brewing industry that gave them their wealth.

St. Louis is a beer city. Not that it hasn't had its share of liquor distilleries and even liquor scandal in the Whiskey Ring of the 1870s. (The abuses of government licensing uncovered in St. Louis boiled all the way to the White House until the investigation stopped just short of former St. Louis resident and President Ulysses Grant.) But the rise of two of the preeminent

Adolphus Busch, the original beer prince, and his wife, Lilly Anheuser Busch. *Missouri Historical Society Collection*

breweries in the country from a notable collection of such put the city on the brewing map from the 1860s on.

The Lemps and the Anheuser/Buschs turned the art of making beer into the craft of making money—until their enterprises ran up against temperance and Prohibition. How each family negotiated the turbulence is an integral part of the St. Louis story. And, apart from stories of the families at the top of the power pyramid are the stories of the people at the bottom, particularly during the dry days from 1920 to 1933.

LAGER AND LEMPS, LIVING AND DYING LARGE

When we say "beer"—as opposed to ale—these days, we often mean lager beer. And we should thank one of two men for introducing lager in the United States, around 1840. The debate among enthusiasts is whether it was a Philadelphian (John Wagner) or Adam Lemp, German immigrant to St. Louis, grocer, manufacturer of beer and vinegar.

Lemp left his brewing family in Germany, immigrating to St. Louis in 1838, where he opened a grocery at Sixth and Delmar. In addition to grocering, he manufactured vinegar and beer, a traditional combination. Before long, one particular beer he offered became so popular that he quit running the grocery and opened a brewery on South Second Street, solidly within the German Soulard neighborhood. What really drew Adam Lemp were the limestone caves below St. Louis. We've talked about those in regard to the pollution of the nineteenth century in chapter 11, but Lemp found a clean one just south of the city limits in 1844.

"Lager" comes from a German word meaning to "store," and it is the primary characteristic of lager beer that it has to be aged to allow the yeast (the very special yeast for Lemp and Busch beers) to settle. Not only does the aging process make the beer less bitter because the yeast settles, but it makes the beer last longer without going bad. Another part of extending the life of the beer is keeping it cool during the lagering process. That's where the caves come in.

The caves below St. Louis were cooler than any aboveground facility in the days before mechanical refrigeration. In addition, Adam Lemp had huge blocks of ice transported from the Mississippi during the winter. Having secured the property at the current intersection of Cherokee and DeMenil Place that provided the entrance to the cave, Lemp enlarged the underground storage to hold more than three-thousand barrels of beer in its first year.

A saloon that served only Lemp beer became widely popular, as did the beer itself—good lager, light with a snowy foam. The brew carried out a theme that the Lemps and the Buschs, in particular, would harp on over the years. Beer was a moderate refreshment, suitable for family beer gardens and light refreshment. It was not the hard liquor that marked the less savory places around town, places more often associated with the Irish gangs from chapter 21. The forces of Prohibition paid little attention to the distinction, as we will see.

Adam Lemp did well and was recognized as the "most substantial" brewer in the city in 1858, giving his son William a brewery of his own at one point. When Adam died in 1862, he left the brewery jointly to his son and to his grandson. The fact that they were not from the same families led to jockeying for control.

It seems Adam Lemp had three wives, one who died back in Germany, one he left in Germany, and one he married in St. Louis. Lemp's grandson by the daughter of his first marriage was given half the control of the Western Brewery and the other half went to William Lemp (Sr.), son of the woman who was left in Germany. William Lemp bought out his half nephew for an amazingly small amount of money. (And the man died not long after that.) Then William Lemp apparently feuded with his stepmother, Louise Lemp, who inherited the family mansion, and her children by previous marriages. It was the start to a very public disintegration of a very public family.

At least William Lemp took the brewing business seriously. Adam's simple brewery grew larger and larger, and William spearheaded the movement to send his lager across the country and around the world in cooled railroad cars. The named brand that got the most exposure was Falstaff, named for and decorated by an image of the Shakespearean character known less for his

If you believe in haunted houses, the Lemp Mansion in south St. Louis offers numerous stories on which to base such a reputation. *Missouri Historical Society Collection*

good character than his happy drinking habits. (The Falstaff brand would be sold in 1921, resurrected after national Prohibition ended, reach another peak in popularity in the 1960s, and decline thereafter.) The Lemp family grew wealthier by the bottle.

On the home front, William and his wife, Julia, had seven children who survived into adulthood, including a daughter who married into the Pabst beer family. Another daughter, Elsa, and their sons, William "Billy" Jr., Louis, Charles, Frederick, and Edwin, would all make news in loud, or unsociably quiet, ways.

Frederick seems to have been his father's favorite, and William Sr. took it hard when Frederick died of heart failure in 1901, age twenty-eight. The senior Lemp was close friends as well with Frederick Pabst, and his fellow beer baron, age sixty-seven, died on the first day of 1904. Before the winter of 1904 was over, William Lemp shot himself to death in the Lemp Mansion. It was the first of a number of tragedies that would lead to the big home/office in Benton Park being labeled "haunted." (Benton Park, the south side's pleasant fourteen-acre greenspace, gives its name to the neighborhood still, with the Lemp Mansion a noted tourist attraction. Of course, it is named for—you guessed it—Senator Thomas Hart Benton.)

Although Louis and Charles had also worked for the brewery, it was Billy Lemp who took over—at least in the legal sense. The stories we have of William "Billy" Lemp Jr. don't reflect hours of work pushing Falstaff and other Lemp beers to new heights. Instead, we have tales of marital difficulties and even more troubling rumors.

Billy was married to Lillian Handlan, daughter of a wealthy St. Louis manufacturer. They had a son, William Lemp III, in 1900. While Lemp partied with friends—the mansion had an underground swimming pool, bowling alley, and theater—Lillian spent money. One story says Billy insisted she spend $1,000 a day or he would cut off her spending altogether. And what did she spend it on? Apparently, anything lavender. Known as the lavender lady, all her garments were that color, and she had multiple carriages, pulled by multiple horses, all with lavender-dyed leather harnesses. The couple also spent freely on art and every other luxury they could imagine, including a country house overlooking the Meramec River south of St. Louis. And Billy had his own obsession as well: other women.

Accusations about the number of women Billy Lemp brought to the mansion surfaced in the divorce proceedings he started in 1908. The particular fight was over custody for the Lemp's young son, William III, and it is said that Lillian almost lost that fight because her husband's attorneys offered a photograph of her smoking a cigarette. Somehow through the swirl of accusations, Lillian got custody and a stipend that would in no way support more lavender harnesses.

The most disturbing story told about Billy Lemp involved another son, this one the illegitimate issue of one of Lemp's dalliances. Over the years, the child's existence has been denied by family and confirmed by servants. It is believed that the boy had Down's Syndrome and was confined to the upper stories of the Lemp Mansion where the servants had quarters. You can imagine the boost this sad story gives to the legends of the haunting. But there's more to come.

Elsa Lemp was the youngest of William Sr.'s children and perhaps the most sympathetic. She was lively, popular, independent, and had interests as diverse as suffrage and spiritualism. (She was a friend of Pearl Curran, whose spiritualist adventure with the ouija board we will explore in chapter 22.) Known as the wealthiest unmarried woman in the city in the decade when Lillian and Billy were fighting it out in court, Elsa lost that status when she married industrialist Thomas Wright in 1910.

It was a tempestuous alliance, marked by the loss of a stillborn child and violent fights. Wright seems to have been as unfaithful as his brother-in-law Billy Lemp, but Elsa responded much more aggressively than Lillian. She is said to have once gotten into her Pierce-Arrow auto and rammed Thomas' Duesenberg—which must have been an early racing version. The couple divorced in early 1919 but remarried in March of 1920, in New York City. They returned home to St. Louis shortly after.

On March 20, according to Thomas, Elsa felt unwell and chose to stay in bed. She reportedly suffered from digestive ailments, so that much is feasible. Thomas went to draw a bath and heard "a sharp cracking sound." When he got to the bedroom, he found his wife dying, with a gun lying on the bed.

Apparently, no one questioned the suicide, although two maids close by didn't hear the shot. One account says Elsa tried to speak but died shortly. A doctor arrived, then a lawyer, and then brother Edwin. Edwin had been having breakfast with a man we'll meet shortly, then assistant city counselor William Killoren. (Killoren was the single candidate to escape the League of Women Voters' "Kill the Ks" campaign, upcoming for him in October of this same year. See chapter 21.) It was Killoren, apparently, who contacted police. Who, of course, wondered why they hadn't been contacted earlier. Thomas Wright is supposed to have been "highly agitated" in the police investigation. But apparently our current habit of suspecting a spouse in questionable circumstances wasn't in play a hundred years ago.

What has undeniably come down through the last hundred years is a comment from Billy Lemp when he arrived at his sister's house. Multiple sources quoted him as saying, "That's the Lemp family for you." That sentiment would resonate more over time, but first we should pull in the other players and the world-shaking events of the 1910s.

"DO COME AND HAVE A STEIN OR TWO UNDER THE ANHEUSER BUSH"

A popular song poking just a bit of fun at your own name. Your own railroad car, "The Adolphus," with every luxury. Advertising so innovative that everyone is talking about Custer's Last Fight. Even a derogatory term aimed at you by St. Louis society: buschy.

And then there's the beer that started out being routinely awful and ended up being the standard for excellence.

In 1852, Eberhard Anheuser was making money in St. Louis making and selling . . . soap. Not beer. Because he had given a $90,000 loan to a brewery making indifferent beer, he picked up that business when it failed, soldiering on to run both companies.

One of the men Anheuser bought brewing supplies from was another German immigrant, a younger man named Adolphus Busch. That's how Busch got to know Anheuser's daughter, Lilly. They married in 1861, Adolphus' brother Ulrich marrying another Anheuser daughter, Anna, in a double ceremony. The other groom and two brides had to wait twenty minutes after the ceremony was supposed to start for Adolphus. He had had to stop to consummate a business deal.

You may recall the story of Camp Jackson and the robust German response that helped turn the tide against secession. Adolphus Busch was one of the Home Guard soldiers, as was his father-in-law, Eberhard Anheuser, surviving, obviously, the shootings of the day. The Germans had signed up for three months and, while other Germans went on to fight

Adolphus III, his father, August Sr., and brother, August "Gussie" Jr., pose with a letter and a case of beer being sent to President Franklin Roosevelt as Prohibition ends. *Missouri Historical Society Collection*

for the Union during the long war, Busch and Anheuser (who was in his mid-fifties) returned to their business interests in the city, with Adolphus working the docks as a mud clerk. A mud clerk met steamboats, looked over the wares, and set about making trades. With the war on, Busch "engaged in the precarious business of handling cotton and Southern products." (Ganey and Hernon)

With the war ended, Adolphus took over the brewing side of the business, and the legends commenced. Armed with a $50,000 loan from Robert Barnes, the only banker in the city who would listen to the young German, Busch built the plant that looks like a castle from a German fairy tale. Today it has morphed into a small city on the south side. Even during the elder Busch's tenure, guides were offering tours. (Years later, the very successful Robert Barnes gave money to Washington University to found its medical school and hospital. Adolphus contributed $850,000 in Barnes' name in appreciation for that early loan. Today's highly-thought-of Barnes Jewish health care system carries on the name.)

Salesman extraordinaire as well as business innovator, Adolphus Busch took care of the bad beer problem by introducing/appropriating a lager based on a German beer from Budweiser. Budweiser not only joined the Lemp beers in the premium lager category, but Busch introduced pasteurization of beer so the aged product traveled and lasted even better. That was good because Busch was advertising it in every way known in the nineteenth century along with a few not yet conceived of. In his increasingly princely travels, he would distribute such trinkets as pocketknives with Budweiser printed on them.

Like other brewers—but maybe more successfully—he supported saloons, buying furnishings and licenses for specific businesses that sold only Budweiser. Close to the end of the century, he came upon a particularly effective piece of promotion: a painting that celebrated "Custer's Last Fight" at Little Big Horn. The only-moderately good piece of art was lithographed some 150,000 times over and graced the backs of bars throughout the country. No mention of Budweiser; no mention of beers. Just Anheuser-Busch printed at the bottom, to be associated with Americana and the West.

Adolphus Busch also built his company up on the supply side, buying up and controlling the secondary industries he needed: barrel makers, glass-bottle companies, businesses providing raw materials, and railroads.

Anheuser died in 1880, and the Anheuser line gradually lost its financial stake in the company. Meanwhile, Lilly Anheuser's husband built an empire. President William Howard Taft referred to him as "Prince Adolphus." In addition to its mansion at Number One Busch Place (not far from the Lemp Mansion), the Busch family had homes in Cooperstown, New York, Pasadena, California, and Bad Schwalbach in Germany. The latter would have interesting consequences in World War I. And, of course, there was the other St. Louis location so closely connected with the Buschs. When they bought it, it was more likely connected with Ulysses Grant: his Hardscrabble farm, close by the family home of his wife, Julia Dent. Today, "Grant's Farm" is toured as well, but under the aegis of the Buschs.

All this emphasis on beer, by the way, assumes that Adolphus was a drinker. He might have been, but it wasn't beer he chose. The story goes that he once asked a news reporter what the man would like to drink during an interview. The reporter thought he couldn't miss by saying, "Budweiser." Adolphus replied, "Ach. Dot schlop?" Adolphus was a wine drinker, who just happened to build a beer dynasty.

Lilly and Adolphus built a dynasty of children as well, with nine of thirteen children surviving childhood. As with the Lemps, their stories became legends. Two of the daughters married Germans and lived in Germany. Two others were the talk of St. Louis society. Of the five sons, Edward, August Anheuser, Adolphus Jr., Carl, and Peter, two made an impact on the company, and one, August A., became the next big Busch presence. Tragedy, often in the form of a bad appendix, took its toll.

Edward, the oldest, was a fifteen-year-old at Kemper Military Institute in Boonville, Missouri, when he died of peritonitis on Christmas Eve of 1879. Carl was disabled from birth, presumably from prenatal injuries suffered when Lilly fell down the mansion's stairs the night her father died. Adolphus Jr. grew up to take an active interest in the brewery, but he died suddenly in 1898 of a perforated appendix, likely related to the illness that had claimed his brother. Peter, the youngest, was the playboy. He was the least interested in the brewery because his interests ran to baseball and spending money. During a stint in San Francisco, he was noted there as the biggest spender on the West Coast. It appears that he also died of something related to his appendix, although one story suggests a girlfriend stabbed him with a hat pin, puncturing the organ. Which would, of course, be quite the anatomical feat.

That left August A., who abandoned his boyhood ambition to be a cowboy and became the steady hand to guide Anheuser-Busch through the very difficult years to come. He would have two sons to help him maintain the Buschs' larger-than-life image: Adolphus III and August Jr.—the Gussie Busch of baseball fame we talked about in chapter 12.

THE DOUBLE WHAMMY: MAKING BEER, BEING GERMAN

When Peter Busch died, his parents were on their way to Germany. When Adolphus himself died in 1913, he was in Germany. When World War I broke out in 1914, Lilly was in Germany, spending time with the two Busch daughters who had married Germans—Germans with ties to the military establishment. The Busch family connection to the Kaiser's Germany wasn't going to be a good look for the rest of the decade.

That problem connected, not so subtly, to the growing prohibition wave.

People often assume that Prohibition started in 1920—as if Congress in 1919 suddenly said, "Let's not drink anymore." But the prohibition, with a little "p," movement had been around for years. States near Missouri, such as Kansas, had voted to go dry in 1880. Of course, the ban wasn't enforced everywhere in the state of Kansas, or Carrie Nation wouldn't have gone about with her ax tearing up bars. And Kansas was an outlier: Open saloons weren't allowed there until 1987. In the 1970s, the state tried to stop airliners from serving alcohol as they flew over.

Still, Missouri had a large number of dry locales. The "local option" meant that an incorporated town or county could vote to prohibit the manufacture and sale of alcohol. By 1910, more than half of those specific locales had done so. A pattern developed: A rural Missouri county would vote dry, but its incorporated county seat would stay wet. Or a group of totally dry counties would surround a wet one. In short, most rural residents supported prohibition; the cities remained wet, wet, wet. Including St. Louis, of course.

August A. always preached that hard liquor was the problem. Beer, with its much lower alcohol content, was the solution. In fact, he would say, eliminating all the beverages men liked to drink was likely to cause trouble, criminal trouble. Most of the American public wasn't buying that argument, and it became tied up with patriotism. Not even General Custer failing to tame the West was patriotic enough to make up for the association of Germany and beer in the minds of many. In fact, the brewers' support of saloons and the saloon culture was seen as a German plot to undermine the country.

When World War I broke out, the United States stayed neutral for most of three years. In name. As a matter of fact, the country sent goods to the allies, Britain and France, but not to Germany. That was largely because Britain controlled the seas early on, but German Americans, including the Busch family, objected. Meanwhile, Germany started using poison gases and its U-boats sank the *Lusitania*. What really turned the US population toward the allies was news of the atrocities German troops committed in Belgium and other areas. There were almost surely unfortunate incidents, but the scenarios were spun, as we would say, by the British propaganda machine. Being German in the United States became more and more problematic.

While the Lemp family had fewer ties to the Kaiser's regime, the Busch ties were strong, and it all became dangerous when the United States declared war on Germany in early April of 1917. Lilly's continuing presence there and the activities of the two Busch sons-in-laws were duly noted. Lilly and daughter Wilhelmina turned one of their properties into a facility to care for injured German soldiers, and the company sent Lilly almost $300,000 to live on in Germany. It was hard for the press—or the US government—to miss.

August A. went from complaining about fake neutrality to displaying his anti-German patriotism at every opportunity. He gave money to the Red Cross and volunteered his diesel engine company to make submarine engines. Brewery workers were abruptly ordered to speak English, German having been the language of the workplace for decades. At the same time that more states and localities were going dry and the conversation about national prohibition was getting louder, Canada and Australia banned the sale of Budweiser because of the Buschs' German connection.

Meanwhile, the US government took control of the financial assets of Lilly Busch because she was living in Germany. "Handsome Harry" Hawes, our dubiously upright head of the Jefferson Club to come in chapter 20, was dispatched to Germany in the midst of the war to bring Lilly home. It wouldn't be easy. She'd have to cross the Alps in the dead of winter, go through neutral Spain, and cross the Atlantic over the growing network of German U-boats that by now were firing on civilians as well as military targets. Behind her, her daughters were begging her to stay; aside from her safety, the German government would seize Villa Lilly if she left. At age seventy-four, Lilly was more fragile than she looked. She spent six weeks recuperating from the rigors of the experience in Switzerland and another ten days in a village on the Spanish border—after watching bombs fall a block from her hotel in Paris.

Because of an uptick in U-boat activity, it took weeks to find a ship that would travel along the west coast of Africa and then cross the Atlantic far south of the action. When Lilly and Harry Hawes finally arrived in Key West, Florida, Lilly was detained and interrogated for nearly two days; the proceedings included a strip search of her and two female traveling companions. August A. was waiting. It was mid-June 1918.

Lilly made it home, but her assets were still held by the government because all "so-called German brewers" were suspect. Those assets were not released until after the war had ended, in December of 1918. And by then, all the so-called German brewers were in economic trouble.

The Eighteenth Amendment calling for Prohibition nationally was passed by Congress over the objections of Germans and a lot of non-Germans who wanted to drink. All of August A.'s efforts—including his financial support of anti-suffrage groups because he feared newly enfranchised women would be particularly supportive of Prohibition—had come to naught. Before the Prohibition amendment was ratified, the government had instituted wartime prohibition to save grain, so the Buschs and the Lemps and the brewers' associations in St. Louis knew what was coming: the total collapse of their businesses.

HAPPY DAYS ARE GONE AGAIN

Both Anheuser-Busch and the Lemp Brewery introduced "near beers"—with greatly reduced alcohol content—in an effort to retain the drinking population. But neither did well after a while because people took up a new drinking interest. The bootleg liquor being made was so bad that the "cocktail" was born, a mixing of liquor with something sweet enough to make the drink palatable. The less-sweet beer fell out of favor.

Faced with little to offer, the two families went in different directions. The Lemps seemed to have lost interest in Falstaff and the brewery operations during the turmoil of 1910s; the brothers Louis, Charles, and Edwin moved on to other careers. One day in 1920, workers showed up at the Lemp plant to find the doors locked. Billy sold the Falstaff brand to another brewer.

In June of 1922, Billy announced he was selling the plant, which had been valued at more than $7 million just before Prohibition went national. He said he was tired of seeing all the weeds in the courtyards. International Shoe Company got the facility at auction for just more than a half-million dollars. And at the end of 1922, Billy took his father's way out, committing suicide in his office at the Lemp Mansion. He was fifty-five years old.

It wasn't the last suicide. While Louis and Edwin went on to live normal life spans, Charles become a recluse in the Lemp Mansion. In 1949, leaving detailed instructions for a non-funeral, he first shot his dog and then himself. Edwin lived to be ninety, dying in 1970. But he had requested that all family heirlooms and art collections be destroyed at his death.

Today, the Lemp Mansion functions as a restaurant and bed-and-breakfast, perhaps especially intriguing for those who think the place is haunted. Much of the brewery still stands amid plans to repurpose it.

Meanwhile, August A. Busch kept up the fight. He and his sons, Adolphus III and August A. Jr. (Gussie), had to give up on near beer, but they kept the plant running by making yeast and canned malt syrup. August A. tried to sell the latter only to pharmaceuticals and food manufacturers, but it is certainly possible some of it ended up in the hands of bootleggers. Speaking of which, August A. kept up a constant barrage of complaints to Washington, charging that legitimate businesses and consumers were being punished while criminals, bootleggers, and gangs benefitted.

In St. Louis, there were plenty of bootleggers and plenty of gang members. Egan's Rats, the gang we will see in chapter 21 on political corruption, became the city's main bootleggers. Another mostly Irish gang was Hogan's; Edward "Jelly Roll" Hogan, the son of a St. Louis cop, managed to get himself appointed a deputy inspector of the State Beverage Department. That meant he could inspect former small brewers now producing soft drinks and exact payment for their continued beer production. The Cuckoo Gang, made up of German, American, and a few Syrian men, ruled Soulard, hijacking and reselling loads of beer and booze and muscling speakeasy owners to buy their product.

There were at least three Italian gangs in Little Italy and on the Hill, the formerly peaceful lower-middle-class neighborhood that was home to Yogi Berra and Joe Garagiola. The Sicilian residents there were particularly adept at building elaborate stills and producing incredible amounts of liquor. As in other cities, the members of the gangs most frequently went after one another, but their threats spilled over into the community, marking the worst outcome of Prohibition—one Adolphus and August A. Busch had predicted.

When Franklin Roosevelt was running for president in 1932, he promised to oversee the end of Prohibition. August A. became a Democrat, promoted Roosevelt, and was grateful to see the end of the scourge in 1933. He may have congratulated himself and his sons for keeping the company afloat. However, the fight had left him exhausted and with serious health issues. In February of 1934, he committed suicide. That left the company in the rather staid hands of Adolphus III, who only had to deal with the Depression and World War II. He died in 1946, and the colorful era of Gussie Busch began, along with more successes for Anheuser-Busch. The decline began with Adolphus IV, who finally sold the company to foreign interests in the early twenty-first century.

But Budweiser and Anheuser-Busch are still firmly entrenched, in the downtown baseball stadium and the sprawling brewery, in the fabric and fame of St. Louis.

A DUBIOUS
CIVIC LEGACY

S t. Louis' boosters have always wanted the city to be in the national eye. The beer and the baseball, the fair, were positives in their day. Come to think of it, beer and baseball still are.

But there have been times in its history when St. Louis took national attention for events that boosters would just as soon no one knew about. Corruption: St. Louis was exhibit number one in Lincoln Steffens' muckraking *The Shame of the Cities* in 1904. Strikes: Many cities were hit by violence, but St. Louis offered up unique twists. Race riots: 1917 was a really bad year in East St. Louis, spilling over across the Mississippi. And prostitution: St. Louis had one of the most progressive approaches in the country. Until it didn't work anymore.

THE SOCIAL EVIL

Most likely, it was cold on December 7, 1871. St. Louis can be both cold and damp in the winter months. But a crowd that eventually grew to five thousand stood around outside a home on St. Charles Street between Fifth and Sixth. A funeral was taking place inside the house, described as a mansion, bought from a Chouteau family member by Mrs. Eliza Haycraft. Occupation: brothel madam. Her story raises questions about prostitution—known as the "social evil" in polite conversation—and the ambitious social experiment underway in St. Louis in 1871.

A SCENE AT A FREE-LOVE MEETING.

THE above is an interesting scene at Lize Haycraft's mansion on Pople
street, during a Free-Love meeting that took place there lately.

A cartoon showcasing Eliza Haycraft, one of the good bad ladies among St. Louis
prostitutes. *Missouri Historical Society Collection*

ELIZA HAYCRAFT, THE GOOD BAD LADY

Not that the house on St. Charles was ever a brothel. Eliza Haycraft had bought it for her retirement home. Her brothels, run by other women at that point, were on Green and Poplar Streets. At age fifty-one, "Little Lize" had evolved from a country girl driven from her home in 1840 to a well-respected philanthropist—on the profits she made from running whorehouses. Although—there were likely those among the crowd outside who had more personal memories than Eliza's generosity.

"Many boys and women and not a few old men" gathered to honor her, according to the daily version of the *Missouri Democrat*, which sent a reporter to cover the funeral. In fact, the reporter managed to get the entire funeral sermon for print in the *Daily Democrat* and in other newspapers across the country.

The *Democrat* reporter saw "a number of poor, forlorn-looking women" and surmised that "they had been the recipients of her bounty at a time when respectable Christian people turned from them with loathing." And men moved slowly outside. "Occasionally a 'veteran' would pass along, casting sad and anxious glances toward the house, as if to satisfy himself that the mistress of the mansion was really dead," according to the *Democrat's* account.

Eliza Haycraft (her married name—although we have little knowledge of the husband) was an attractive young woman who legend said was seduced at age twenty and thus thrown out of her home in Callaway County. Supposedly, Eliza came to St. Louis by canoe or skiff in 1840 and embarked on the only profession open to her: prostitution. Unlike many in the trade, she must have saved enough money to move into management. By 1851, she had two houses. By the time the Civil War ended, she managed five bordellos.

There may have been up to six sisters and a brother at the funeral in 1871. However, if sister Sarah was there, she had to have snuck into the state. Apparently having joined her sister in St. Louis and possibly joining the profession, Sarah killed a man described as "her seducer" with a knife through the heart in December of 1855. A judge sentenced her to hang, but Eliza paid $500 to an attorney to petition the governor for clemency. The governor came through, but it took more than that to save Sarah. Both the original trial judge and the Missouri Supreme Court refused the stay of execution. Then, the city marshal refused to carry it out. More than two years after the deed, Sarah was pardoned with the provision that she leave Missouri. Meanwhile, Eliza, our businesswoman extraordinaire, refused to pay the attorney who had originally filed for clemency; the Missouri Supreme Court ruled that was okay because you can't pay for a pardon.

To explain the wealth accumulated by Haycraft and a few other madams, it helps to know that the city's population increased by tenfold from 1840 to 1870. And that doesn't count the number of men who passed through on their way west or because the war brought them temporarily to the city. So, Eliza made money on the increased traffic. And then there were the number of properties she bought as investments. Fearing banks, she put her money into commercial real estate—including a warehouse located near Second and Poplar, excavated by a highway work crew within the last ten years. In fact, the city excavated a number of structures for the Poplar Street Bridge, including Haycraft's brothels.

Haycraft used the money from her brothels and investments to help individuals and charities. When she died on December 5, 1871, she still had an estate estimated at just less than a quarter of a million dollars, or just more than $6 million in 2020 dollars. The *Daily Democrat* thought she left a good deal to family and friends, but she "did not forget the church and charitable institutions."

Dead of a liver disease, she would be buried on December 7 in Bellefon-taine Cemetery, the resting place of St. Louis elite, the original homestead of Steven Hempstead, the burial ground where headstones already read Lisa and Benton and Charless. However, she would not have a headstone herself. The cemetery committee had denied her access, but she went over their heads . . . to meet with their wives, who amazingly brokered an agreement. In the months before her death, she was allowed to buy a huge plot, enough for twenty bodies, as large families often did. But hers was the only body that would be buried there, and there would be no headstone. Furthermore, it was at the back of the cemetery at the time. The main entrance has since moved, and now the large plot is "up front."

THE SOCIAL
EVIL ORDINANCE

S t. Louis is an especially interesting case because, unlike other American cities, it came up with answers to some of the questions raised by prostitution. In 1870, St. Louis legalized and regulated the trade. The fact that the experiment lasted only until 1874 indicates that the answers may not have been the best. Or maybe, that there are no good answers.

Well-defined red-light districts evolved in the 1870s and on into the early twentieth century in many US cities. Their names still resonate today in the Tenderloin districts of New York City and San Francisco, the Levee in Chicago, Storyville in New Orleans. St. Louis' red-light district was less nameable because it was large and fluid. A downtown corridor from the river wharf as far west as Twelfth and later on to Jefferson was implicated. And the reason for that was reflected in the kind of wealth Eliza Haycraft amassed.

Prostitution was highly profitable, and the "best" madams were astute businesswomen. They could afford to outbid almost anyone for property. And when they moved into a new neighborhood, other property values fell.

Stories from the mid-nineteenth century tend to center the trade close to the river. Almond Street, which ran from the southern wharf only to Fifth Street (now Broadway), was often used as a shorthand for bawdy houses and crowds of revelers. But as madams sought to establish safer, and marginally quieter, houses for a better clientele, they could afford to move away from streets like Almond.

Besides property values and the perceived nonsexual crimes that accompanied the houses, the issue of disease had to be in the minds of nineteenth-century citizens. Not as often discussed in the papers, except in advertising from doctors who claimed to have cures, syphilis and other venereal diseases were drawn out and deadly. As a disease, syphilis advances in stages from merely nasty skin sores to severe pain to possible dementia or cardiovascular decline. By the mid-nineteenth century, the methods of treating it were almost as bad as the disease because they involved mercury—meaning many victims died of mercury poisoning. Moving into the twentieth century, physicians mixed arsenic and bismuth with lesser amounts of mercury, to "mixed" results. Penicillin was the answer—but it wasn't available and used to treat syphilis until 1943.

Syphilis and gonorrhea were often seen as the particular scourge of men, and of military men at that. Efforts to control prostitution in Europe, frankly, were efforts to maintain the health of soldiers. But, of course, the family man in peacetime who visited Almond Street or a more upscale brothel could bring disease home to his wife. And that could result in babies born with congenital syphilis. Plus, there was the danger to prostitutes themselves. Eliza Haycraft's story reminds us that there was a fine line between respectability and destitution, between dying young of disease and living long enough to escape the many-faceted dangers of the job.

So: health, crime, and hits to property values. St. Louis needed a several-pronged solution.

Radical legislation called on police to catalog the prostitutes, the ones who worked from brothels, the ones who used "houses of assignation"—largely hotels—and streetwalkers who took men to their own flats. In order to corral their activities, the police were to issue permits for women to move into new quarters. And perhaps most amazingly, the city was going to organize a group of physicians who would check the health of the (duly registered) prostitutes. If a woman was ill or showed signs of any sexually transmitted disease, she would be admitted to a special hospital.

And how would this be paid for? Every prostitute examined would have to pay a monthly fee of $6 (a bit over $150 in 2020 dollars); an additional $10 monthly (more than $260) was levied on brothels. All of this proceeded, we should note, with the approval of the state legislature, which had issued a new charter for the city of St. Louis for the purpose.

At first, the city simply used a special ward of City Hospital. But that wouldn't do. Women could "escape" too easily. Soon the city decided to open The Social Evil Hospital and House of Industry a good ways from downtown, in a pleasant country home at Arsenal and Sublette Streets. It was a half mile from the county insane asylum and "a good rifle shot away from any other house," according to a newspaper report. Policemen were on guard to "keep the patients in and strangers out." (*The Missouri Republican*) Women were invariably taken from their houses or flats without notice— because if they'd had notice, they wouldn't have stayed in town.

Although they paid the license fees, women relegated to the hospital also paid for their care there. We have to wonder what "treatment" meant before there was a satisfactory remedy. For that matter, there is no record of an efficient diagnosis other than the sores beginning to appear. How long would a woman need to be in confinement to be cured? As for the House of Industry, attempts to find new careers could hardly have gotten far when there were few careers for women—and none that paid so well.

A reporter from the *Missouri Republican* interviewed forty-some-odd women at the hospital and reported on conditions in late December 1872. He said it looked like a pleasant-enough girls' boardinghouse until the patients "commence to talk." They offered an earful. The licensing, they said, constituted meddling in their business, although the health care was of some benefit. Most were not looking for reform or another job. The managers wisely did not force or even offer any sort of religious service. "The majority of their class know religion only as a scourge," the reporter said. The women "ask no outside sympathy, and . . . want no outside meddling."

Police Chief James McDonough—soon to become part of the problem—estimated that there were 5,000 prostitutes in the city before the ordinance. At their best, the police never registered more than 1,300 women a year. Of course, some may have decided to take their businesses outside the city rather than be registered and inspected. A few may have, as they told police, "reformed." Others simply became hard to find.

Meanwhile, the matter of permits for moving must have taken up a lot of police time. Despite the low number of women registered, the police issued thousands of moving permits—up to nine per woman in one year.

And the moving didn't always go smoothly as far as property values were concerned. At one point, police allowed Madam Vic DeBar a permit for a new brothel to be located in a house near Sixth and Elm. That was the location of St. Luke's Hospital, one of at least six private hospitals in the city. The Episcopalian hospital board decided to vacate the premises and move elsewhere. But who to rent the building to? Who could pay a sizable rent? Madams, of course. Two more brothels moved in when one wing of the hospital was rented to well-known-madam Kate Clark. The other side of the building went to Clark's competitor, Lizzie Saville.

Residents began to flee. A few other brothels got permits to scoop up the property, but the bawdy houses could fill up only so much of the neighborhood, and by August 1873, the *Republican* reported houses "standing vacant."

Some St. Louis clergymen objected. By 1873, the Reverend William Greenleaf Eliot, who pastored the Unitarian Church and had helped found Washington University, made medical, social, moral, and legal arguments against the scheme. Medically, the "cures" were suspect, he said, it being well known, "the poison continues in the blood and may be implanted in its worst forms." Socially, condoning prostitution threatened marriage by "making it safe" for married men to have sex with prostitutes without penalty. Morally, the policy made "the most unjust discrimination between equal offenders," condemning only the women who were "instruments of the legalized lust of habitually profligate men." Legally, the St. Louis experiment denied women the same freedoms granted men, who Eliot claimed were "equally culpable and often times more diseased." (Sneddeker)

On top of that, the Reverend Eliot questioned the numbers. How did 653 women registered in 1872 square with 2,684 arrests? Of course, it does square if each woman was arrested, on average, 4.4 times. Which would explain why the police were increasingly busy enforcing the ordinance.

In June of 1873, Eliot tested the constitutionality of a city ordinance violating state law, or, to be more exact, the capacity of the state legislature to let that happen. In doing so, he named names. Kate Clark and Lizzie Saville, the women who were renting pieces of the old St. Luke's Hospital as bordellos, received complaints saying they violated state—not city—law. The two wealthy madams promptly hired a good attorney who said the legislature could do as it pleased. A local court agreed with Eliot, the judge adding that the law was unjust because it applied to only one gender, not both. But the women won on their appeal to the state Supreme Court.

What Eliot couldn't do on his own, local politicos managed. The two biggest supporters of the plan were Police Chief James McDonough and Mayor Joseph Brown. Chief McDonough fell afoul of public opinion when he went after his neighbor, a former prostitute named Fannie Carnivan. She hosted a party one night that raised complaints of undue noise from the chief, who she told to "watch his own doorstep." (Sneddeker)

The chief said Mrs. Carnivan's subsequent arrest was justified because she had once been a prostitute—blowing the whole argument that women were reforming and leaving the trade. At some point he entered her property, rousted Carnivan's servant girl out of bed, refused to leave while she got dressed, and then threatened to arrest her as a prostitute if she didn't testify against Carnivan. The newspapers had been passing on complaints of police using their expanded powers to harass women regardless of their professions or immediate activity. The chief's actions against Fannie Carnivan were particularly "bad press," as we would say.

Meanwhile, Mayor Brown had problems of his own involving corruption in hiring city contractors. He tried to distract the public by going after critics of the prostitution policy, namely the city's now-aroused clergy. He called them hypocrites for not trying to reform the women in the Social Evil Hospital. Brown took it upon himself to visit the women, reading from the Bible and from popular literature—Edgar Allan Poe and Robert Burns presumably being uplifting to their condition. We can imagine from the interviews what the women thought of that piece of politics.

Mardi Gras of 1874 was the last straw in the eyes of many. Because of the publicity the ordinance had shed on prostitution, it became public record that many of the masked women on the arms of the St. Louis elite at the annual festivities were leading madams and practitioners of the regulated but legal prostitution profession.

It became a partisan political issue, and the legislature in Jefferson City was deluged with petitions from Eliot and others in 1874. Repeal finally happened, but only when the two sides agreed on a "no-raid" bill that would protect women who had registered in good faith. The legislation prohibited police from raiding brothels except for especially defined complaints, forbade police from trying to extort bribes or favors, and, in a sense, made St. Louis an exception once again. Brothel-keeping was not prohibited as it was in the rest of the state.

The predictable happened. Madams with the money to do so kept up with the westward movement of the population. More neighborhoods were unofficially declared no longer respectable, and property values fell. By 1879, the city and state relented. The laws against raids were repealed; keeping a brothel was declared a misdemeanor. And St. Louis was back where it had started in the 1860s: Brothels were a no-no, but they existed under a system of discretion on the part of police and politicians.

MEET ME BY
THE STATION

By the 1880s, residences along Market, Chestnut, and Pine as far out as 15th Street were being bought up. Neighborhood associations blossomed to encourage people not to sell to madams. Clergy supported the associations less from a moralistic stand than a practical one. If residents moved away from a neighborhood, they hollowed out the churches located there. Selling a church building in a neighborhood overtaken by prostitution couldn't have been easy. Re-establishing a church farther west wasn't easy either. The Rev. W. W. Boyd of the very prominent Second Baptist Church actually proposed a segregated vice district, got the proposal through the state legislature in 1894, and saw the governor veto it. When the idea was revived after the fair in 1904, the ministers couldn't agree on where the district could be, given that none of them wanted it in their neighborhoods. (We will meet the Reverend Boyd in chapter 21, where he airs his view of women.)

Starting in 1893, there was a new magnet for attracting clientele. The majestic Union Station, between 18th and 20th on Market, touted as being among the most elegant of the new rail facilities in the country, was now the source of transient men as the river had been before. Union Station offered hundreds of men with "lay-overs" daily. All sorts of businesses grew up to serve that trade, but brothels, both Black and white, were primary among them.

That meant that families, elite and otherwise, had to pass by everything from tacky trinket shops to barely dressed women posing in windows as the decent folk came and went from Union Station. And if it was bad in 1893, it was going to be a lot worse in 1904 when the city wanted to impress arriving tourists for the World's Fair. Plans were floated to simply tear down the shops across Market, but it would take years for that plan to come to fruition. The city managed to convince prostitutes to keep a low profile for the duration of the fair.

They may not have paraded as brazenly, but prostitutes were certainly active at the time of the fair in the "Badlands," the neighborhood across from the station, also known as Chestnut Valley. And there was at least one last scandal to be had: City police were taking bribes to help prostitutes rob clients.

By late 1905, an investigation was underway into police graft. The most sensational explanations came from the "Queen of the Badlands," a madam named Ollie Roberts. Roberts herself wasn't operating during the fair, having been imprisoned for shooting a man in her brothel, but she was offered a parole for her testimony against a Sergeant John Connors and three patrolmen.

Robbery of men using the brothels was common. Roberts explained how she could spy on men through holes in panels to gauge when and how the robberies could occur—robberies of "suckers" as she routinely referred to the men. Those men would sometimes complain to the police; we can imagine that other times they were too embarrassed to do so. But the ones who did complain often did so to policemen who were in on the scheme.

When she first met Connors, for example, he and Roberts "fixed it up then that he should have half the take when a sucker hollered." She went on to testify that, "When a man was touched [stolen from] and made a kick [complained to police], the officer would ask him his name, whether he was married, what kind of job he had, whether he lived in the city, and about his family. Then he'd take him to all the other houses on the street and try to make him pick out the girl who had robbed him. If he was positive as to the house, the officer would give a tip, and by the time they got there everybody would be gone." (All juicy quotes from *Post-Dispatch*, March 1906)

The prosecutor wanted to know how much money Ollie Roberts had stolen in her house alone: might it be as much as $100,000 [more than two and a half million today]? Roberts allowed as how that was too low a figure. She recalled that the biggest haul she took from one man was $2,045. Asked what happened to that particular sucker, she replied, "Oh, he killed himself, I believe."

Another suicide was associated with the case as well. As the case had gathered steam in January of 1906, a Sergeant George Colestock shot himself in a hotel room. Colestock had "arrested" Roberts some time before when a "square" cop happened to be the one to hear the complaint of a robbed "sucker." Colestock reported back to Roberts that the good cop had raised a stink with the captain, who was "getting sore and she'd have to stand for a pinch." Colestock had arrested her on a charge of wandering, which she easily avoided serving time for—because, as the Queen of the Badlands said, "I was never arrested in my life without my consent."

When the investigation concluded, at least fourteen cops and other public officials were implicated—and Sergeant Colestock's family were widowed and orphaned. Ollie Roberts violated the parole she'd gotten and was back in the penitentiary. It was a long way from the relatively benign prostitution of Eliza Haycraft with her legacy of philanthropy to Robert's deadly version of the profession. That's probably why a musical has been written about Haycraft. But not Roberts.

ON STRIKE

Labor unrest roiled American cities in the late-nineteenth and early twentieth centuries, and St. Louis put an exclamation mark on the turmoil when prominent citizens took up arms against striking streetcar workers.

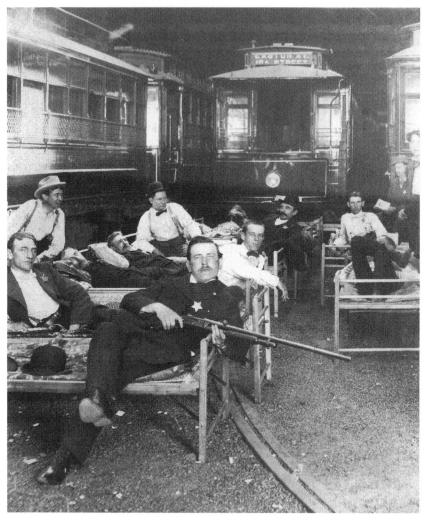

Upper-class St. Louisans who responded to the call for a posse wait in a car barn to confront striking streetcar drivers. *Missouri Historical Society Collection*

THE MAJESTY
OF THE LAW

The nation was in the waning days of a depression that had started in 1873 when the big rail lines decided to reduce workers' pay by 10 percent in the summer of 1877. An observer sympathetic to management would say the rail companies were barely staying afloat themselves, and they either had to let men go or reduce everyone's pay. An observer sympathetic to labor would say the rail barons could have easily afforded to avoid paying men less, imposing speed-ups, blacklisting union activists, and letting dangerous conditions multiply. Either way, the strikes on the Baltimore and Ohio rail started in West Virginia and Maryland and spread west, bumping up against worker complaints in East St. Louis on July 22 and in St. Louis on July 23 of 1877.

The Workingmen's Party, the forerunner of the Socialist Labor Party in the United States, took control of what soon enough became a general strike. That alone would have led St. Louis mayor Henry Overstolz to call for help. But what really frightened and infuriated the city's establishment was the inclusion of Black levee workers in the group alternatively described as a protest and as a mob.

The strike leaders called on various businesses to join the protest, widening the stakes beyond rail workers. The Workingmen activists wanted eight-hour workdays and a ban on child labor. We can read two different interpretations on how the breadth of the strike played out. Sources sympathetic to the strike say that workers, including the Blacks, marched through the city asking workers at mills, foundries, bagging factories, and more to join them. And that men did so, swelling the march as it continued. The *Missouri Republican* said, "It is wrong to call this a strike; it is a labor revolution." (Johnson)

Historians less sympathetic to labor paint a different picture, asserting that the railway workers only wanted to stop trains, but that, "as is always the case, the turbulent and unruly, the vicious and idle gathered around the strikers, swelled their forces, and could not be restrained from violence and outrage." (Scharf) From this perspective, the marchers were a mob that threatened manufacturers and businesses, forcing them to close. Most outrageous, to the owners, were the Blacks, always reported to be at the fore of the workers pushing into buildings and running off other workers.

As usual, the police numbers were hardly sufficient to control the crowds. Mayor Overstolz called on "law-abiding" and "prominent" citizens to form a Committee of Public Safety, organized into various companies and armed. Soon, the group numbered about five thousand, summoned as a "posse comitatus"—the Latin phrase for the good-old posse assembled by outnumbered sheriffs in numerous Westerns.

Overstolz, in his proclamations, said, "It is earnestly desired to avoid the necessity of resort to force, but the majesty of the law will be asserted." It was fine for men to strike, "to abandon their employment," he said, but that they had no right to interfere with those who were content with their wages. (Scharf)

It is said that the events of those few days in St. Louis constituted the first general strike in the country's history.

The Workingmen leaders sent messages to the governor and mayor asking for, in addition to work hour–shortening legislation, a program to procure food for destitute workers—for which the labor organizations would pay. The letter to Overstolz stated that, "We, the unfortunate, toiling citizens, desire to faithfully maintain the majesty of the law while we are contending for our inalienable rights." (Scharf)

The battle over the majesty of the law was short-lived. The leadership of the strike, in contrast to the men on the street, pulled back from the conflict, the posse raided their headquarters, and the first general strike ended. The Illinois National Guard occupied the railyards in East St. Louis. In St. Louis, the names of the prominent citizens who'd joined the posse were reported in self-satisfaction.

Back in chapter 5, we unveiled the Veiled Prophet event. Not by accident, the first and only officially revealed "prophet" was the first: police commissioner John G. Priest. Priest continued to lead a group of posse members after the strike, a physical presence that announced the determination of the "prominent" to police the proletariat. The first Veiled Prophet parade featured Priest in white robes with a revolver, a rifle, and a bowie knife. Even the *Missouri Republican* noted that a "villainous-looking executioner" stood behind Priest.

The Veiled Prophet extravaganza of the elite went on for more than a century, its ominous beginning likely losing some of the urgency of the message over time. But the posse comitatus strategy wasn't forgotten by the elite, who would send their sons to protect the city in deadly confrontations almost twenty-five years later.

WHEN THE STREETCARS STOP RUNNING . . .

I t is easy to assume that corruption and monopoly power don't make much difference in everyday lives. Who controls what in the city might just seem a game among the elites. But streetcars were essential. As St. Louis spread west, people relied on streetcars, noted for obvious safety precautions, sensible schedules, and reasonable fares, to get to work. On the flip side, streetcar workers wanted shorter shifts, steady pay, freedom from harassment if they chose to join a union, and relief from pressure to short customers on stops, seats, and safety. The third leg of the stool was owners who wanted less competition and more profits. You can guess who got what.

More than the General Strike of 1877, the situation in 1899, leading to events of 1900, smacked of corruption—or what was called "boodle" in St. Louis. That meant paying off the city officials to get privileges that included everything from utility contracts to low tax assessments. One popular name for the association of West End and downtown elite was the Big Cinch. Former mayor, former governor, future fair director David Francis was one example, but there were more, maybe a dozen or more names that would appear over and over as financial beneficiaries of each other's firms: bank directors, utility company vice presidents, commodities and dry goods magnates, and real estate moguls. And brewers. Adolphus Busch of beer fame served on bank and utility boards. (St. Louis had its own boss, Edward Butler, and we will hear a lot more about him in chapter 20 on corruption in the city.)

The name "Big Cinch" may have come from William Marion Reedy, an Irishman from the city's Kerry Patch who gained renown editing a highly influential political and literary magazine, *The Mirror*. The idea of a clique of men who ruled the city financially and ran roughshod over middle- and lower-class needs came as well from Joseph Pulitzer; the *Post-Dispatch* seldom failed to attack the group. And, in 1899, journalists watched the Big Cinch extend its influence to Jefferson City and the Missouri Legislature, as it scored a coup on the streetcar business.

Although numerous legislators and the governor had run on antitrust platforms in 1888, they promptly approved legislation in the spring of 1889 that allowed the several St. Louis streetcar companies to merge. One behemoth formed—St. Louis Transit—along with the slightly smaller Suburban company. The Amalgamated Association of Street Railway Employees saw the handwriting on the wall and tried to secretly recruit drivers and other employees, a local for each company. Predictably, the companies found out and started firing union members.

And just as predictably, the companies went high-handed. The worse was St. Louis Transit, which increased fares, cut back on the number of cars, and changed routes to produce long wait times. Other money-saving measures resulted in dirtier and more crowded cars and more dangerous operations: The frequency of accidents rose—as did public ire, fueled by the angrier papers and magazines, including the *Post-Dispatch*.

In early 1900, the locals were set to strike, starting with the Suburban lines. Suburban was ready with nonunion outsiders who manned the cars. The cases of violence—supporters would throw rocks, scab conductors would fire pistols above the protesters' heads—were sporadic and routinely condemned by the union. Accidents were up: a child killed while playing on the tracks, a woman run over on her way to work, a produce wagon driver knocked to the ground. The union blamed the replacement workers. Strikers organized horse-drawn wagons to move customers who sided with them.

In early May, the transit ownership pushed workers to fourteen-hour workdays, threatened to reduce wages, and harassed known union members. When the transit union local responded, everything that had happened relatively mildly in the Suburban strike flared into violence.

The day the strike started, May 8, 1900, the headliners were members of the Garment Makers' Union, young women who formed a human barricade in front of a transit car at Fifteenth and Washington. The most dramatic moment came when one young woman broke from the crowd and begged the conductor not to continue. It turned out he was her brother. We don't know how that one ended, but other confrontations that day resulted in a young man wounded when a conductor fired into a crowd. Police were assaulted as they dashed from one stoppage to another. The unions denied inciting any violence and, indeed, much of the stoning and stopping came from angry citizens.

By the third week of the strike, sympathizers were getting more sophisticated. They dynamited cars and built bonfires on the tracks. The predictable response was a posse numbering 2,500 men, all drawn from the "better elements" of the city.

It should be noted that a good many families among the better elements had no great love for the rail companies that ran dangerous and inefficient lines. A surprising number of men called to posse duty discovered disabilities. Still, the violent reactions by ordinary citizens seemed to have convinced sufficient elites that class warfare was at hand to motivate their participation. The upper-class posse men positioned themselves in car barns in various working-class neighborhoods with arrest powers and orders to shoot anyone who resisted.

They constituted a powder keg, awaiting a fire source. Strikers inadvertently provided one on June 10, a rainy and otherwise peaceful Sunday morning. That day, some eight hundred strikers, unarmed, crossed the Eads Bridge to enjoy a picnic offered by the Belleville, Illinois, rail local. When the strikers returned home that afternoon, led by a drum and bugle players, headed west on Washington Avenue, the posse was waiting.

A streetcar headed west passed between the parading picnickers and the jeering posse. Something sounded, maybe a rock thrown at the car. Three posse men charged into the crowd of strikers with guns drawn, and a shot was fired. That led other posse men to open fire from the ground and from the upper windows of the barracks. By the time the shooting stopped, three strikers were dead and fourteen injured. William Marion Reedy apparently watched and thought the posse men "were more than half glad the music had begun." (Young)

The outrage, from Reedy's readers and others, was sufficient to lead to the gradual withdrawal of the posse from the city's streets. The strikes ended in arbitration saying it would preserve union jobs but didn't. Several outcomes resonate. One was the rise of public outcry that would hobble the boodlers, largely in the presence of a young man who had helped in the negotiations, one Joseph Folk. (More about "Holy Joe" Folk soon.) Unions would continue to organize and make a difference. The other, less favorable, outcome was the hiring of men and women from the "countryside" who were expected to be more docile and less inclined to union involvement. In East St. Louis, the "countryside" workers were all too often Blacks from the Deep South. That trend may be said to have sparked one of the worst race riots in US history.

DEADLY RACE
AND GENDER

The city across the Eads Bridge from St. Louis, Missouri, was a factory town. The main reason for moving to East St. Louis was a job. The main reason for offering a job there was the near absence of taxes and regulation.

By 1917, many of the biggest national corporations had a presence. In some cases, a satellite community actually carried the name of the company. There was the precisely named Monsanto. Andrew Mellon's Aluminum Ore Company called its suburb Alorton. Jay Rockefeller's Standard Oil called its town Wood River. National City held the National Stockyards, convenient to the companies run by Mr. Armour and Mr. Swift. Meanwhile, Jay Gould controlled the railroads that bottlenecked in East St. Louis before crossing the Eads Bridge, controlled by J. P. Morgan. It was well-recognized that East

A victim of the St. Louis mob awaits the ambulance appearing at left. The leader of the mob is the one being restrained by the police officer. Members of the state militia hold back other mob members. *Missouri Historical Society Collection*

St. Louis existed only for the products it provided and the profit it promised. Civic life was meaningless. The city ran on corruption, noxious operations, and greed. St. Louis' Big Cinch looked downright benign by comparison.

The factory leaders (and therefore the city government) in East St. Louis allowed and might have encouraged the migration of Blacks to the city for one purpose: as a reserve workforce to break strikes, to do the absolute worst, unskilled jobs in meatpacking plants and the furnaces of the steel companies, to be the threat. Stay in line, the companies told its preferred white workers, or a Black man will take your job.

Before World War I, the Black population was small and set in segregated ways, even though Illinois law since 1874 prohibited segregated schools and facilities. Whites in East St. Louis resoundingly rejected those innovations, stating in various ways that the city was a white man's town. However, World War I so increased the demand for products made in East St. Louis—munitions and food products sent to Europe even before the United States joined the war in the spring of 1917—that Black migration was inevitable. The word "colonization" began to be used.

THE DEADLY
SUMMER OF 1917

In the 1916 elections, Democrats charged Republicans with colonizing, importing Blacks from the South and signing them up to vote. Of course, Republicans who figured prominently among factory owners may well have recruited Southern Blacks, but not to vote—only for labor supply reasons. But the Democrats hoped to turn out the white supremacist vote by portraying the Black influx as a serious threat to white safety. Tales of Black crime spread, despite the lack of jail records to back it up, and whites began to say that it wasn't safe for their women to go out at night. Vote fraud was alleged, but never proven, in part because the Black vote never materialized. But the stage was set for increasingly strident white newspaper stories of Black violence.

A strike at the Aluminum Ore plant in late May and June of 1917 was the spark. With the United States now at war against Germany, and with many whites who had German heritage on the picket lines, the company held off the strike with patriotic rhetoric and Black replacement workers. The threats from whites increased and became public. Blacks began to arm themselves.

On July 1, white men drove a Model T Ford through a Black neighborhood and began shooting into houses. Police officers made the unfortunate decision to take an unmarked Model T—they were all identical for the most part—into the neighborhood to see what was happening. When Blacks fired to stop the second incursion, they killed the two officers.

Word spread fast, and Black workers who were getting off work the morning of July 2 met a mob that grew to more than a thousand white men—and white women. Black men were shot as they walked down streets; they were pulled off streetcars and beaten. Dead bodies were burned in the streets and hoisted on lampposts. White women pulled the clothes from Black women they found outside their homes, shot at them, and forced them to flee into houses that wouldn't be safe for long. As the riots stretched out over the next several days, Blacks who tried to hide in their homes were shot as they fled fires. Some fled to white neighbors. While some Black families were protected, others were kicked out and killed.

News made its way across the country, and activists responded. Journalist Ida B. Wells appeared, as did W. E. B. DuBois, investigating for the NAACP. Their oral accounts tell story after story of terror. The only possible escape for many Blacks was to get across the Mississippi pedestrian bridge to St. Louis, but at one point, whites were waiting for them and shot to kill. By July 3, militiamen had managed to escort several hundred Blacks across the bridge, according to a newspaper account. Many stayed permanently on the west side.

The headlines from the two largest St. Louis newspapers tell the contemporaneous story. The morning edition of the *St. Louis Globe-Democrat* on July 3 spread its headline across the page: "100 Negroes Shot, Burned, Clubbed to Death in E. St. Louis Race War." Subheads said, "Women of Lowest Type Torture Negresses While an Axman Cleaves Skull," and "Chicago Printer Declares He Saw Militiaman Shoot Blacks and Police Officers Incite the Mob," and "Captive Being Dragged to Lynching Post Is Beaten Down by Rain of Bricks." In an editorial comment, the *Globe-Democrat* asserted that, "The lust of murder turned the mob into savages."

Even more eloquent were comments from *St. Louis Post-Dispatch* writer Carlos F. Hurd, identified on the front page of the July 3 evening edition, an unusual attribution in the days before bylines. He opened by saying, "For an hour and a half last evening I saw the massacre of helpless negroes at Broadway and Fourth Street, in downtown East St. Louis, where a black skin was a death warrant."

Referencing well-reported war atrocities, he continued. "I do not believe that Moslem fanaticism or Prussian frightfulness could perpetrate murders of more deliberate brutality than those which I saw committed, in daylight by citizens of the State of Abraham Lincoln."

Official death estimates ranged from thirty-nine to forty-eight, but that only counted bodies that could be found. Other deaths occurred in the three hundred buildings, including homes, burned to the ground. Other bodies were dumped in the Mississippi and never found. Riots followed in other American cities in the next three years, but the official death toll from East St. Louis was not exceeded until the Rodney King riots in Los Angeles in 1992.

WOMEN WORK TOO

The labor-related race war in East St. Louis was easily the most violent event of the labor era, but we should note the surprising role St. Louis women played in labor activity in the 1910s and 1920s. At least two died in connection with their work.

The Women's Trade Union League (WTUL) was an attempt to join working-class women with upper-class women who could, perhaps more effectively, argue the cause. In many cities, the upper-class women led the way. But in St. Louis, a young woman who had worked in garment factories from the age of thirteen, one Hannah Hennessy, led Local 67 of the United Garment Workers of America (UGWA) in a fight that got the attention of St. Louis men.

Hennessey started the WTUL chapter in St. Louis. A few West End matrons, notably Cynthella Knefler, suffragist and activist, held offices, but it was the efforts of working women who built an organization that would make a difference in an upcoming fight.

Women workers were the core of the garment industry that had, ironically, moved to St. Louis from New York City and Chicago seeking cheaper workers. In St. Louis, Marx & Haas was a major garment manufacturer, with its two factories at Thirteenth and Washington and Sixteenth and Market. Because it employed women for all jobs except cutting the cloth (which required the strength to cut through thick layers of fabric as well as the skill to waste as little cloth as possible), Marx & Haas made its money by paying as little as possible for piecework. Women would work as quickly as possible to turn out as many garments as possible—and then the boss would lower the piecework rate. Few women made anything like a living wage. Furthermore, the shops' lint-filled air and close quarters were breeding grounds for tuberculosis. When, in 1909, Marx & Haas laid off a tubercular man who had tried to use an elevator, the UGWA local struck.

One of the leftovers from the 1900 strike was a Citizen's Industrial Alliance of St. Louis, made of leading manufacturers—the "alliance" referring to deals they had struck with skilled locals to keep them from striking during the World's Fair. Once the fair closed, the alliance went on the offense against unions, using legal tactics, blacklists, and the city's most notorious detective agencies, companies that infiltrated unions and provided strike-breakers. Marx & Haas particularly favored the Kiely Secret Service Agency, whose director was former police chief Matthew Kiely, fired because of his shoot-to-kill order during a 1903 teamsters' strike.

One month into the strike, Hannah Hennessey died of the tuberculosis that killed so many garment workers. We don't know her age. We only know that she handed the reins over to Fannie Sellins, another St. Louis Irish woman and a charter member of the local. Sellins in turn recruited another Irish worker, Kate Hurley, and the two took the campaign against Marx & Haas national. They went to big national conventions and small labor hot spots and raised enough money to sustain the striking workers in St. Louis for two years. Furthermore, Sellins managed a boycott of Marx & Haas goods that was so effective that the company closed its Sixteenth and Market Street operation. In October of 1911, the company signed a contract with the UGWA.

Ultimately, though, Sellins fought the UGWA. The conservative, male-oriented union failed to back a 1912 strike against another St. Louis factory. The struggle in St. Louis continued until the 1930s when larger numbers of garment workers unionized. Meanwhile, Fannie Sellins gave up on the UGWA and the fight in St. Louis. She went to work for the United Mine Workers as an organizer in Pennsylvania and West Virginia. At one point, she counseled Black workers who had been brought in from the South to work as scabs in a Pennsylvania strike. She was successful enough that three operatives of the Allegheny Coal Company chased her from a picket line in Pennsylvania and shot her in the back. An Allegheny county coroner's jury ruled it self-defense on the part of the shooters: self-defense from "the Anarchy and Bolshevist Doctrines instilled into the minds of the unamerican and uneducated Aliens." (Faherty)

Women's labor became a theme of the 1910s in St. Louis. In 1913, the state Senate held hearings in St. Louis to determine the need for minimum-wage legislation for women. They heard from women working in laundries who fainted from the heat, from women injured making envelopes sent to city dispensaries for treatment on the public's dime, from women who bought clothes on credit. A minimum wage for women was widely discussed and even found its way into some political platforms, but we have no evidence that it ever passed in Missouri.

The "Hello Girls," telephone operators for Southwestern Bell (one of two St. Louis telephone companies) went on strike in 1913. They were associated with the IBEW, the International Brotherhood of Electrical Workers. Locals got over their surprise at the better-dressed, respectable women picketing; the women were arrested with other union members protesting strikebreakers brought in from out of town. The women were making progress in launching a boycott when the strike was suddenly settled with no relief other than the pledge to reinstate the operators. The male members of the IBEW local had decided to settle without talking to the women.

Still, Southwestern Bell instituted an eight-hour workday and raised some wages in order to head off more union trouble. It worked for a few years.

By 1919, the women's Telephone Operators group within the union went on strike again. Southwestern Bell brought in not only strikebreakers, but union spies. This time, the men of the IBEW local supported the women and helped organize a boycott. After six weeks, a compromise was reached in which the women won more pay and other benefits but again failed to get Bell's recognition of their union. Luckier women worked for the smaller Kinloch Telephone Company, which had recognized the union and worked through contract negotiations earlier. (Unused to telephone lines as we are, it is particularly hard to imagine two sets of wire crossing city streets and every business advertising not one but two telephone numbers, one for each exchange.)

The 1919 effort had occurred against a backdrop of a second general strike, recalling the efforts of 1877. In February of 1918, some 30,000 workers were on strike in St. Louis. One historian has counted 5,000 department store clerks, 3,500 workers from Wagner Electric, 3,000 garment workers, and 4,000 tobacco workers. Employers organized and fought back; their real victory in the labor wars waged by both men and women lay in the national politics of the 1920s.

DECADES OF TOIL

Most labor efforts fell by the wayside in the 1920s as companies managed to associate labor concerns with Marxism and the Bolshevik government that had taken over in Russia—as evidenced by charges leveled at Fanny Sellins. In St. Louis, one effort in the 1920s was mounted by a Black man who had worked many years as a porter for George Pullman.

George Pullman produced the Pullman sleeping cars in the days when railroads were the standard method of travel. Porters on those sleeping cars made beds and generally looked after the welfare of the traveling and sleeping public. Almost all porters were Black; all were chosen for servility and a ready smile; all were called "George" by passengers who didn't care to find out their servers' names. The Brotherhood of Sleeping Car Porters was founded in 1925, and one of its leaders was E. J. Bradley in St. Louis. He quit his long-standing porter job and maintained an office close to Union Station's busy train traffic for years.

His job was made particularly difficult not only by Pullman's clout but also because many Blacks distrusted labor unions for their white bias. Pullman at one point fired people who spoke to Bradley in St. Louis; in another power play, the company sent advertising dollars to one of St. Louis' Black newspapers, the *Argus*, which opposed the Brotherhood. Still, Bradley persevered for years and, in 1937, the Brotherhood managed to sign a contract with Pullman.

Just to remind ourselves that dubious organizations occasionally do good, if small, deeds, we should include the story of the Society for the Prevention of Calling Sleeping Car Porters (SPCSCP) "George." Yes, indeed. Founded as a joke in 1914, it was open to anyone, presumably whites, whose name was George. At one point, it had 31,000 members, including Admiral George Dewey, Britain's King George V, and George Herman "Babe" Ruth. Although there is no indication that the SPCSCP cared about Black identities in the least, it did convince the Pullman Company in 1926 to put a card rack in each sleeping car, so each porter could be identified by his real name. We don't know how much use the card racks got, but it potentially was a lot. In 1926, there were 12,000 Black Pullman employees and only 362 were named George.

A MORALITY PLAY
OF CORRUPTION
IN FOUR ACTS

A campaign button associating Joe Folk with good government as he ran, successfully, for governor in 1904. *Historical Society of Missouri Collection*

THE CHARACTERS

E d Butler, the bad guy—boodler-in-chief and "boss"

Joe Folk, the good guy, elected circuit attorney in 1901

Henry Hawes, pretending to be a good guy, leader of the Jefferson Club of the divided Democratic Party

Rolla Wells, something of a good guy, elected mayor in 1901

Lincoln Steffens, leader of the Greek chorus of press righteousness and author of *The Shame of the Cities*, joined by local reporters

THE SETTING: "MISTER, YOUR SALOON'S ON FIRE"

Lincoln Steffens traveled to St. Louis in 1902 to research one of his articles for *McClure's Magazine* on corruption in American cities. What he found in St. Louis was fraud that started at the top with an elite that "misused politics." He put the starting date about 1890, when the elite (the Big Cinch) went after public franchises, utilities and railways, as loot. Walking around St. Louis in 1902, Steffens found streets poorly paved and covered with trash. City Hospital was an overflowing firetrap. Four Courts (which housed police, city courts, the jail, and—out back—the hanging scaffold) smelled of formaldehyde and insect powder to keep vermin at bay. Taps in the hotels issued liquid mud. Tax money to fix such problems was diverted to line the pockets of boodlers, boodle being the name for both the practice of bribery and the actual money exchanged.

The Municipal Assembly was home not to the elite but to their tools, men Steffens assailed as illiterate and lacking in ordinary intelligence. The power brokers, rather than serving in political office themselves, had taken to backing men who would do their bidding. A large number of the officeholders were saloon owners. Steffens started a fun story with his very serious recounting of a practical joker who paid a boy to enter the House of Delegates and yell, "Mister, your saloon is on fire." The kid had to dodge out of the way as delegates rushed out of the chamber.

The Municipal Assembly had two chambers, a Council made up of nine members and the House of Delegates, with a representative from each of the twenty-eight wards. They were organized into "combines," which oversaw the selling of legislation. The designated leader of a combine at any given time received cash and distributed it to legislators in return for their votes, positive or negative, on a particular piece of legislation.

The combines had a set list price for everything from a sidewalk to a space on the wharf. New tracks were charged by the linear foot, depending on where they were located. Any privilege or improvement, legitimate or not, sat on a sliding scale according to how much opposition was expected. Boodle was not a matter to be administered incompetently.

The sums involved were considerable. When a grand jury finally heard testimony, a delegate said the combine had paid him $25,000 in a year; a councilman put his take at $50,000. It explains why men of fairly ordinary means went into debt to pay the powers that could put them into office.

And who were those men with power?

ED BUTLER

First of all, there is St. Louis' own boss, not so well known as Tweed in New York City or Pendergast in Kansas City, but amazingly effective for many years. Sometimes called Colonel Butler although we have no evidence of a military career, Butler came to the United States from Ireland when he was twelve years old and worked for a blacksmith, the trade he reimagined as the basis for his bossism when he moved on to St. Louis just before the Civil War. A big man who resembled a gorilla according to some, Butler made his mark on St. Louis quickly. Streetcars were horse- or mule-drawn at the time, and the colonel wanted the contract for shoeing them. So, he bribed local politicians to get it. That led him to think that the real wealth wasn't in shoeing horses. It was in providing votes.

According to Butler's own telling of the legend, his first big operation was gathering up a thousand men from St. Louis to travel to Indianapolis to vote—it was a hard day as they moved around the city voting ten times each—for the pay from two mysterious Indiana gentlemen. Whatever the election was, Butler's men clinched the vote. Thereafter, Butler's loyal corps of voters and henchmen was called Butler's Indians. They almost always carried St. Louis elections as well, usually for Democrats.

However, Butler's allegiance to the Democratic Party could shift if the pay was right. While appearing to support a Democrat in the 1897 mayor's contest, he actually promoted Republican Henry Ziegenheim (of "We've got a moon yet, ain't we?" fame) by directing his Indians to vote only once for the Democrat.

Butler's size and demeanor, along with his derby and his $1,200 diamond stickpin, always identified him to political types in the know if not to the general public. Worth several million dollars, he never sought office himself; he merely controlled whoever did. He desired, however, that his son, James, be part of the elite and be elected to Congress in 1900. That would play into Butler's calculations in the politics of that year.

HARRY HAWES

awes—"Handsome Harry," as he was known—was the Police Board head who tried to stay out of the fray during the streetcar strike. At the same time, he was head of the Jefferson Club, basically a group of upper-class Democrats who supported William Jennings Bryan. That meant they opposed the "goldbug" Democrats such as fair director and former governor David Francis, who favored "sound money." William Marion Reedy of *The Mirror* liked Hawes and described the Jefferson Club as a "crowd of young men of education and gentlemanliness." Although—the club's numbers were strangely swelled by a good number of policemen who apparently also recognized the leadership of their Police Board director. The Jefferson Club publicly stood for reform.

In reality, the Jefferson Club stood for minor reforms that wouldn't jeopardize the interests of its educated and gentlemanly members. And Hawes didn't hesitate to align himself with enforcers from the more political gangs. (See the next chapter.) After the 1900 strikes, Hawes struck a deal with Butler, involving the mayoral and circuit attorney candidates.

ROLLA WELLS

The mayoral candidate of the Jefferson Club, supported by Butler in his deal with Hawes, was the elite Rolla Wells. Wells owned the American Steel Foundry and was a director on the boards of two banks. His father had founded the street railways, but Wells made headlines when he vowed to divest himself of his interest in the United Railway company and the North American Company, which owned the gas and electricity providers. Reform, at last!

Wells would be mayor during the World's Fair. The city's elite favored him for the job in part because he would cut a dignified figure in dealing with equally elite visitors. He walked a line between reform and not-reform, but mostly he must have watched in wonder as the other candidate in the deal, Joe Folk, became circuit attorney.

JOE FOLK

The story goes that when Harry Hawes came to Butler's office one day and suggested the lawyer Joe Folk for the candidacy, Butler said he really didn't know Folk. So Butler had Folk drop by his office and saw "nothing wrong" with the quiet young man who was popular with the unions and agreed to "give him" the job. The fact was Hawes wanted Folk, and Butler wanted Hawes' upper-crust support for his son, James Butler, who was running for Congress in the fall of 1900.

It was the major miscalculation of Butler's career.

Joe Folk had come to St. Louis from Tennessee to make his living as an attorney. He wore conservative suits and a pince-nez—those amazing little glasses that balanced on a nose without aid of earpieces. Folk was notably deadpan and serious, a man of detail and long hours, as unassuming as Butler and Hawes were outgoing. Folk's attempts to settle the streetcar strike, undercut by deviousness on the part of the transit owner, had gotten Folk the approval of Unionists. He was an early member of the Jefferson Club, Hawes' predecessor as president, as a matter of fact. It's not obvious that circuit attorney was Folk's dream job; he had to be asked twice. When he finally accepted, he warned Hawes that if elected, he would do the job right and that he would brook no opposition in going after lawbreakers. Hawes likely thought that was just the usual reform rhetoric. He was wrong.

THE GREEK CHORUS
OF MUCKRAKERS
AND JOURNALISTS

William Marion Reedy criticized St. Louisans for not caring about the good name of their city. Meanwhile, he had a comment on virtually everything happening in the city, which we know because we've found him in several previous chapters and we'll see him in more to come. He had firm opinions on who Joe Folk should go after.

In the story that follows, several reporters make appearances to uncover corruption. James "Red" Gavin of the *St. Louis Star* sniffed out one boodle. Frank McNeil of the *Post-Dispatch* actually journeyed to Mexico to bring back a witness. And Claude Wetmore of the *Post-Dispatch* helped the writer who did the most to light the back rooms of St. Louis, Lincoln Steffens.

Lincoln Steffens was a muckraker—one of the writers whose goal was to expose the seamy side of American life. You know them for detailing conditions in the meatpacking and patent medicine industries, for investigating business fraud and exploitative working conditions. Steffens' passion was corruption and, at the very start of the twentieth century, he was publishing articles in *McClure's Magazine*. Steffens didn't hesitate to name names or generalize about the state of the body politic. When people complained that politics should be run more like business, Steffens pointed out that businessmen were the source of corruption in politics: "He is a self-righteous fraud, the big businessman," Steffens wrote. "The politician is a businessman with a specialty." As for bosses such as Ed Butler, Steffens said, "The boss is not a political, he is an American institution, the product of a freed people that have not the spirit to be free."

Steffens combined seven stories on six cities into a book called *The Shame of the Cities*. St. Louis, he was considered so corrupt that it got two chapters. The first St. Louis chapter was hopeful of change because it was about Joe Folk.

ACT ONE: MR. FOLK GOES TO THE COURTHOUSE

The election that put Joseph W. Folk into office as circuit attorney was corrupt enough that Steffens could have written about it alone. Butler's Indians "repeated" repeatedly. Hawes' goons ran their own operations. Gangs intimidated voters and election officials sufficiently that precinct returns were held up to make sure all the Democrats had sufficient ballots in. Wells and Folk may have looked good in hindsight, but the election itself was so bad that it boomeranged on Ed Butler. His son, James, elected to Congress on the repeated ballots, had the seat taken away when the stench of the election reached Washington. A House of Representatives committee decided that both Republicans and Democrats in St. Louis had cheated, but the Democrats more so.

So, Folk took the oath of office in early January 1901 and promptly outraged Ed Butler by picking his own assistants as opposed to the ones Butler had lined up. The next thing Folk did was call a grand jury to investigate the very election that had put him into office. By the time that played out, seventeen Democrats and fifteen Republicans were indicted for election-related misdemeanors—not serious charges but certainly enough to get the attention of everyone in St. Louis and others around the country. It was a warm-up for the real thing.

Soon enough, Red Gavin of the *Star* suggested that Folk check out a short newspaper item about the large amount of money that had shown up in a bank. Gavin thought it was an unpaid bribe, a case of miscommunication and mistrust between the Assembly's combine and the Suburban Railway

Company. It took Folk an hour to give the sheriff one hundred names, men subpoenaed to appear before the grand jury. The list included assemblymen from both branches, officers of the Suburban, and bank employees from presidents to cashiers.

It goes without saying that a mere rumor about a bribe wasn't going to shake Butler's system. So, Folk got creative. Charles Turner was president of the Suburban Railway; the name of Philip Stock, who represented brewery interests, had come up as a possible legislative agent. (Steffens described Stock as a man-about-town and, sarcastically, a good fellow. Turner was a descendant of the French elite.) Folk ordered them both into the grand jury room and lied to them. Presumably in his low-key, matter-of-fact way, Folk told the two men he had enough evidence on them to send them to the penitentiary for bribery involving the passage of a rail-related ordinance. He graciously gave them three days to offer their stories to the grand jury; if they failed to do so, Folk said he would issue warrants for their arrests.

Stock's attorney tried claiming that the agent wanted to appear but couldn't because of poor health. Folk offered his sympathy but said that if Stock failed to appear, he'd be "arrested before sundown." Stock and Turner were before the grand jury the next day.

Their story was both predictable and extraordinary. During the rail workers' strike described in chapter 18, the Suburban was clearly angling to be bought out by the much larger St. Louis Transit Company. Turner wrote the sweeping House Bill No. 44 that would allow for the sale and, in the process, double the value of his Suburban lines from $3 million to $6 million.

Passage of a bill involving that much money was clearly a job for Ed Butler, who said he could guarantee its passage for $145,000. Because there was apparently competition among boodlers, Turner found a member of the House of Delegates who promised to get the bill through for $135,000. Stock put $75,000 for the necessary number of House of Delegate members into a safe-deposit box at the Lincoln Trust Company and gave a key to a delegate/combine representative. The rest, $65,000, went into a safe-deposit box for councilmen at the Mississippi Trust Company, with the extra key given to a council combine member. The boxes could be opened only when Stock and a representative of each body appeared with the appropriate keys.

All would have gone without notice except that a member of the council held up the proceedings for thirty-two consecutive meetings. He wanted Stock to buy $9,000 of junk shares he happened to own. Stock finally did so. If you're keeping track, that raised the cost of the deal to $144,000, just a thousand short of what Butler had asked. And Butler may have had his say because, oddly enough, the Circuit Court, acting on behalf of "adjacent property owners," ruled that the House of Delegates' approval of the Sub-urban deal couldn't stand. Turner, furious, wasn't about to hand over the money in the safe-deposit boxes because he hadn't gotten the legislation. The combine wasn't about to give up the money; the Assembly had voted as requested and had no control over court action. The talk was that the combine members tried to spread just enough rumors so that Turner would give up the money. That's when word got out.

Meanwhile, Folk wanted the actual proof to back up what Turner and Stock had told the grand jury. With a group of grand jurors trailing him, Folk demanded that the bankers allow him access to the safe-deposit boxes. The bank presidents themselves insisted that couldn't be done, until Folk threated to issue warrants charging the men as accessories to fraud. That did it. The boxes were open, the money counted: $75,000 at Lincoln Trust and $65,000 at Mississippi Trust, just as reported.

Turner and Stock had immunity for their testimony, but other arrests followed quickly: those of the assemblymen involved in the combine and two wealthy brewers who had cosigned the $135,000 note.

All made bail, of course, and at least two assemblymen fled to Mexico. Ultimately, someone in St. Louis must have heard from one of them, under-taker John Murrell, who was reportedly homesick in Mexico. *Post-Dispatch* reporter Frank O'Neill fetched him back home, and Murrell got a reduced sentence for testifying for Folk. The result was some fifteen members of the House of Delegates indicted for bribery. At least three got significant sentences. One of the brewers was acquitted on the basis that he didn't know what the loan he cosigned was for.

Folk faced condemnation from a wide range of St. Louisans. Death threats came his way. Word from Tennessee said investigators hired by someone in St. Louis were trying to dig up dirt—which was apparently unavailable, Folk being as straight as his public persona suggested. Mayor Wells offered faint support. Historians believe Wells avoided corruption himself, but he was surely friends with the men Folk had targeted. At the Jefferson Club, Hawes must have objected angrily. The club didn't want reform of its own members; persecuting small-fish Republicans was its reform goal. Hawes stopped socializing with Folk.

Butler, meanwhile, was enjoying himself. His assessment of the Suburban affair has survived: "There wouldn't have been any safe-deposit boxes if I had handled the matter. I am not a cheap man but when I get my fee the delivery of the goods is certain and expeditious." (Kirschten) A businessman with a specialty, indeed.

ACT TWO: THE OUT-OF-TOWNER

The role of the newspapermen tells us that they had not been ignorant of the situation. Claude Wetmore, a city editor for the *Post-Dispatch* relieved of duties after the streetcar strike, seems to have actually written the chapter on St. Louis for Lincoln Steffens, with Steffens editing. When Steffens wrote his second chapter on St. Louis, he did it on his own, implying that Wetmore's inside knowledge also made him sympathetic to some of the men involved. Another tip from a newsman reportedly started Folk on his second big investigation. Oliver Kirby "OK" Bovard had replaced Wetmore as city editor at the *Post-Dispatch*, the start of Bovard's crusading career in the paper's management.

Bovard called Folk's attention to a case the *Post-Dispatch* had tried to make a couple of years before involving a company called Central Traction, another situation involving the lucrative streetcar system. An out-of-towner from Kansas City, named Robert Snyder, came to St. Louis seeking a city-wide franchise in 1898. It would usurp the multiple-company lines running in the city at the time. In order to get the bill allowing the franchise passed in the Assembly, Snyder would have to out-bribe councilmen and delegates; seven councilmen were already getting $5,000 a year in bribes from the associated rail companies, with one councilman, Frederick Uthoff, receiving $25,000 to keep the others in line. Ed Butler coordinated the ongoing boodle.

Snyder is said to have offered Uthoff $50,000 to help breach the Butler defenses, and Uthoff was ready to take the money, returning the $25,000 as evidence of his honesty. That allowed Snyder to set about bribing sufficient assemblymen to get the Central Traction bill passed.

Snyder ended up paying out $250,000, a cool quarter-million in pre-1900 dollars, to assemblymen to get his legislation passed in April of 1898. And, of course, Snyder didn't even attempt to consolidate the railways himself. He sold to another company for $1,250,000, making a million dollars on the whole deal and explaining why he could pay so much boodle. The new owners did indeed consolidate, leading to the formation of the St. Louis Traction Company that was struck in 1900.

Folk's problem was the age of the deal. The Missouri statute of limitations protected the boodlers after three years, provided they were residents of the state during those years. Snyder, though, had lived in New York City for a good part of that time. At his trial in 1902, Snyder claimed that he wasn't a fugitive, having returned home to Kansas City on several occasions. The jury seemed to be accepting that until Snyder's lawyer's closing argument, in which he casually asserted that bribery isn't a serious crime. "It is a conventional offense, a mere perversion of justice," the man insisted. Folk argued that bribery is "treason, and the givers and takers of bribes are traitors of peace." (Primm) The jury liked that. Snyder was sentenced to five years in prison.

ACT THREE:
EDUCATION IS A
HELL OF A BUSINESS

So far, Ed Butler had managed to avoid Joe Folk's crusade. Butler continued to socialize and politicize with Hawes, who was cutting Folk out of such events. But Butler had a skeleton in a closet in the form of a personal contract.

Butler had invested in the St. Louis Sanitary Company years before, back when he first started making money in St. Louis. By 1901, his was the only firm that had the technical process conveniently required by city ordinance to dispose of garbage. Also conveniently, the 1901 Council delayed authorizing the city's Board of Health to advertise for bids, so St. Louis Sanitary was the only company in the running for the next three-year contract. So confident was Butler that only his company could get the contract that he doubled the annual charge to $130,000. Just to make sure it would go smoothly—because Butler was thorough— he called on two members of the Board of Health, a Dr. Merrell and a Dr. Chapman, and offered them $2,500 to make sure of their vote. They indignantly refused the money and went directly to Joe Folk. Of course, they also approved the contract because someone had to deal with the trash and St. Louis Sanitary was the only garbage collector in sight. They didn't know, at the time, that Mayor Rolla Wells had another thought on the matter.

His "insurance" exposed, Ed Butler was indicted for attempted bribery and got a change of venue. That put his trial in Columbia, home of the University of Missouri. Butler is said to have arrived in front of the ramshackle courthouse accompanied by a small army of press, lawyers, and his appropriately demure family, including a young granddaughter. He dressed himself as a prosperous farmer or cattleman, avoiding ostentatious displays of wealth. By this time, the whole country was watching events in Missouri, Joe Folk having become something of a real Folk-hero. Butler was playing to the crowds as well but blew it when he looked around and asked what people in Columbia, Missouri, did for a living. Told that the city housed the state university and two other colleges, Butler was incredulous. "That's a hell of a business," he said. (Kirschten)

With the senior class of the University of Missouri law school in attendance at each session, Butler's attorneys argued that bribery was highly unlikely given that Butler's firm was the only one seeking the contract. To counter the defense arguments, Folk timed another grand jury revelation back in St. Louis that jurors in Columbia would hear about.

It seems Butler had been involved in a street-lighting legislation deal in 1899. When a bill was offered for a ten-year contract, delegates blocked it, feeling they hadn't been given enough boodle. Butler offered $47,500, but the combine held out for more until Butler appeared on the House floor one evening to pass the word that "everything was all right." The bill was approved unanimously, and delegates gathered afterward at a "birthday party" thrown for one of the members. The host passed out the presents, not only to the birthday boy, but to all the delegates present, a monetary total that approached what the combine had asked for.

Folk's strategy in this case was to use John Murrell, the delegate who had fled to Mexico and been returned by the *Post-Dispatch* reporter, Frank McNeil. Keeping Murrell's return quiet and sequestering him in a small, nearby town, Folk used the man's reappearance to good effect. While questioning a House of Delegates member, who rejected all knowledge of the combine, Folk asked if the man would like to see Murrell again. The delegate, assuming Murrell was still in Mexico, thought that would be fine, and he was shocked when Folk opened a door, revealing Murrell. Who was willing to tell all. The shocked delegate told all he knew as well. That was the information that flowered in the grand jury during Butler's trial. The grand jury news and the very credible testimony of the two medical men led to a guilty verdict and a sentence of three to five years for the boss.

ACT FOUR: HOLY JOE GOES TO JEFFERSON CITY

In all, the man now called "Holy Joe" Folk managed to get sixty-one indictments and twenty-three convictions. Only eight of the men convicted went to jail—and that did not include Ed Butler. The Missouri Supreme Court stepped in to overturn many of the convictions, including Butler's on the most incredible of grounds: Butler had tried to bribe the wrong people. Never mind that the Board of Health had been the body that issued the sanitation contract for years. The Supreme Court ruled that such action was in the jurisdiction of the Board of Public Improvements, so Butler's attempted bribery was of no consequence.

In the sanitation fight, it was ultimately Mayor Wells and not Joe Folk who put Butler out of business. Wells used his own money to buy an island in the Mississippi River, twenty-odd miles south of the city. Butler didn't object when Wells then bought up Butler's hauling company at a very good price. That was all the mayor needed. He promptly announced that the city would take over garbage collection. Butler, aroused, said he could live with a reduced price. The mayor said "too late"; the city would simply use the hauling company to move garbage to barges, which would then move the garbage to the island where Wells' new colony of hogs took care of the rest. Later on, in Wells' second term as mayor, a new firm not controlled by Butler took over the garbage collection business, the hogs not being voters.

The decisions by the Missouri Supreme Court were largely thought to be political. For one thing, the wealthier men on trial had their convictions overturned on a variety of suspect grounds. The less wealthy assemblymen were the ones who went to jail. Furthermore, Justice James Gantt wanted to run for governor. And by 1904, Joe Folk was running for governor as well.

In addition to his boodle prosecutions, Folk had gone after police graft (angering Hawes even more), insurance fraud, and gambling operations in St. Louis. William Reedy complained that Folk was offering only negative St. Louis publicity when the city needed the more positive sort. In St. Louis, Folk was consistently supported by the *Post-Dispatch*, which had actually run a public campaign to raise money for Folk's investigations when the House of Delegates turned down Wells' request for more funding—unsurprisingly. Other newspapers, including the *Republic* and the *Star*, wavered. The ever-Republican *Globe-Democrat* opposed Folk, but then it opposed Hawes, Butler, Francis, and Wells too. Folk did have the support of the *Kansas City Star* and the population across rural Missouri. His enemies might have called him "Holy Joe," but that didn't dent his outstate popularity.

Hawes and Mayor James Reed of Kansas City tried to block Folk's Democratic nomination for governor to let Gantt slip in, but they failed. Folk was the only Democrat to win in the state, which went for Theodore Roosevelt in 1904. By all accounts, Folk enjoyed a very successful governorship, continuing to root out nasty politics in Jefferson City. He and his attorney general lengthened the pesky statute of limitations on bribery to five years, passed legislation restricting freight rates, established two new teachers' colleges, and adopted new labor laws: an eight-hour workday in mines and smelters and restrictions on women and children's working hours.

Back home in St. Louis, Ed Butler folded. "I have been stealing elections from the Republicans for thirty years, and I have decided to quit," he said. "I'm like them boodlers who got conscience-stricken and confessed. I've put in many a queer lick for the Democratic party, but I ain't going to do it any more. In other words, I've got conscience-stricken, too." (Kirschten) Butler died in 1911.

THE BAD, THE UGLY, AND THE SURPRISINGLY GOOD

Nat Goldstein was clerk of the Circuit Court and head of the Courthouse Ring, accused of corruption in the selection and functioning of judges. *St. Louis Post-Dispatch*

Corruption in St. Louis was aided and abetted by gangs, the toughs who delivered the votes for the political bosses. The story of corruption is their story as well.

But in 1920, when a group of Republicans operated a more civilized but equally corrupt Courthouse Ring, a new force arose to fight for the public good. Women.

THE GANGS OF ST. LOUIS—POLITICS' VIOLENT UNDERBELLY

est you think that all this was politics as usual, just a little dirtier than what we are used to in the twenty-first century, we should dig deeper than Steffens managed. How did Butler actually deliver votes? Did no one oppose him in his vote-gathering/ballot-box-stuffing endeavors? Steffens noted that many lawmakers were saloon owners. What he didn't point out was how many saloons were headquarters for St. Louis gangs, and how violent those cultures were; which gangs worked for which politicians; and which politicians were actually gang leaders themselves. Because almost every workingman had a regular saloon he visited on his way home, there was ample opportunity for an adept saloon owner to gather a political following.

For the quarter-century stretching roughly from 1894 to 1919, the dominant gang in St. Louis changed names, known, over time, as the Ashley Street gang, Kinney's gang, and Egan's Rats. They were led by fast friends (and later brothers-in-law) Thomas Egan and Thomas Kinney, the latter known as Snake Kinney—until he became known as Senator Kinney. Snake Kinney at one time and another owned a saloon at the corner of Second and Carr, a business formerly owned by Egan's father. It epitomized the northside Fourth Ward saloons that delivered reliably Democratic results. (It's the area dominated today by the Dome arena.)

As a matter of fact, most local ward politicians in the 1890s—both Republicans and Democrats—had a small army of thugs recruited from the saloons of their districts who were experts at charging into polling precincts and voting often as well as intimidating anyone who would vote differently. Election days simply were a change of pace from their usual rounds of robbery, assault, and copious drinking.

At first, Egan and Kinney were Butler men, Butler Indians, who helped assure votes. Both men were frequently arrested but usually got off on pleas of self-defense—and police indifference to one crook offing another. Kinney was by far the more pleasing personality, while Egan was simply violent. Once Egan took after a suspect member of his own gang with a hammer used to break rocks while both were in the workhouse. The man survived a crushed skull and remained loyal to Tom Egan thereafter.

By the critical election run-up in 1900, as Hawes was making deals with Butler to put Folk on the ticket, Snake Kinney decided it was time to step into politics himself. Deciding to run for the House of Delegates from the Fourth Ward, Kinney broke with Butler and went over to Hawes' organization. Hawes would wield Egan and Kinney's gang extensively in the upcoming election.

The Walnut Street gang, led by two of Butler's blacksmiths and former police detective Jack Williams, stepped into the void on Butler's behalf, setting off gang warfare. Their particular turf was the Badlands, the area anchored by Chestnut and fronting Union Station. Not that the gang members didn't roam the polls on election day. Williams was accused of killing two men when the gang tried to invade a polling place in the Nineteenth Ward, located at North Grand and Natural Bridge Road. Of course, Williams was acquitted. Meanwhile, bad blood between the two gangs resulted in several shootings and at least two killings.

The election of 1901 saw violence at the polls and between the gangs. Snake Kinney became one of the saloon owners of the House of Delegates, winning the seat by an amazing four thousand votes, to his opponent's one hundred. His younger brother was elected a constable—meaning he could carry a gun legally. Perhaps, it was the gun he used later in 1901 to shoot a Walnut Street gang rival.

The goings-on continued for the decade, with a brief hiatus for the World's Fair. When Joe Folk was elected governor in 1904, Snake Kinney was elected a state senator, and he actually had a reputation as a good one.

He helped Folk with the labor legislation, set up a system of convict labor that improved Missouri roads, and even helped pass a law forbidding saloons near the University of Missouri campus in Columbia. Apparently, that was okay with a new Kinney ally, the powerful Lemp brewery family. Back home, Egan's Rats kept the city under their thumbs, the new gang name gaining credence when the *Post-Dispatch*'s Weatherbird asked "Who'll put a bell on one of Egan's Rats?" (The Weatherbird, a cartoon mascot, has offered Post-Dispatch readers forecasts and the occasional political comment since 1901.)

Kinney died in 1912 from tuberculosis. When Tom Egan died in 1919 of natural causes, he was Democratic committee chairman in the city. He only glimpsed the beginning of a business ploy he had been anticipating for years: Prohibition. The cagey Egan knew that Prohibition wouldn't dissuade most drinkers; he had been making plans for years to capitalize on bootleg booze, as reflected back in chapter 16.

A NEW DAY DAWNS.
FOR A WHILE.

Corruption evolves. By the late 1910s, with Ed Butler's boodle a memory, the new threat to public morality came in the person of a Republican committee operative and clerk of the Circuit Court, one Nat Goldstein. Goldstein started out as a harness maker. Much like Butler, he went on from a fairly limited occupation to excel in the business of making friends and making himself useful to those friends.

Mayor Ziegenheim gave Goldstein a job in the water rates office back in the 1890s. From there, Goldstein became a deputy sheriff under a Republican and moved on to being a deputy in the circuit clerk's office in 1909. All of this fit a pattern of Republican committee members holding appointive office under elected Republican officials. Goldstein was head of the party in the Nineteenth Ward. His deputies held office in five other wards.

Most importantly, Goldstein headed the Courthouse Ring, a local machine that offered its own slate of judges for election. Presumably, the judges so elected listened when Goldstein suggested that certain men be excused from jury duty or that others' sentences be adjusted—for good cause, of course. Newspapers, primarily the *Post-Dispatch*, editorialized against the Courthouse Ring to no effect, charging that its operation increased crime in the city. Nationally, claims that Goldstein and one of his deputies, acting as Republican delegates to the national convention, had taken money from a presidential candidate bounced off Goldstein, even after he was called before a congressional hearing on the matter.

In the election of 1920, Goldstein's ring wanted to elect its own slate, as usual, including William Killoren and Karl Kimmel to the Circuit Court and Chauncey Krueger to the Court of Criminal Correction. All might have proceeded according to plan except for one new element.

The Nineteenth Amendment, allowing women to vote at all levels of government, was passed by the US Congress in 1919. Missouri was one of the states that rushed to ratify, surprising given that one of its senators, the same James Reed of Kansas City who had opposed Joe Folk in 1904, was considered the most adamant foe of woman suffrage in the country. But it took thirty-six states to ratify and, by the August primaries of 1920, that hadn't happened yet.

The magic moment came later that month. Tennessee ratified in mid-August, and St. Louis women sprang into action, switching their membership from the Equal Suffrage League to the League of Women Voters. They taught women how to vote—in 1920, you scratched the name of the person you were voting against—encouraged women to go to the polls, and took a controversial stand.

The league had three presidents, a Republican, a Democratic, and an Independent, to prove that they were nonpartisan. But the group claimed it could have a voice in elections that the women thought should indeed be for nonpartisan positions. And that included the courts. So, the brand-new League of Women Voters took a stand against the Courthouse Ring.

They gave their campaign the rather violent name of "Kill the Ks," as they went after candidates Killoren, Kimmel, and Krueger. Needless to say, they drew immense publicity. Women going to the polls would be a show in itself. Women carrying "Kill the Ks" banners upped the ante several notches.

As the election neared, one of the candidates, William Killoren, publicly decided to abandon his association with the ring. Catholic organizations sprang to the defense of one of their own. It worked for him. He was narrowly elected, but Kimmel and Krueger were defeated in the face of a Republican landslide.

The vote had three distinct results. First of all, Killoren had a long career, credited his moral turnaround to the league, and was praised by those women over the years as a good judge. (His presence in the Elsa Lemp Wright saga took place the year before his election. See chapter 16.) Secondly, the press trumpeted that the newly enfranchised women had managed in weeks what their pages had failed to do for years. The *Post-Dispatch* asked, "Who can doubt that suffrage for women has brought us to a time of new and better political incentives, new and better campaign methods and more certain and vastly improved election results?"

Thirdly, not everyone was happy. After all, those were Republican judges that had gone down to defeat. Members of the Republican Women's Club objected. There were reports of women elites refusing to speak to each other. The husband of the Republican League president, "a practicing lawyer of high standing," was the target of threats that he would be driven from the city. He publicly replied that his wife's opinions were her own business. (Dobkins)

The league's sudden standing in fighting the machine gave it some say in upcoming events, particularly regarding Nat Goldstein. In 1921, the political patronage machine looked to be promoting Goldstein for the vacant post as St. Louis postmaster. Republican senator Spencer Selden of St. Louis, who had supported suffrage and the League, also supported Goldstein, so the women leveled their complaints at the senator. The nomination fell apart when the city's Republican mayor, Henry Kiel, feared that the governor would appoint a political opponent to the vacant clerk's position. But the women had made a point of the power of their opposition.

Nat Goldstein retired from politics in 1922, headed for one of the "splendid offers" that had been made him in private business. (*St. Louis Post-Dispatch*)

Meanwhile, the league exercised more power. In 1921, it insisted that the school board should also be nonpartisan, even though its membership was usually decided by Democratic and Republican leaders agreeing to a joint slate. The league's support of a nonpartisan slate angered the union element, who had a representative among the partisan nominations, and put the women at odds with Mayor Kiel, who supported business as usual.

The nonpartisan slate included four of the five people elected, another victory for the women. But they lost the support of labor unions and some Kiel backers. And not everyone lauded the women. The Reverend Boyd we've met in several social conflicts was quoted as saying the women couldn't have written reports attributed to them. "Anyone acquainted with grammatical construction can see at a glance that the record never originated in the minds of the women. Women haven't brains enough to originate it." (Dobkins)

In 1922, it was more difficult for the women to claim nonpartisanship when they opposed the re-election of Senator James Reed. The hard-line-against-suffrage senator and former Kansas City mayor was up for his third Senate term. He faced plenty of other opposition, including that of former president Woodrow Wilson, who disliked Reed for opposing the League of Nations. Technically, the St. Louis women argued that they objected to Reed for the same reason, the national women's group having taken a stand for the international peace organization. But most people read the St. Louis League's opposition to Reed as payback for his stance on the vote. Reed overcame the opposition within his party, the women's attacks, and a Republican opponent to gain a third term.

By this time, the league had lost a good many Republican women, Kiel backers, labor activists, and now staunch female Democrats. Focusing on educational campaigns and getting out the vote seemed the only way to maintain any presence at all in St. Louis, and the women remaining in the organization did that, becoming the League of Women Voters we know today. Nevertheless, they were on the forefront of the political scene in St. Louis, and acknowledged boodle was a thing of the past.

THE COMPELLING
PERSONALITIES OF THE
TWENTIETH CENTURY

The first half of the twentieth century was famously marked by wars and depression. But people's day-to-day lives went on, marked, as this section shows, by equally storied local events. Three women—four if you believe in spiritualism—offered wonder at a ouija board and shocking crime in the very real world. And there are multiple stories of courage: St. Louis priests battling Satan in an exorcism and young Black St. Louisans battling Jim Crow.

PEARL AND PATIENCE

Pearl Curran spent a good part of her adult life taking dictation from a spirit named Patience Worth . . . or from deep within her own subconscious. *Missouri Historical Society Collection*

A ouija board sits on a table, and people gather around, anxiously putting their fingers on a triangular piece of wood they hope will move of its own volition. If someone asks the right questions or is open to heeding unearthly voices, the pointer might carry the living hands from letter to letter to spell out a message from . . . beyond.

St. Louis is home to two well-documented experiences that put us face-to-face with the world beyond our physical dimension. One, told in this chapter, is the most fully fleshed example of spiritualism, the act of communicating with the dead. The other, topic of the next chapter, is the best-recorded case of an exorcism, of the priestly battle for the body and soul of a young man. And both started with a ouija board.

FROM A PLAYTHING TO A PASSION

The story goes that Pearl Curran was bored with her friend Emily's interest in this silly ouija board craze. But she indulged her friend as they sat in St. Louis' upper-middle-class West End on a July night in 1913. Ouija boards were a common plaything for adults, being the commercially produced version of more ancient means of supposedly communicating with the dead. Perhaps to encourage a wider audience than fringe spiritualists, the company had named the board for the French and German words for "yes": *oui* and *ja*. Put together, they sounded sufficiently exotic to attract people who wanted to contact dead family members or any other spirits waiting to be called upon.

While Pearl and Emily's husbands played pinochle in another room, the two friends put their hands on the planchette, the triangular moving piece of the board. If a spirit "spoke," the planchette would move under their hands, going from letter to letter in the alphabet printed on the board. Pearl's mother, Mary Pollard, waited patiently with a pencil and paper, ready to write down any message the dead decided to send.

And then, to Pearl's surprise, if not to Emily's, the planchette began to move and the letters Emily called out to Mary actually spelled words and made sense.

Many moons ago I lived. Again, I come Patience Worth my name.

This was more than the occasional identifiable word or sentence that the women had "received" in nearly a year of playing with what Pearl considered a toy. It was the first time they had a sense of someone communicating directly—and a name.

None of the three women had ever known a Patience Worth. But that was about to change. Despite Emily's belief in spiritualism—and her background as a professional writer—it wasn't Emily to whom Patience was speaking. Experimentation over the next few months made it clear that Patience Worth, whoever or whatever she was, had decided to speak only to Pearl Curran.

And, Patience had a lot to say. Over the first few weeks, Patience offered epigrams and carried on conversations, as if she could hear what the women were saying to her and about her. Personality emerged. Patience was godly but not always polite, eager to say her piece but not always . . . patient . . . with questions she considered trivial. Early on, she responded to Mary Pollard's comments as "Much clatter from a goose." (Litvag)

Patience sounds like a name from the 1600s and America's Puritan heritage. Certainly, Patience's language seemed to hail from that period—but not exactly, as scholars would point out. It might have been what someone from another period thought Puritan-era speech sounded like. The picture of Patience that emerged from hints she dropped was that of a spinster who left England to immigrate to the colonies early on, likely to die in an attack by Native Americans.

We know all this because John Curran, Pearl's husband, stopped playing pinochle as the women worked the board over the next months and took up recording the sessions. Emily tended to add her own interpretations and words and was gradually excluded from the proceedings. John Curran had years of note-taking ahead of him.

For a taste of Patience's writing, here are her most-often-quoted lines. The poem is called "Patient God," the name the Currans gave it.

> *Ah, God, I have drunk unto the dregs,*
> *And flung the cup at Thee!*
> *The dust of crumbled righteousness*
> *Hath dried and soaked unto itself*
> *E'en the drop I spilled to Bacchus,*
> *Whilst Thou, all-patient,*
> *Sendest purple vintage for a later harvest.* (Litvag)

She didn't always use the eighteenth-century thees and thous. Here is another example.

Who said that love was fire?
I know that love is ash.
It is the thing which remains
When fire is spent,
The holy essence of experience. (Simon)

Patience dictated epigrams, stories, and plays, finally graduating to lengthy novels, including one set in Biblical times. The highly regarded *The Sorry Tale* runs 325,000 words, delivered in chunks of dictation, one letter at a time, chunks running about the length of an average chapter in this book (which totals some 80,000 words, for comparison). The book was published in 1917 and acclaimed for its knowledge of place and time as well as story. (The main character is a discarded son of Tiberius Caesar, a baby born in Bethlehem the same night as Jesus. Their paths cross several times before the character becomes one of the two thieves crucified beside Jesus.)

During the almost-two-year span of that book's dictation, Patience came up with a startling proposal. Even more startling was the fact that the Currans followed through on the request: Patience wanted a daughter. Meaning the Currans should adopt one.

Patience wanted the Currans to seek out a little girl who was in need of a good home. John and Pearl located a woman whose husband had just died in a mill accident and who had no way to support their child, as yet unborn. We don't know what the Currans would have done about their agreement to adopt the child had it been a boy. But it wasn't. The child was not only a girl, but as she grew, she had the red hair and brown eyes that fit Patience's much-earlier description of herself. Skeptics hooted; the Patience Worth fan club was crazy for Patience Worth Curran—or Patience Wee as the little adopted girl would be known in her youth.

Patience clearly considered the child somehow an extension of herself and offered Pearl plenty of advice as the child grew. In fact, she "spoke" with Patience Wee herself as the girl matured—and offered profuse congratulations and a farewell when the girl married years later.

The adoption is one of the odd aspects of what could, of course, have been a hoax. Most famous spiritualist encounters had been proven just that. But those women had almost always made a profit from their efforts; they were often paid by people desperate to speak with a departed loved one or to receive some tip for the future—which Patience almost never predicted. In fact, the Currans gathered some fame, but it didn't translate into wealth, by any means. They spent as much entertaining the ever-increasing numbers of guests they let into the sessions as they made from Patience's books.

EXPLANATIONS–OR NOT

The obvious question is whether this was really just the writing of Pearl Curran. If so, it must have come from deep within her subconscious. She was not particularly well-educated, having left school at age thirteen. Her skills were musical; at times she taught piano and voice. In talking to her, no one ever noted a tendency to the poetic or historical—or the dishonest. Furthermore, if she had the skill to write, she likely would not have done so in an awkward and archaic tongue. Years later, after the birth of her own daughter—Pearl was thirty-nine and John Curran had died six months earlier—Pearl went on a speaking tour to make what money she could. It was never much.

Plenty of people plumbed the mystery. Most notable was William Marion Reedy, the editor of *The Mirror*. Reedy always remained a skeptic, but like many others, the famous and the mere friends, he sat at a table with Pearl Curran and had no explanation for what he saw unfolding. He spoke to Patience, and Pearl's hands skimmed out the answers. In the pages of *The Mirror*, he reprinted pieces of Patience's works and applauded them. He considered *The Sorry Tale* "the most remarkable piece of literature" he had ever read. (Litvag) Occasionally, he regretted that he was associated with "spook literature," but he liked Patience Worth, and she liked him, offering up words of tribute when he died in 1920.

Another well-known St. Louis writer dedicated even more time to the Currans and to Patience. Casper Yost was an editor at the *Globe-Democrat*, religious indeed, but a well-respected and likely cynical newsman. He sat in on sessions at the Curran house, wrote a good many words in the *Globe-Democrat* on the subject, and helped the Currans publish Patience's novels. In fact, he wrote a book about Patience.

Skeptics of all varieties, from those who laughed at the notion of communicating with the dead to neurologists who sought a scientific answer, talked to Pearl Curran over the years. Because she refused to be hypnotized, most of them remained doubters, but none of them ever came up with a good explanation. Was Patience a discarnate spirit or a piece of Pearl Curran's deep subconscious—and if the latter, how could Pearl Curran be so utterly unaware of any such literary parts of herself?

The best psychic researcher who examined Pearl, Dr. Walter Prince, wrote in 1926 that, "Either our concept of what we call the subconscious must be radically altered . . . or else some cause operating through but not originating in the subconsciousness of Mrs. Curran must be acknowledged." (Litvag)

Pearl Curran remarried and moved to California and continued working with friends to record Patience's words. In mid-November of 1937, Pearl reported to a friend that Patience had, for a change, predicted the future; she had shown Pearl "the end of the road." On Thanksgiving Day, Pearl caught a cold that morphed into pneumonia. She died in early December of 1937.

Others have claimed to channel Patience Worth in the years after Pearl Curran's death, but none of that was ever widely credited. For twenty-four years, the team of Pearl and Patience fascinated and entertained St. Louis and the world.

THE EXORCISM

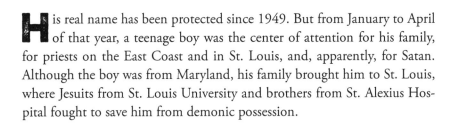

His real name has been protected since 1949. But from January to April of that year, a teenage boy was the center of attention for his family, for priests on the East Coast and in St. Louis, and, apparently, for Satan. Although the boy was from Maryland, his family brought him to St. Louis, where Jesuits from St. Louis University and brothers from St. Alexius Hospital fought to save him from demonic possession.

St. Francis Xavier, the College Church of the Jesuit's St. Louis University, was pastored by Father William Bowdern when he was called to soldier through an exorcism. *Missouri Historical Society Collection*

WE'LL CALL HIM R

R was an only child who found a friend in his aunt, his father's sister from St. Louis. Let's name her Aunt A. She visited often at the family home in Maryland and introduced R to her hobby, spiritualism. She taught him how to use a ouija board, and he had one she'd left or that his parents had gotten him. R's mother always had an interest in spiritualism, although not on the scale of her sister-in-law.

While Pearl Curran became a spiritualist by accident, Aunt A was an active member of a well-recognized movement, one that could precisely state its beliefs. The aunt would have asserted confidently her ability to communicate with the dead and, most importantly, that there was no reason to see that activity as diabolical. Spiritualists identified themselves as good Christians—ones who were willing to put their belief in a Christian afterlife into practice. Others outside the group identified attempts to contact the dead as opening a gateway to evil. That is the starting point of some explanations of the events of 1949.

Descriptions of R vary wildly. Some describe him as a quiet, non-athletic boy, probably weighing less than a hundred pounds when he was age thirteen in January of 1949. He would turn age fourteen by the time the story ends in the spring of 1949. Other reports say he was a prankster who liked to intimidate neighborhood children. All the accounts are after-the-fact because where would you find a description of a middle-class, law-abiding young teenager before trouble overtook him? And once the incident was over, everyone's description of R is colored by what they think was going on in the house in Maryland.

R's grandmother and the boy were alone in the house on January 15 when they heard scratching and water dripping and then saw a picture of Christ moving on the wall in the grandmother's room. The family chalked it up to rodents in the walls, and an exterminator put out poison. But the noises didn't stop in the grandmother's room until January 26, when Aunt A died in St. Louis.

We can imagine that R pulled out his ouija board and tried to contact Aunt A. That's when the noises moved to R's room, changing subtly. He reported hearing squeaking shoes and moving feet for several nights. Finally, his mother and grandmother joined him one night and heard the marching feet as well.

His mother was convinced it was Aunt A and asked for a sign, three knocks—something Aunt A had taught was one way to communicate with spirits. They heard three knocks. So, the mother asked for a confirmation of four knocks. And got them. And then the scratchings began closer to hand.

It felt, they said, like something was in the mattress, scratching to get out. Sometimes, the bedclothes, usually tucked under the mattress, would unfold, standing out to the sides of the mattress, rigid. The nighttime-scratching and mattress-shaking went on for several weeks, during which the daytime hours became eventful as well. Bibles flew, vases were shattered against walls, chairs R was sitting on capsized and sent him to the floor—chairs too heavy for the grown men in the family to tip when they sat on them.

And the mayhem followed R to school. His desk moved, as he said, like the planchette on a ouija board, bouncing into other desks. Of course, R was blamed by teachers and fellow students despite his denials. His parents let him stop attending school until they could get help.

Where that help would come from wasn't obvious. The family was Lutheran, and they first turned to a Lutheran pastor who had an interest in parapsychology. Not a believer in demonic possession, he immediately thought of poltergeists and psychokinesis, the part of ESP (extra sensory perception) that allows people to move objects without physically touching them. Because the Lutheran assumed it might be easy for R to cause these things to happen in his own home, the pastor had R stay at his home for a night.

After R's parents left, R and the pastor settled into twin beds. Soon enough, R's bed began vibrating. The pastor suggested R try sleeping on a chair. Within moments, the chair moved and then slowly tipped over. As when the bed was vibrating, R seemed to be in some sort of trance. The pastor next tried a pallet on the floor for R, but the man awoke to find the pallet levitating with R on it.

Back home the next night, R's problems got worse, with claw marks appearing on his body. Not sure whether the problem was psychological, parapsychological, or supernatural, the Lutheran pastor suggested the family contact a Roman Catholic priest, saying, "The Catholics know about things like this." (Allen)

R and his parents found Father Hughes, a youthful cleric, unlikely, in hindsight, to be the best choice for an exorcist. The Roman Catholic ritual recommends an exorcism be done by a particularly pious and studious priest, which didn't fit Hughes' profile. But he gave it a shot. He got R admitted to Georgetown University Hospital, assigned to a room under an alias, and strapped to a bed. In between prayers and reported flying objects, R slipped his hand from under the restraints, ripped loose a piece of bedspring, and raked it down Father Hughes' left arm. Hughes, seriously injured and bleeding profusely, fled, and that was the end of that attempt.

R's family needed to find help and needed to get out of town. The neighbors were more than anxious, embroidering the rumors swelling across the community. St. Louis was an obvious retreat because R's parents had siblings there. We can debate whether the next twist led to wise action. Once R's mother had mentioned St. Louis to him, the next scratches/welts appearing on R's body spelled out "Louis." Apparently reverting to her spiritualism experience, she actually asked, out loud, "How long?" And scratches indicating three and a half weeks appeared on R's chest.

If it were Satan's work, one wonders why R's family would take that advice. Maybe they thought it came from Aunt A. But then, it's not clear they had an option. Not only were the nightly visitations getting worse, but the marks on R seemed to erupt from inside his body, causing the boy physical as well as emotional pain.

THE ST. LOUIS SAGA

In St. Louis, the family moved in with another of R's aunts, uncle, and cousins. On arrival, some of the family actually tried a ouija experience, using a kitchen table instead of an actual board. Somehow, the family got the message that it was Aunt A talking to them. But that didn't end the nightly violence. In fact, the first night R tried sleeping in the room with a male cousin, in a house in Bel-Nor suburb, the adults ran to the bedroom when the scratching noises began. Both boys lay unmoving on a mattress that was flopping and shifting.

There are suggestions that the family thought it was Aunt A reaching out, causing the outbreaks. Or that R had reached out to her, via his ouija board, starting the visitations.

The key moment came when R's female cousin, a student at St. Louis University (SLU), said she intended to talk to one of her professors.

We have a name here we can use: Father Raymond J. Bishop, Jesuit, education professor at SLU, keeper of the diary that surfaced years later. Father Bishop listened to the young woman and visited the family. The holy water and sacred relic he left near R's bed were thrown across the room that night. On his next visit, Bishop brought the rector of what is locally called College Church, the towering St. Francis Xavier house of worship that rises on Lindell on the SLU campus. An army chaplain during World War II, Father William Bowdern was highly respected, as much for his kindly toughness as his holiness. After hearing his report, Bowdern's superiors determined that he was the man to do what was seldom attempted in the modern church: an exorcism.

By this time, it was mid-March. Bowdern and a team including Bishop and a young scholar named William Halloran—a former football player valued for his strength in controlling R along with his Jesuit training—began a nightly fight. R would go off to bed, no doubt still exhausted from the previous night's lack of sleep. The priests would begin the old rituals, the prayers, the threats, the commands to Satan to leave the boy. Increasingly, R reacted violently, spitting—never missing a target even though his eyes were closed—cursing at the priests, urinating in response to questions, requiring restraint. One night he broke Halloran's nose. The strange welts on his body sometimes rippled across his skin, sometimes were bloody, often spelled out words, such as "Hell." Sometimes he sat up, seemingly calm, but singing in an odd voice—singing being something he never did normally, oddly, or otherwise. On one occasion, the singing was beautiful, almost professional.

Bowdern carried on the ritual night after night. Along the way, during days when R was calm, the priest suggested that the boy might want to become a Catholic. R agreed and took up the learning with alacrity. During the days. At night, he was anything but religious. In fact, his baptism as a Catholic and his first communion made the situation worse.

R would alternate between being a normal if listless young man during the days and a violent, insufferable personality at night. Father Bowdern lived on bread and water and barely managed to keep up his duties as head of a large parish. As Easter of 1949 approached, everyone involved was exhausted.

On Palm Sunday of 1949, R was taken in by the Alexian brothers. The brothers had maintained a hospital in St. Louis since 1869, always dedicating a wing to the treatment of mental illnesses before that was common. R went about chores with kindly monks during the day and was locked in a room on the fifth floor at night. Brothers kept up a vigil of prayer in their chapel, while the priests repeated the exorcism ritual over and over. Some nights, other patients and staff heard screams as the fight intensified.

Alexian brothers began to note that the room itself was chill, not to mention that it stank. And the young man who could occasionally be pleasant became more violent, harder to restrain, punching brothers, throwing plates and other objects.

On the night of April 18, Bowdern changed tack and issued his prayers in English. He put religious medals around R's neck and forced the boy to hold a crucifix. After his most violent writhing since it all began, R fell silent until a new voice emanated from him, one proclaiming to be St. Michael and commanding Satan to leave. R awoke and described a battle scene to Bowdern, the other priests and brothers. St. Michael had beaten Satan, he said.

By the next afternoon, R seemed himself. As he awoke from a nap, asking where he was and what had happened, an explosion is said to have sounded, reverberating through the hospital, heard and felt by everyone. There was no damage; there was only an awesome sound. Bowdern took it as a sign. The possession had ended. The "case" was over.

The Alexians sealed the room. The Jesuits sealed accounts of the events as well as the lips of its priests. Several copies of Father Bishop's diary were kept in order to provide guidance in case another Jesuit needed—ever needs—to perform an exorcism. All the Catholics involved kept the silence.

But back in Maryland, the Lutheran pastor was eager to talk about the event, now that R and his family had returned home. He was likely shocked that the three had converted to Catholicism. The pastor's story lingered. Twenty years later, a student at Georgetown University heard rumors, got interested, and accumulated enough specifics to write a book that was turned into one of most terrifying and impressive movies of twentieth-century America: *The Exorcist*. The author changed R to a young woman and put the scene entirely in Washington, D.C. But family and clerics in St. Louis recognized the source of the story.

R returned to school. Although his name is not revealed in records of the event, it is said he has led a happy, normal life with his wife and children and has retired. He would be eighty-five years old as of this writing.

The case is, of course, still debated today. Thomas Allen, another writer, got hold of the Bishop diary and struck up a friendship with Father Halloran. Both Allen and Halloran have never stated that it was a true case of possession by Satan. They simply state that they can't know—Halloran because he didn't feel qualified to say, Allen presumably because of his agnosticism. On one side are the critics/skeptics who insist it can all be explained as a nasty young man playing pranks. Another school says it is all a matter of psychology, and R never had the right psychologists to get to the heart of the matter. These perspectives don't explain why R was either cured of a troubled psyche or cleaned up his behavior overnight on April 18, 1949.

Another group believes firmly in the possibility of possession and points to the ouija board as an opening, even suggesting that R's mother was eager enough to contact Aunt A that she virtually used R as a human ouija board, at least early on. All the priests involved are now dead; all of the buildings except the house in Bel-Nor have been razed. The diary was snatched from the old Alexian Brothers hospital as it was being torn down in 1978.

Today, there remains only a boy now grown old who knows as much truth as can be known. And the spirit of Father William Bowdern, who believed in the fight. And won it.

RICH GIRLS
BEHAVING BADLY

Two women, one the glamorous, middle-aged wife of a St. Louis physician, the other the spoiled, teenaged daughter of a respected businessman, set tongues wagging in the 1930s and 1940s. The question, then as now, was does crime pay?

NAUGHTY NELLIE

I t is un-feminist to begin Nellie Muench's story by describing her husband and father and brother. Nellie was decidedly her own woman. But the male connections made her actions all the more brazen.

Nellie Tipton Muench was from Mexico, Missouri, a county seat about a hundred miles west of St. Louis, north of today's Interstate-70 route. Her father was a prominent minister in Mexico. Her brother was Ernest M. Tipton, a justice on the Missouri Supreme Court. She met her husband, Ludwig Muench, who would become a medical doctor, when she was at Stephens College and he was at the University of Missouri, both in Columbia. They were a musical couple: He played the violoncello and she the piano well enough to draw members of the St. Louis Symphony to join them for musical evenings at their home in the Central West End.

Nellie was not the typical Central West End matron, however. She owned a dress store called Mitzi's Shop, located in the three hundred block of North Euclid Avenue. There she sold some of the most expensive outfits in town, among elegant furnishings and with comely models. Some of the customers were men, buying expensive dresses and other items for wives and, perhaps, for courtesans.

The shop was near "fashionable establishments of ill-repute," as Nellie put it in a book she wrote around 1929. The women from those establishments patronized Mitzi's, and it was a matter of amusement to Nellie that they may have rubbed shoulders with the wives and daughters of the houses' male patrons. (In some books, the writer is anonymous; in this one, the printer refused to enter his name.)

The shop went under in 1928, before Nellie wrote about it, leaving debts of more than $75,000. The bankruptcy left debtors with a fraction of their investments. (Presumably the Republican politician she had once accused of charging her 46 percent interest when she was desperate for a loan escaped.) Nellie had a history of more than poor financial management. Another dress shop owner had alleged that Nellie stole dresses worth several hundred dollars; Nellie had been questioned by police about jewels that disappeared from a hotel room; Nellie had tried to get $17,000 from a businessman's estate on the pretext that he had purchased that much in clothing from her before his death.

Nellie's response to many of these charges was that her brother's political opponents—and particularly the press—hoped to embarrass him. In making that defense, she bluntly and approvingly stated that her brother was affiliated with Kansas City boss Tom Pendergast; the Pendergast men lined up against monopoly and greed, she said. Pendergast, of course, made Ed Butler of St. Louis (in chapter 20) look honest.

THE FINGER-WOMAN

All of this was readily recalled in St. Louis when, in 1934, Nellie was implicated in a kidnapping in association with various crooks and gang members from St. Louis County and East St. Louis. It was an association she had publicly avoided for three years.

As Prohibition seemed destined to end and as the Great Depression began to throw a different pall over the country, kidnapping became a pastime of local toughs. St. Louis was rocked when, on the night of April 30, 1931, Dr. Isaac D. Kelley was called out of his home to treat a child with a severe earache—and wasn't seen again for eight tense days. Dr. Kelley had taken a telephone call from a man who said he'd just moved from Chicago where a physician there had given him Dr. Kelley's name. Apparently, it was a name Kelley recognized.

But as the doctor got to the Clayton subdivision—said to have been lured into the county because the kidnappers were more afraid of St. Louis City detectives and prosecutors—he was kidnapped by men who took him first to a moonshine distillery in St. Charles County west of St. Louis and then across the river to East St. Louis. Somehow, the negotiations broke down, and the kidnappers arranged for a police reporter they respected, from the *Post-Dispatch*, to come across the river and pick Kelley up on an empty road. The doctor had been threatened repeatedly but not seriously harmed. Unfortunately, the case went cold there.

In 1934, a county gangster offered to sell the *Post-Dispatch* the story of the kidnapping. Names of a variety of shady characters, one of whom was in jail on another kidnapping case and three of whom had died in an East St. Louis gangster killing in 1932, were named. But the real bombshell was the mastermind of the crime: Nellie Muench. Muench and her husband would have moved in the same circles as Dr. Kelley. And she would have known the name of the Chicago doctor. It came out later that Nellie danced one night at the Coronado Hotel with one of the kidnappers, passing close enough by Dr. Kelley and his wife on several numbers so that the kidnapper could recognize him. She was, therefore, the "finger" in the case.

The political clout of the sister of a state supreme court justice should not be underestimated. First off, a judge in St. Louis county allowed a change of venue to the Tipton's home county. The sheriff was a family friend; he was said to have put only names of his friends on the jury list. A coterie of clever attorneys appeared to be defeating the local prosecutors when the big announcement came, the announcement designed to cement the jury's sympathy for the country girl ensnared in the crimes of the big city.

Nellie Muench was pregnant. Everyone who knew her was shocked; everyone watching the circus in Mexico expected her to bring the newborn into the courtroom.

Nellie was in her forties in 1934 and had been married for twenty-two years, childless, when the birth of a son was dramatically announced. The *Post-Dispatch* was on it. The paper reported that a male child had been taken from City Hospital in July and delivered to the Muench home. Unfortunately, the baby was ill and died a few days later. Almost as unfortunately for Nellie, the *Post-Dispatch* dropped two other bombshells. The baby was the child of an unwed mother in Minneapolis. And Nellie had gone to another socialite physician, a Dr. Pitzman, who shared an office with her husband, accusing Pitzman of being the father of her child and actually extorting money from him.

Of course, with a dead child, Nellie set out to find another, because having a live infant was part of her scheme for the upcoming trial. The story here was taken up by the *Star-Times*, whose staff connected with a woman named Anna Ware, mother of the new child. In a serialized story, the *Star-Times* reported that Anna was from Philadelphia, where she had worked in the household of a Mrs. Giordan and where she had a child as a result of an affair with Mrs. Giordan's husband. As it turned out, Mrs. Giordan was the daughter of a St. Louis woman, and Mrs. Giordan persuaded Anna to travel to St. Louis to have the baby, promising her an adoption within the family.

Anna later testified that an attorney named Jones had met her at Union Station. He took her for a ride with a woman who he said had lost a baby and was looking to adopt another. By the time Anna gave birth, she was asking if she could keep the baby if she could raise the money for expenses, but Jones told her no. She held the baby for an hour when Jones appeared with a nurse to take the baby away.

As it turned out, the baby was not needed at the October trial in Mexico, where the prosecution failed to put into evidence either Nellie's career or the stories circulating in St. Louis about the child. It actually was less exciting than the hearing in St. Louis in which Anna Ware fought for the return of her child.

Nellie now brought the child into court, but instead of eliciting sympathy, the scene elicited boos from spectators. Anna Ware was the one who garnered sympathy. Jones, the attorney, claimed he had gotten both the deceased infant and the Ware baby for couples in Memphis. The nurse who had helped Jones spirit the baby away claimed to have been with Mrs. Muench when the baby was born.

The St. Louis Court of Appeals had appointed a special commissioner for the case. Rush Limbaugh Sr. of Cape Girardeau called eighty-seven witnesses and took a month to write the report. In it, he concluded that Nellie was not the mother and had procured the Ware baby for purposes of her trial. Anna Ware got her child back, and she fled with the child just before Christmas of 1935. (This Rush Limbaugh, by the way, was an active jurist until shortly before his death in 1996 at age 104. He was the grandfather of conservative radio commentator Rush Limbaugh III.)

So, Nellie, her husband, Jones, and the nurse went to trial in 1936. Dr. Pitzman testified that Nellie had gotten $16,000 from him and persuaded him to leave a third of his estate to the baby. The nurse got confused on the stand. So did Nellie. They were convicted in the state court and, by the end of the year, faced another charge in federal court on using the US mail to defraud. All four were convicted there, including Dr. Ludwig Muench, although Nellie insisted her husband had no part in the events. Nellie was sentenced to ten years in a women's prison in West Virginia; the nurse was sentenced to five years there. Dr. Muench was sentenced to eight years in

Leavenworth; the attorney Jones was sentenced to ten years there. Muench divorced Nellie just as she got a conditional release from prison. She changed her name and moved to Kansas City.

Nellie Muench was mature, sophisticated, vivacious, and calculating. The case that rocked St. Louis in the next decade featured a younger woman who duplicated only the calculating part.

REMORSELESS MARY CATHERINE

The one thing everyone could agree on about Mary Catherine Reardon was that she was spoiled. Friends reported that the fourteen-year-old's father doted on her. He not only gave her anything she asked for but also suggested parties and events to entertain her.

He could afford it. J. Vincent Reardon owned a paint manufacturing business; he and his wife and only child lived in tony Ladue, one of the wealthiest of the St. Louis county suburbs.

Leona Reardon, Mary Catherine's mother, seemed much less interested in her child. Perhaps it was because of her alcoholism, which put her in a hospital at a critical point in the events of 1947. Because of her relationship with her mother, Mary Catherine described her home life as "lousy."

The principal of the school she attended, Wydown, had a description for her as well: a "semi-truant" who did poorly in school despite having an "excellent mentality." In fact, he was describing both Mary Catherine and another ninth-grader, Michael D'Arcy, age thirteen.

Michael wasn't much into girls, according to his mother, being more interested in sports and photography. But he had been talking about Mary Catherine Reardon for a couple of weeks when the two decided to skip school on Friday afternoon, February 7, 1947. They bummed around town for several hours, ending up at Union Station, from where Michael called his mother. The conversation was along the lines of "Guess you know we skipped school," and "Come home right now and we'll straighten it out." Michael said he would do so.

Instead—according to the story offered by Mary Catherine the next day—they called the St. Louis County Cab Company, with which the Reardon family had an account. A cabbie drove them out in the county to a restaurant in Wentzville, a town some forty miles west of Union Station. The two waited until the cab was out of sight and then walked to the Travelers' Auto Court, "auto court" being a common name for a motel in 1947.

According to Mary, the two had decided to run away, although she made it clear that marriage was not in their plans. She thought she could get a job in New York City or Chicago, possibly working as a waitress. She stayed outside while Michael went in to tell the motel's co-owner that he and his sister had just arrived from East Orange, New York, and that their father would be arriving that night to pay the bill. Although the man was a bit suspicious given that East Orange is in New Jersey, he took the young man at his word. For what it was worth, both Mary Catherine and Michael looked much older than their ages, Michael being 5'10".

Meanwhile, the D'Arcy and Reardon families were talking to each other by telephone. Mrs. Reardon had contacted the cab company, which gave them trip details, but the Reardons didn't pass that on to the D'Arcys until after midnight. Vincent Reardon headed out to Wentzville at about seven Saturday morning.

Mary Catherine told investigators later on Saturday that her father had struck Michael in their initial confrontation at the Travelers' Auto Court, but apparently Reardon cooled off and the three headed for his auto, Mary Catherine and Michael taking the back seat. At some point on the road home, the story goes tragic. In confessions to police, Mary Catherine said she asked for Michael's gun—why a thirteen-year-old had carried a gun to school the day before is unclear—waited for a stretch of road where there were no other cars, and shot her father in the back of the head.

Vincent Reardon lost control of the car, which overturned into a steep ditch. The coroner later said he died, not of the gunshot wound, but of a crushed chest. Michael was pulled from the car with serious injuries and died of them hours later. Mary Catherine was pulled from the car with a scratch to her forehead, asking the county officer, "How is the young guy?" and "Is the old man dead?" She seemed to have no serious injuries.

At police headquarters, she told the whole story and added that she shot her father because she was afraid he would get more strict with her and maybe even send her to all-girls school. Reporters who got to the scene in time to hear all this described her as "remorseless." The one person who didn't get to the scene before she signed a six-page confession was her attorney.

The papers were full of details, of course, identifying Mary Catherine as a young murderer. Reporters were able to find plenty of folks who would say that spoiling the young woman had led to the tragedy. The stories continued with the legal debate about whether she would be tried as a juvenile, which judges decided to do. The trial in juvenile court, before a jury, came swiftly, on March 28.

Reporters described the fourteen-year-old as "plump," "calm," "poised" — and as it turned out, unshakable on the stand. Despite six different people recalling her confession, she said she remembered nothing of saying any such things. And, of course, the official copy was thrown out because her attorney hadn't entered the room before she signed it. Both a county law officer and a policeman heard the confession, along with the coroner, two reporters, and a nurse who heard the whole story over again at a hospital. That many people recalling her story should have counted for something, but the defense had a new angle that overrode Mary Catherine's first tale.

It seemed—according to dramatic defense accounts—that Michael did the shooting. Elaborate scenarios were demonstrated to show how that could have happened. And on top of that, Mary Catherine herself was shot! A bullet grazed her arm, passed through her armpit, and lodged in her back! Where it had resided since the shooting and during the trial! Jurors were invited to feel the bump as Mary Catherine—calmly—lifted her sweater. Her attorney ridiculed the hospital staff for not finding the bullet. So, the jury acquitted her, even though the judge insisted that there was enough evidence to find her guilty.

Mary Catherine stood to inherit considerable money from her father. And, of course, Leona did inherit a good amount. Not long after the shooting, Mary Catherine moved to Los Angeles with an aunt, telling the press she was tired of people in St. Louis staring at her. The St. Louis juvenile caseworker assigned to her could only write long letters of advice, which we may assume Mary Catherine ignored. At some point, her mother joined her in California, in time to object to Mary Catherine's new romance.

Mary Catherine, now age seventeen, eloped with Gabriel Gueci, age eighteen, to Nevada. Leona had actually called in a missing persons report to stop the elopement, but clearly not in time. It was not a happy marriage. The young couple obviously didn't want to live with Leona, and Gabriel's parents came to dislike Mary Catherine. That came out in the papers after Mary Catherine was arrested for shoplifting clothes in a Los Angeles shop on Wilshire Boulevard—claiming she had no money but she liked pretty things and was used to getting them. Headlines that spread across the country called her "the poor little rich girl." The predictable divorce happened in 1951, with Mary Catherine still too young to inherit her father's money. From there, she disappears from the papers' pages.

Perhaps she went on to become another Nellie Muench, but this poor little rich girl was lost to history.

25

A RICH HERITAGE: BLACK LIVES IN TWENTIETH-CENTURY ST. LOUIS

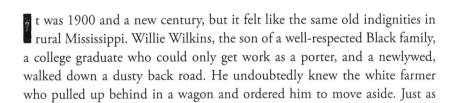

t was 1900 and a new century, but it felt like the same old indignities in rural Mississippi. Willie Wilkins, the son of a well-respected Black family, a college graduate who could only get work as a porter, and a newlywed, walked down a dusty back road. He undoubtedly knew the white farmer who pulled up behind in a wagon and ordered him to move aside. Just as undoubtedly, the "request" was a standard collection of racial epithets. It was the last straw for Willie Wilkins.

He jumped onto the wagon and hit the farmer several times before heading home. Once there, he told his story, and his family debated their options. At the same time, the farmer was telling the story to his family and friends, and their option was fairly clear. It was time for a lynching.

By the time friends appeared to warn the Wilkins, Willie's father was bundling Willie and his new wife, Mayfield, into a wagon headed to the next train station up the line. By morning, they were on their way north, taking the Illinois Central into St. Louis. The railroad cars they rode would have been segregated, likely meaning there

Roy Wilkins' definition of the color line in St. Louis early in the twentieth century must have resonated through his life and work as he headed the NAACP in the turbulent 1960s. *Library of Congress*

was only one car Blacks could ride on. When the train stopped, they would have had to find the colored toilets. Hopefully, the Wilkins family sent food with them because there was no using white eateries along the way.

And then the Illinois Central pulled into the colossal Union Station in St. Louis. Willie and Mayfield went looking for the colored toilets and couldn't find them. Someone likely told them to use the integrated facilities. Had they looked for food in Union Station, they might have found at least one lunch counter that wouldn't serve them, but the mere fact that they could share a washroom with whites was talked about in the family for a generation. And then the world tilted even more.

The bustle inside St. Louis' Union Station rivaled any terminal in the country, but the Wilkins managed to find a Black face, a janitor busy sweeping. They showed him the slip of paper they had gathered up at the last minute in Mississippi, the paper with the address of a friend on Papin Street. They were dismayed when he said he'd never heard of it. And then dismay turned to astonishment when an elderly white man stepped into the conversation and asked if he could help.

The man offered directions to Papin Street, but the complexity was overwhelming. So, he led them out onto the streets of St. Louis, went to a trolley, explained their destination, and ordered the white conductor to get them there. Then he tipped his hat and left.

That left the Wilkins to move toward the back of the trolley, but they immediately realized that it wasn't necessary. Blacks and whites seemingly sat wherever they chose. Willie and Mayfield must have looked at each in disbelief. They had few possessions, very little savings, and a scrap of paper for a welcome, but the Illinois Central had carried them a distance greater than the miles would indicate. The folks at the house on Papin Street made the welcome a warm and concrete thing.

The Wilkins almost certainly didn't know the history of St. Louis and integrated streetcars. Still living in the city at that point was the aging Captain Charlton Tandy, not long ago admitted to the Missouri Bar, headed to living out his days as a Republican committeeman in the Tenth Ward. Well-known in St. Louis, Tandy had raised up a volunteer Black militia during the Civil War, headed relief efforts for families like the Wilkins headed north and west, stood up for quality Black education in the city, and made sure public transportation was integrated. Tandy is said to have grabbed the reins of the horses pulling street trolleys in the late 1800s and stopped the trolleys' progress until everyone who wanted to board, Black, immigrant, poor native white, could do so. He was arrested for his actions, but Erastus Wells, owner of the trolley franchise (and father of soon-to-be-mayor Rolla Wells, of chapter 20 fame) backed Tandy and paid his fines.

As might be expected, life did not continue to be rosy for Willie Wilkins. His older son, writing years later, reported that Willie discovered the color line in St. Louis the next morning and that it "started at the pay window." Willie could find nothing in St. Louis in 1900 and ended up taking a job at a brick kiln factory across the river in East St. Louis. And, of course, a home in St. Louis carried the Jim Crow restrictions that hadn't been as obvious that first day. Theaters, hospitals, and schools were all segregated or restricted, unlike the trolleys and the station. The house the Wilkins found on Laclede Avenue was near an integrated district but still in one of the city's Black enclaves.

In 1901, the Wilkins had a son, Roy, followed by a daughter, Armeda, and another son, Earl. Willie became increasingly depressed with the work in East St. Louis, understandable given the situation leading up to the 1917 race riot, and turned to the African Methodist Episcopal Church, one of the largest Black denominations. Roy remembered Willie reading endless passages from the Bible while the biscuits and gravy cooled at dinnertime.

Meanwhile, Mayfield had developed consumption, her coughs worsening month by month. Roy was five when his mother died. Willie would have still had his job, but he couldn't come up with the $70 for the funeral. At that point, an angel of mercy from farther north arrived. Mayfield's sister had moved all the way to Minnesota. She apparently assessed Willie's despair, assumed payments for Mayfield's funeral back in Mississippi, and decided that the children needed a home Willie couldn't provide. At first, she went for the typical solution: She'd take baby Earl back to her own childless home and send Roy and Armeda back to Mississippi to be raised by their grandparents. But her husband objected, saying he wouldn't split up a family. So the three Wilkins children moved to St. Paul. Roy was promptly enrolled in a school in which he was the only Black student.

We know all this because Roy Wilkins went on to become executive director of the NAACP, shepherding the organization through the civil rights era of marches in the South and of legislative and judicial action in Washington, D.C. Readers who remember those tumultuous days picture Wilkins working with every president from Kennedy to Carter and opposing Black militancy. His posthumous biography outlined the differences between the Mississippi of his parents, the St. Louis of his childhood, and the Minnesota where he worked his way through college.

The fact is that all Blacks in St. Louis, even descendants of the early city's freed slaves who formed a Black aristocracy, faced Jim Crow restrictions and prejudices that ranged from annoying to deadly. But the Black experience in the twentieth century is not homogenous. There were poor, middle-class, and upper-class Black families. There were successes and failures. We know enough of a select group of children from the first half of the century to paint a picture that ranges across socioeconomic circumstances, highlighting unique individuals.

At the turn of the century, the color barrier had been drawn at Grand Avenue. West of Grand, wealthy and less-wealthy whites fought to keep their neighborhoods free of Black residents, regardless of what those Blacks might have been able to afford. In fact, St. Louis became the first city in the country to pass a segregation law in 1916. It was immediately made inoperative in a Supreme Court case, but the city persisted in allowing covenanted neighborhoods, which achieved the same end. The physical problem was not only that Blacks were restricted to older housing east of Grand, but that there wasn't enough of that housing. Old buildings were divided and redivided, and rents soared. It became much more expensive to live east of Grand than west for the same square footage—and, of course, the color line at the pay window that Roy Wilkins described meant that Blacks had trouble earning enough to pay those higher rents.

Two Black neighborhoods are of note, the poorer one centering on the old Mill Creek Valley. As the century progressed, Black students who managed to stay in the schools of the Valley went to Vashon High School. (Its first building is still in use as part of Harris-Stowe State College, and the newer building is still in operation as a high school.) The first and older school, Sumner, is known as the first Black high school west of the Mississippi, and it once included the teacher preparation college now centered in Harris-Stowe. In 1910, a stately Sumner High building anchored the Ville, the more middle/upper class Black neighborhood.

The Ville's other anchor was another kind of college, a school of cosmetology. Annie Turnbo Malone was in her thirties when she moved to St. Louis from small towns in Illinois to take advantage of the World's Fair. She had already developed her formulas for shampoos and other hair products, the first to specifically fill the needs of Black women. Thousands of women sold her Poro products. The college that spread over a city block in the Ville offered classes, business space, labs, and public areas. The space housed refugees from the 1927 tornado and provided other public services over the years. Annie Turnbo Malone is said to have been the first Black female millionaire—as well as first citizen of the Ville.

SO MANY WAYS
TO BE BLACK

Some of our stories come from the Valley, some from the Ville. Some of the names you will recognize from the vantage point of the twenty-first century; others have faded but were renowned not so many years ago.

Josephine Baker's family sat at the poorest end of the scale in St. Louis. Her mother was a laundress and her father was on relief; the bed in the one-room shack held the entire family. Josephine's energy and talent and determination overflowed the place. When she could scrape together the fifteen cents, she went to the Booker T. Washington Theatre, the Tom-and-Charlie-Turpin enterprise a block west of Union Station on Market. Charming her way into an audition and lying about her age, she managed to get a job performing with a vaudeville group called the Dixie Steppers, and she left St. Louis with the group in 1921. That led to a career in New York City and Paris, where her singing, dancing, and general flamboyance were a huge hit.

Josephine eventually renounced her US citizenship to become a French citizen and was later honored by that government for her role in the French resistance during World War II. When she returned to the United States to perform, she was horrified at the racism that still marked the country and refused to perform before segregated audiences. She participated in the 1963 March on Washington, a major event in the civil rights movement. She died during a performance in 1975, survived by a dozen children adopted from countries around the world.

Lloyd Gaines moved to St. Louis from Mississippi when he was young, became valedictorian at Vashon High in 1931, and graduated from Lincoln

University, the state's Black liberal arts college in Jefferson City, with honors and as class president. The headlines began when he applied to law school at the University of Missouri in 1936. The university's refusal became a legal landmark, resulting in a Supreme Court decision that said the state of Missouri had to either let Gaines in or provide a separate but equal education in-state. The state responded by taking over the now-largely-unused Poro Cosmetology School in the Ville and setting up a law curriculum in 1939. But Gaines never attended.

Although the NAACP had called on Lloyd to speak before various groups and promoted his case, he had no permanent job or support. In March of 1939, he was in Chicago, staying with members of the fraternity he had joined while at Lincoln. He went out one night, saying he needed to get stamps, and never returned. His family in St. Louis knew him to be a loner and one who could take care of himself. A final letter told his mother not to worry about him. Outside the family, no one in an official capacity seemed to know he was missing until the NAACP went looking for him in the fall of 1939 in order to file another suit, contending that the hastily thrown together program in St. Louis wasn't equal to the university law school program. Gaines was nowhere to be found.

The first assumption was that he came to some harm, either randomly or because of the case's notoriety. But another interpretation is that Gaines lost patience with the legal process and his inability to find and keep a job while he was in legal limbo. The family rarely spoke of him, it seems, either out of grief—or some knowledge they never shared.

If you know jazz, you know the name Miles Davis. Davis was born in 1926 to an upper-class East St. Louis family; his father was a dentist there. Early on, Miles took lessons from the German who played first chair trumpet in the St. Louis Symphony. Young Miles started playing with groups in the area early on, explaining that he didn't have much time for sports—or gangs. He went on to Julliard in New York City after graduating high school but left there to play with jazz great Charlie Parker. For that matter, Davis had actually performed with Parker, Dizzy Gillespie, and Sarah Vaughn in St. Louis. From there on out, he pioneered "progressive" jazz and became one of the greats himself.

His description of Blacks from his high school days offers a different take. From the perspective of a New Yorker, Davis saw the St. Louises on either side of the river as "real square" country towns, "racist to the bone." The "hipness" of the area came from its Black population. In his autobiography, Davis explained that, "A lot of [Black] people from that area had a whole lot of style back then," possibly because there was a steady exchange of musicians between Chicago, New Orleans, Kansas City, and St. Louis. On the other hand, white audiences made up of men who worked in slaughterhouses and such wouldn't put up with anything less than a musician's best—which Miles Davis always delivered.

You won't find Goode Street on a current St. Louis map; it's been renamed Annie Malone Drive. So, it's appropriate that rock and roll great Chuck Berry was born on Goode Street, also in 1926. One of Berry's hits was "Johnny B. Goode"; he supported himself at one point as a hairdresser, a trade he learned at Annie Malone's Poro College. One of his early-stage successes was a blues number for a recital at Sumner High—all of which makes Berry the quintessential Ville product.

It was Berry's genius to pull together country and blues rhythms to define rock and roll guitar. His autobiography filled in details of a happy early life. He performed his "duck walk" while playing guitar because he had entertained his family and visitors retrieving a ball from under the kitchen table using the move. He learned music and poetry growing up because his mother and father both sang at the Antioch Baptist Church and because his father read poetry to entertain the Berry children. He had a solid though not easy economic advantage, due to his father's construction skills, which would have led to a very middle-class existence without the tribulations of the Great Depression. And, he early on had a lively interest in sex that led to legal troubles, including a three-year prison term for transporting a fourteen-year-old girl across a state line.

Through the prison terms—he was also convicted of armed robbery when young and tax evasion when he was older—Berry set standards for rock and roll in the 1950s and continued to perform in the St. Louis area until his death in 2017. He was one of the original eleven inductees into the Rock and Roll Hall of Fame in 1986.

When Maya Angelou read one of her poems at President Bill Clinton's first inauguration in 1993, she was the second poet to do such a recitation, the first woman, and the first Black. She is known for her poetry and autobiographical fiction, but her life was far more varied and intriguing than that.

Born in St. Louis in 1928, her parents sent the three-year-old Maya and her older brother, Bailey, to live with her paternal grandmother in Stamps, Arkansas. Their father suddenly reappeared when Maya was seven and took the two children back to St. Louis to live with their mother and maternal grandmother, the father himself disappearing back to California. Of all the stories of Black childhoods in St. Louis, the story Maya told in her book *I Know Why the Caged Bird Sings* is one of the most unusual as well as tragic. That's because her maternal grandmother was a political boss, not with the clout of an Ed Butler but still a force to be reckoned with in her ward.

Angelou describes "numbers runners, gamblers, lottery takers, and whiskey salesmen" sitting in the living room politely waiting for Grandmother Baxter. Mrs. Baxter's status as a precinct captain and her pull with the police meant that she could get favors for the men and ask a favor in return: that they deliver the votes. Add to that that Grandmother Baxter's sons, Maya's uncles, had reputations for meanness that rippled through the Black community.

The young girl's life changed when she was raped by her mother's boyfriend the next year; her testimony against him in court was as scarring as the event. The man was convicted but released immediately. Maya was terrified when a white policeman came to her grandmother's house the next day, "taller than the sky and whiter than my image of God," to respectfully explain that the convicted rapist had been found dead, likely kicked to death. Maya took the moral responsibility on herself, although the speculation has always been that her uncles had carried out their own sentence. Maya went mute for several years, speaking only to her brother, even as the two were returned to Stamps.

Her careers ranged from being the first Black female cable car conductor in San Francisco to involvement in sex trades to singing and dancing to civil rights activism to receiving numerous awards for her writing. Maya Angelou was a resident professor of writing at Wake Forest University—although she had never received a bachelor's degree—when she died in 2014.

Dick Gregory's mother was desperately poor, raising her six children on what she could make working in the homes of white folks for twelve hours a day, seven days a week. The problem with that was she had to explain to the social worker why she hadn't bothered to keep her own house clean: She had to pretend she wasn't working or she couldn't draw relief money. Dick, the second oldest, born in 1932 during the Depression, always worked himself, shining shoes and selling newspapers. But their three-room house on North Taylor was always cold and never clean. He tells the story in his autobiography about the woman who came to the door one Thanksgiving with a basket for the needy. He slammed the door in her face; it was easier than explaining that the Gregory family had no way to cook a raw turkey.

Dick Gregory turned his frustrations and energy into running and became a track star at Sumner High. It got him a college scholarship in Illinois, although his career there was interrupted by military service. In the military, he began the stand-up comedy routines that would make him a household name—often a controversial one—across the country in the 1960s, using humor to skewer racism. He was known for his civil rights activism, advocating for Blacks as well as for women and Native Americans, along with his promotion of vegetarianism and animal rights. In 1968, he ran for president.

This routine is frequently quoted—in internet stories and in Gregory's autobiography to suggest the revolution in humor that was Dick Gregory:

> We tried to integrate a restaurant, and they said, "We don't serve colored folk here," and I said, "Well, I don't eat colored folk nowhere . . . bring me a whole fried chicken." And then the Klan walked up to me when they put that whole fried chicken in front of me, and they say, "Whatever you do to that chicken, boy, we're going to do to you." So, I opened up its legs and kissed it in the rump and tell you all, "Be my guest."

Dick Gregory dealt creatively with the fact that Sumner High served not only very poor Blacks but also the children of the Black upper class, doctors and lawyers and such. A young woman who moved to St. Louis as a teen-ager said the latter group made her feel like an outsider. Anna Mae Bullock, raised in Nutbush, Tennessee, and transplanted to St. Louis when she was sixteen, arrived at Sumner for the 1955–1956 school year.

She was also raised by grandparents, parents flitting in and out of her life. Unlike classmates, she found a life outside Sumner across the river in East St. Louis, listening to and then singing with rock groups there. That's where she met Ike Turner before her graduation from Sumner in 1958. We know her as Tina Turner, another rock and roll great, and the only one of this group still alive as of this writing. Her story, including her marriage to, and escape from, Ike Turner, is still unfolding.

We could count many others. There are the two opera singers, Robert McFerrin Sr. and Grace Bumbry (both Sumner grads). Robert was the first Black man to sing with the Metropolitan Opera. You may know his son, Bobby McFerrin, also of musical note.

And then there are the actors, including Robert Guillaume, who you would know if you remember sit-coms from the 1970s and 1980s. Redd Foxx, stand-up comedian and actor, was born in St. Louis and raised in Chicago.

Baseball players abound. James "Cool Papa" Bell moved to St. Louis as a teenager and became a Negro Leagues legend as one of the fastest men to ever play. He was a mentor to Quincey Trouppe, another Negro Leagues standout and the first Black scout for the St. Louis Cardinals. Elston How-ard, a noted athlete at Vashon, played in the Negro Leagues until he became the first Black to play for the New York Yankees in 1955. He played outfield and back-up catcher to another famous St. Louisan, Yogi Berra, of the Italian Hill neighborhood.

If you're into boxing, you might recognize the names of three champi-ons of the last century: Henry Armstrong, Archie Moore, and Sonny Liston. Armstrong read a poem at his graduation from Vashon. St. Louis offered Moore and Liston a different kind of education on mean streets in the Valley.

All of St. Louis' Black children, the ones destined for fame and the ones we know little of, could not ignore, as they grew up, the racial turmoil. St. Louis Blacks did not accept the status quo quietly. The city's Urban League, made up of both Blacks and whites, fought against the restrictive covenants and the high-rent, crowded housing, along with Jim Crow indignities. The latter included segregated playgrounds and swimming pools. The Urban League joined the local NAACP chapter in seeking to open both, leading to a major confrontation that symbolized the end of the first half of the century.

In 1949, the St. Louis Parks Department director announced one day that, henceforth, the nation's largest open-air swimming pool, the one the department maintained in Fairgrounds Park, would be open to children of any race. Word spread and Black teens joined white teens to enter the pool when it opened that day, June 21. It would not be a play day of any sort.

Crowds of whites of all ages were waiting when Blacks left the pool; it was largely white teenagers who attacked. The fight was on, and every police officer and detective on the evening shift were called to the park. One estimate put 5,000 people at the scene as the evening wore on. One white man and one Black man were seriously injured, with a score of others being punched, kicked, and assaulted with baseball bats. The mayor quickly countermanded the parks head's announcement, agreeing that there was no legal excuse for segregation but arguing that everything worked better when Blacks kept to their own pools (all indoor at the time) and whites to theirs (which included both indoor and outdoor pools).

The next summer, the pools were integrated by a federal court. Angry groups of whites again gathered but police controlled the situation. Increasingly, however, summer after summer, whites either boycotted the huge Fairgrounds pool or simply moved away from the city to points west. By 1956, the city apparently decided it wasn't worth the cost to maintain an inner-city pool used only by Blacks. The country's largest open-air pool was filled with concrete, and a smaller pool was built in the park.

FURTHER READING

Chapter One

Charles van Ravenswaay, in *Saint Louis: An Informal History of the City and its People, 1764–1865*, 1991, for the traditional story of the city's founding and later feuds between Chouteau and Laclède descendants.

Katharine T. Corbett on Marie Thérèse in "Veuve Chouteau, a 250th Anniversary," in *Gateway Heritage* magazine, 1983. Corbett also as author and editor of *In Her Place: A Guide to St. Louis Women's History*, the essential source on everything female in St. Louis history to its publication in 1999.

Jay Gitlin in "Constructing the House of Chouteau," in *Commonplace* (a journal of early American life), 2003.

William E. Foley in "The Laclede/Chouteau Puzzle: John Francis McDermott Supplies Some Missing Pieces," in *Gateway Heritage* magazine, 1983.

Two standard histories: James Neal Primm's *Lion of the Valley: St. Louis, Missouri, 1764–1980*, 1981; and *Missouri: The WPA Guide to the "Show-Me" State*, 1941.

For the revisionist history, Carl J. Ekberg and Sharon K. Person, "The Making (and Perpetuating) of a Myth: Pierre Laclède and the Founding of St. Louis," in *Missouri Historical Review*, 2017.

Chapter Two

Kathryn Corbett on both Mitain and Mary Hempstead Lisa in *In Her Place*.

Richard Edward Oglesby for his biography, *Manuel Lisa and the Opening of the Missouri Fur Trade*, 1963.

The explorer quoted, Edwin James, *Account of an Expedition from Pittsburgh to the Rocky Mountains*, of the 1819 expedition.

Jay Gitlin again, *Commonplace*, 2003.

Interpretations of the Native American experience from Tanis Thorne in *The Many Hands of My Relations: French and Indians on the Lower Mississippi*, 1996.

Descriptions of Lisa and his exploits from van Ravenswaay (*Informal History*) and James Neal Primm (*Lion of the Valley*).

Chapters Three and Four

Adam Kloppe, for the Missouri Historical Society, "The Louisiana Purchase and the Rise of Dueling in St. Louis," 2014.

Elbert Smith in "Now Defend Yourself, You Damned Rascal," for *American Heritage*, available online, but originally from the magazine in 1958.

Primm again, in *Lion of the Valley*.

Andrew Wanko, *Great River City: How the Mississippi Shaped St. Louis*, 2019.

"Bloody Island: Honor and Violence in Early Nineteenth-Century St. Louis," Charles van Ravenswaay, in his *Informal History* and as an article in *Gateway Heritage*, 1990.

J. Thomas Scharf in his monumental *A History of St. Louis City and County*, 1883.

Jim Winnerman, "Death and Honor on Bloody Island," from *Wild West Magazine*, April 2020, reprinted on HistoryNet.

"Crack of the Pistol: Dueling in 19th Century Missouri," from the Education site of the Missouri State Archives and Missouri Digital Heritage.

Dick Steward on Biddle and Pettis, and Kenneth H. Winn and Lawrence O. Christensen on Brown and Reynolds, respectively, in *The Dictionary of Missouri Biography*, 1999.

Beverly Bauser, "The Abraham Lincoln–James Shields Duel, September 22, 1842," on the Madison County, Illinois GenWeb site.

Chapter Five

Again, Primm in *Lion of the Valley*.

Ernest Kirschten, a *Post-Dispatch* editorial page writer, in *Catfish and Crystal: A Story of St. Louis, U.S.A.*, 1989.

Charles C. Clayton's *Little Mack: Joseph B. McCullagh of the St. Louis Globe-Democrat*.

Homer King, *Pulitzer's Prize Editor: A Biography of John A. Cockerill*.

Versions of the shooting story all over the internet: "The Slayback Homicide" in a 2014 issue of the website "Murder by Gaslight"; for the Missouri Historical Society, Brittany Krewson, "Tragedy in the Newsroom" in 2018; Kerrigan Chapman, "The Veiled Prophet: A History of Bigotry in St. Louis" for Odyssey in 2017; Kirby Ross on "James O. Broadhead: Ardent Unionist, Unrepentant Slaveholder" for the website Civil War St. Louis in 2002.

For good, but very short, biographies of major St. Louis players buried in its elite graveyard, Carol Ferring Shepley's 2008 *Tales from Bellefontaine Cemetery*.

"Mack" McCullagh in the *Globe-Democrat*; and a staff-full of writers for the *Post-Dispatch*, October 12–16, 1882.

Chapters Six and Seven

Writers we've met before: Scharf, Primm, Ravenswaay, Kirschten, Shepley, and Wanko.

Also: Katherine Douglass, writing in Katharine Corbett's *In Her Place*, on Harriet Scott.

Robert W. Tabscott, "Elijah Parish Lovejoy: Portrait of a Radical: The St. Louis Years, 1827–1835," in *Gateway Heritage*, Winter 1987–1988.

John A. Bryan, "The Blow Family and Their Slave Dred Scott," *Bulletin of the Missouri Historical Society*, 1948.

John Wright, *Discovering African American St. Louis: A Guide to Historic Sites*, second edition, 2002.

Robert Moore Jr., "A Ray of Hope, Extinguished: St. Louis Slave Suits for Freedom," *Gateway Heritage*, Winter 1993–1994.

Bonnie E. Laughlin, "Endangering the Peace of Society: Abolitionist Agitation and Mob Reaction in St. Louis and Alton, 1836–1838," *Missouri Historical Review*, October 2000.

For the matter of Hannah's death, *General William S. Harney, Prince of Dragoons* by George Rollie Adams, and a book edited by abolitionist Theodore D. Weld, *American Slavery as It Is: Selections from the Testimony of a Thousand Witnesses*, 1839.

Frederick A. Hodes, whose large volumes on St. Louis history describe everything from such major events as McIntosh's burning to how many people celebrated St. Patrick's Day in a particular year, specifically, *Rising on the River: St. Louis 1822 to 1850*, published in 2009.

For details on the Scott lawsuit, Louis Gerteis, *Civil War St. Louis*.

Chapter Eight

James Neal Primm for details on riots.

Thomas Scharf's 1883 history, with eyewitness accounts of riots.

Ernest Kirschten and Frederick Hodes again.

On the Know-Nothings, an older source not specific to St. Louis: J. C. Furnas' *The Americans: A Social History of the United States, 1587–1914*.

Father William B. Faherty, S.J., *The St. Louis Irish: An Unmatched Celtic Community*.

John C. Schneider in "Riot and Reaction in St. Louis, 1854–1856," in *Missouri Historical Review*, January 1974.

And still here:

Soulard Farmers' Market bills itself as the oldest west of the Mississippi, a phrase you hear a lot in St. Louis. Several buildings have occupied the site, but they seem to have been continuously busy for at least two centuries.

Chapter Nine
Primm, Charles van Ravenswaay, and George Rollie Adams.

For an eyewitness account, Galusha Anderson's *The Story of a Border City During the Civil War*, published in 1908, from a pro-Union Baptist minister.

For the most detailed account, Louis S. Gerteis, *Civil War St. Louis.*

And still here:

Lyon Park today is incorporated into the grounds of the old arsenal. Fittingly, it is located in the historically German Soulard neighborhood, near the Anheuser-Busch Brewery.

Chapter Ten
Joan Cooper on the cholera epidemics and the role of women in 1927 tornado, both in *In Her Time* articles.

John M. Barry, *The Great Influenza: The Story of the Deadliest Pandemic in History*, 2004 (and 2018)

Primm, again. Ravenswaay for details on the fire of 1849. Hodes for details on both the fire and the 1849 cholera epidemic.

For the Kansas flu, see a two-part article in *Missouri Medicine*, Summer 2018, "The 1918 Influenza in Missouri: Centennial Remembrance of the Crisis," by David S. McKinsey, Joel P. McKinsey, and Maithe Enriquez.

For the 1925 tornado, Andrew Hurley, Shuron Jones, and Eliza Murray, in the Spring 2020 issue of *Gateway.*

Chapter Eleven
Andrew Hurley, editor of a collection called *Common Fields: An Environmental History of St. Louis*, 1997; his introduction and chapter on the nuisance trades; Walter Schroeder on geology; Eric Sandweiss on streets; Katharine Corbett on sewers; Craig Colten on unbridled

corporate pollution in East St. Louis; and Joel Tarr and Carl Zimring on smoke control.

Walter Johnson's scathing *The Bloody Heart of America*, 2020, about East St. Louis.

On River des Peres, Michael Allen, director of Preservation Research, on that group's website in 2010.

On the Mill Street Sewer explosion, John Dietzler in the *Bulletin of the Missouri Historical Society*, January 1959.

Stu Beitler, on a genealogy site, called GenDisasters.com.

And still here:

Mayor Kiel gave his name to the Kiel Auditorium, located on Market between City Hall and Union Station. The auditorium cleverly featured opera and other stage entertainment on the Market Street side and sporting events on the south side. That side has been rebuilt as the Enterprise Center; the 2019 NHL Stanley Cup champion St. Louis Blues play hockey there. The Market Street side has been renovated as the Stiefel Center.

By all means, visit the Missouri Botanical Garden, in sun or shade, and the Muny Opera, now safe from flooding sewage.

Chapter Twelve

On all things baseball, Peter *Golenbock's The Spirit of St. Louis: A History of the St. Louis Cardinals and Browns*, 2000.

George Lipsitz, *The Sidewalks of St. Louis: Places, People, and Politics in an American City*, 1991.

Jon David Cash, "Chris von der Ahe, the American Association versus National League Culture War, and the Rise of Major-League Baseball," *Missouri Historical Review*, October 2014.

Jim Rygelski, "Baseball's "Boss President" Chris von der Ahe and the Nineteenth-Century St. Louis Browns, in *Gateway Heritage*, 1992.

Anthony Lampe on "The Background of Professional Baseball in St. Louis," *Bulletin of the Missouri Historical Society*, 1950.

And still here:
Today's baseball park downtown is Busch Stadium III.

Chapter Thirteen
Edward Berlin's detailed biography, *King of Ragtime: Scott Joplin and His Era*.
Walter Johnson again, in *The Broken Heart of America* on Scott Joplin, Stagolee, the murder ballad genre in general, and African American frustrations.
Nathan B. Young's *Your St. Louis and Mine* on Charlie and Tom Turpin. Quotes from, and the section about, Nathan Young in *Ain't But a Place: An Anthology of African American Writings about St. Louis*, edited by Gerald Early.
"Frankie and Johnny" information abounds on the internet.

And still here:
Check out the Scott Joplin State Historical Site on Delmar Boulevard and its re-creation of Turpin's Rosebud Bar.

Chapters Fourteen and Fifteen
On the native groups at the fair, a masters' thesis by Jeffrey D. Gauss, on "The Department of Anthropology at the Louisiana Purchase Exposition," 1994, William & Mary College.
And another thesis-writer, Andrea M. Fowler, on "Building an Image: Japanese Influence on the Perception of Western Countries, A Study of the 1904 St. Louis World's Fair," a 2019 submission to West Virginia University.
Walter Johnson, *The Broken Heart of America*, on imperialism at the fair.
Sue Bradford Edwards on "Imperial East Meets Democratic West: The St. Louis Press and the Fair's Chinese Delegation," for *Gateway Heritage*, 1996.
Martha R. Clevenger on "Through Western Eyes: Americans Encounter Asians at the Fair," in *Gateway Heritage*, 1996, as well as context for the memoir of Edward V. P. Schneiderhahn in *Gateway Heritage*, 1992.

On the 1904 Olympics, Mark Dyreson's "The Playing Fields of Progress," in *Gateway Heritage*, 1995. On George Poage's achievements, June Wuest Becht in *Missouri Biography*, 2004.

Karen Abbott, "The 1904 Olympics May Have Been the Strangest Ever," *Smithsonianmag.com*, 2012.

Russell M. Magnaghi's "America Views Her Indians at the 1904 World's Fair in St. Louis," *Gateway Heritage*, 1998.

In *Gateway Heritage* about the Philippine Reservation, Sharra L. Vostral's "Imperialism on Display," 1993; Clayton D. Laurie's "An Oddity of Empire," from Winter 1994–1995; and Nancy J. Parezo's "The Exposition within the Exposition," 2004.

Dawn Raffel on *The Strange Case of Dr. Couney: How a Mysterious European Showman Saved Thousands of American Babies*, 2018.

Michael Lerner on the Black experience in "Hoping for a Splendid Summer," in *Gateway Heritage*, Winter 1998–1999.

Robert Moss in seriouseats.com in 2016 entitled, "The 1906 World's Fair: A Turning Point for American Food."

Pamela J. Vaccaro, *Beyond the Ice Cream Cone*, 2004.

An overview from Aisha Sultan of the *St. Louis Post-Dispatch*: "Secrets, Scandals, and Little-Known Stories about the 1904 World's Fair," October 13, 2019.

For a general sense of what St. Louis expected of the fair, "A Mirror Held to St. Louis: William Marion Reedy and the 1904 World's Fair," by Jeffrey E. Smith, in *Gateway Heritage*, 1998.

And still here:

Forest Park survives, of course, its ecosystem restored to the extent nature and the city have allowed. The primary remain of the fair is the St. Louis Art Museum on "Art Hill." The St. Louis Zoo, also located in the sprawling Forest Park, contains the Flight House, the magnificent birdcage that belonged to the fair. A popular feature in the park is the World's Fair Pavilion, but it was built in 1909 with proceeds from the fair.

Chapter Sixteen
Usual sources: Kirschten, Shepley, and Primm.

Terry Ganey and Peter Hernon, *Under the Influence: The New Edition of the Unauthorized Story of the Anheuser-Busch Dynasty*, 2012.

William Knoedelseder, *Bitter Brew: The Rise and Fall of Anheuser-Busch and America's Kings of Beer*, also 2012.

Stories about the Lemps all over internet publications, including Audrey Webster on "The Lemp Mansion Curse," in the-line-up.com, February 2019; Chris Naffziger, on Falstaff beer for the *Riverfront Times* in 2014 and about the Lemp family intrigues for stlmag.com, including an article in July 2019. Information on the Lemps from Donald Roussin and Kevin Kious in several forms, including an article reprinted on beerhistory.com. Troy Taylor, on Elsa Lemp through his Facebook page, authortt. Tim O'Neill, stltoday.com, February of 2020, about the closing of the Lemp Brewery. And numerous stories about the Lemp Mansion as a haunted destination.

Daniel Waugh, *Gangs of St. Louis*, 2010.

Gary Mormino, "A Still on the Hill: Prohibition and Cottage Industry," *Gateway Heritage*, 1986.

Chapter Seventeen
Reporters for the *Missouri Republican* (no bylines at the time!) on December 29, 1872.

Stories in the *St. Louis Globe-Democrat* and the *St. Louis Post-Dispatch* on the police graft trials of 1906.

James Wunsch, "Protecting St. Louis Neighborhoods from the Encroachment of Brothels, 1870–1920," *Missouri History Review*, 2010.

Duane Sneddeker, "Regulating Vice: Prostitution and the St. Louis Social Evil Ordinance, 1870–1874," *Gateway Heritage*, 1990.

Michael J. Meyer, involved in the archeological excavations of the 2010s, on "Brothels Uncovered: The Madams of St. Louis," for *Gateway*, 2019.

Andrew Wanko, in *Great River City*.

Bill McClellan and Joe Holleman of the present-day *Post-Dispatch* on the legacy of Eliza Haycraft and her grave in Bellefontaine Cemetery.

Fly North artistic director Colin Healy and Bluff City Theatre for information about the musical *Madam* in 2019.

Chapters Eighteen and Nineteen
Thomas Scharf, for whom the 1877 strike was recent, in his 1883 *Encyclopedia*.
Walter Johnson, for whom it was vintage, in *The Broken Heart of America*.
Primm for the 1900 strike.
James F. Baker, "The St. Louis and Suburban Streetcar Strike of 1900," *Missouri Historical Review*, 2007.
Dina M. Young, "The St. Louis Streetcar Strike of 1900," *Gateway Heritage*, 1991.
Johnson also on the 1917 East St. Louis race war.
Elliott Rudwick, *Race Riot at East St. Louis July 2, 1917*, 1972.
Harper Barnes, *Never Been a Time*, 2008.
The two stalwart dailies, the *St. Louis Post-Dispatch* and the *St. Louis Globe-Democrat*, of July 3, 1917.
Rose Feurer, labor expert and editor of *The St. Louis Labor Tour*, a booklet that identifies sites in the city associated with union activity, on Hennessey and Sellins.
William Barnaby Faherty on *The St. Louis Irish*.
State Senate hearings reported in the *St. Louis Post-Dispatch* of May 23, 1913.

Chapter Twenty
Lincoln Steffens, *The Shame of the Cities*, 1904.
As usual, James Neal Primm and Ernest Kirschten.
James Markham, *Bovard of the Post-Dispatch*, 1954.

Chapter Twenty-one
Daniel Waugh, *Egan's Rats*, 2007, and *Gangs of St. Louis*.
Linda Harris Dobkins (pen name Jo Allison) for the story of Goldstein and the league in "What Men Expected, What Women Did," *Missouri Historical Review*, 2014.

Chapter Twenty-two

Irving Litvag, *Singer in the Shadows: The Strange Story of Patience Worth*, 1972.

Ed Simon, in an essay for *The Public Domain Review*, 2014, "Ghostwriter and Ghost: The Strange Case of Pearl Curran and Patience Worth."

Chapter Twenty-three

Thomas Allen for the definitive book, *Possessed*, with Bishop's diary in the second edition.

Steven LaChance of St. Louis asserting demonic possession in *Confrontation with Evil*; Joe Nickell in "The Skeptical Inquirer" for a counterpoint.

John McGuire of the *Post-Dispatch* for new information, April 17, 1988.

Internet articles on a topic that won't go away; like the demons exorcised by Jesus in the Gospel, they are legion.

Chapter Twenty-four

Ernest Kirschten, in *Catfish and Crystal* on Nellie Muench.

For Mary Catherine Reardon's story, numerous newspapers, including the *Globe-Democrat*, the *Post-Dispatch*, and others carrying Associated Press reports from Los Angeles.

Chapter Twenty-five

Histories from Primm and Johnson, along with autobiographies:

Standing Fast by Roy Wilkins.

Josephine by Josephine Baker.

Chuck Berry: An Autobiography, unassisted by a co-author.

Miles: The Autobiography by Miles Davis and Quincy Troupe (son of the baseball player who spells his name differently).

nigger, by Dick Gregory.

I, Tina, by Tina Turner.

The many autobiographical works by Maya Angelou, particularly *I Know Why the Caged Bird Sings*.

Excerpts from these works (and much more), in *Ain't But a Place*, edited by Gerald Early.

Details of the Fairgrounds Park riot from the *St. Louis Globe-Democrat*, June 22, 1949.

Update on the story of Lloyd Gaines by Chad Garrison in *The Riverfront Times*, April 4, 2007.

On Tandy and keeping up with locations, John A Wright, *Discovering African American St. Louis*.

INDEX

ABOUT THE AUTHOR

Jo Allison (the pen name of Linda Dobkins) grew up in Missouri and spent ten years as a journalist, mostly for newspapers. She was the first woman to do television news in her hometown of Joplin, Missouri. Although she went on to teaching and researching, she believes reporting was the best education she could have had.

Allison writes historical fiction as well as nonfiction including a mystery series that begins in 1910 St. Louis.